Forgotten Essays
H. Stanley Redgrove

Editor
Darrell Jordan

Publisher
Athenaia

2024

FORGOTTEN ESSAYS H. Stanley Redgrove - Compiled with graphics and edits by Darrell Jordan, Copyright © Second Edition 2024. All rights reserved. No part of this book may be reproduced in whole or in part without the written permission from the publisher, nor stored in any retrieval system or transmitted by any means, electronic, mechanical, photocopying, recording, or other, without the written consent of the publisher.
For bulk purchases, please contact the publisher.
Enquiry@Athenaia.Co

Library of Congress Cataloging-in Publication Data
Names: Redgrove, Stanley | Jordan, Darrell
FORGOTTEN ESSAYS H. Stanley Redgrove K, Darrell Jordan, MPS
Description: Second U.S. edition. | Coeur D'Alene, Idaho: Athenaia [2024]
Identifiers: LCCN (pending) |
ISBN 979-8-88556-053-5 (Second Edition hardcover)
Subjects: OCC042000 / BODY, MIND & SPIRIT / Alchemy |
OCC016000 / BODY, MIND & SPIRIT / Occultism|
OCC012000 / BODY, MIND & SPIRIT / Mysticism
LC record available at https://lccn.loc.gov

On the internet: Parallel47North.com/collections/esoteric-books
Managing Editor: Darrell Jordan
Original Author and Essays: H. Stanley Redgrove
Executive Producer: Yuka Jordan
Book Cover Design by Yuka Jordan
Book Cover Art and Illustrations: Darrell Jordan
Image Credits: H. Stanley Redgrove and Darrell Jordan's personal collection
Printed and bound in the United States

Publisher: Athenaia, LLC
2370 N Merritt Crk Lp, Ste 1, Coeur D'Alene, ID 83814
The United States

It may be that when we no longer know which way to go that we have come to our real journey. The mind that is not baffled is not employed. The impeded stream is the one that sings.

~ *Wendell Berry*

About H. Stanley Redgrove

H Stanley Redgrove was born in 1888 and attended London University, where he attained a BSc in chemistry. He became a fellow of the Institute of Chemistry, a member of the Society of Public Analysts and author of more than a dozen books. He was a lecturer in Mathematics and Chemistry and in 1938 moved to Pangbourne where he manufactured Berkshire Beauty products. On March 11th 1943, he suffered a brain seizure and died on March 13th at the age of 56.

H. Stanley Redgrove

INTRODUCTION

In all departments of human activity in politics, in science and religion, principles, formerly accepted without question as fundamental, have been thrown down into the arena of controversy and subjected to a rigorous examination. And the results of this sifting process are a profound discontent, a restless chafing at the bounds of our present knowledge, which find expression in, and are peculiarly characteristic of the art of the period. "Light, more light!" were the dying words of Goethe, the pioneer of the nineteenth century, and the dying 20th century re-echoes them.

Nothing is more remarkable than the change which has come over our habits of thought within the last few years. Until quite recently, it was considered a sign of intellectual superiority to rest content with the position of an *Agnostic* in regard to the most important subjects which can engage the attention of man. It was asserted that not only do we not know anything about God, the soul, or a future life, but that it is idle to enquire; that true wisdom consists in denial of the possibility of any such knowledge, and that every revelation which professes to give information on these subjects is the product of a distempered fancy. But this curious form of intellectual pride led the Agnostics, like the Puritans in Hudibras, to "Compound for sins they were inclined to, By damning those they had no mind to," and did not hinder them from indulging in the wildest speculations about the origin of life on the planet and gravely asserting that the chief difference between a man and a monkey is that phosphorus is present in larger quantities in the brain of the former.

It was inevitable that the pendulum should swing back in the opposite direction, and the reaction from Agnosticism has resulted in a very strange phenomenon, the recrudescence of Gnosticism, a veritable revival of Alexandrian thought.

During this life, we are each of us "imprisoned in the five senses," and, though thought reaches out far beyond them, its range is limited by the capacity of the physical brain. In time, that capacity will expand. Ideas easily grasped by the man of modern culture are beyond the comprehension of the savage.

The improved intellectual mechanism of future generations will no doubt deal freely with conceptions which present culture cannot appreciate. Spiritual science, however, is an infinitude, and no attempt to interpret it in physical plane language will ever be more than suggestive and alluring.

Herbert Stanley Redgrove 1887-1943, was an Occultist, Chemist and founding member of the Royal Society of Chemistry. The insight so proffered by this learned Occultist, will perhaps lift the veil just enough, that more Light is shined on the Mysteries.

H. Stanley Redgrove

ABOUT H. STANLEY REDGROVE	I
INTRODUCTION	II
ON THE INFINITE	- 7 -
ON MATTER AND SPIRIT	- 12 -
ON THE SELF-EXISTENT	- 19 -
ON CREATION	- 25 -
THE THEORY AND PRACTICE OF MAGIC	- 31 -
1. The Doctrine of Emanations	- 31 -
2. Medieval Ceremonial Magic	- 34 -
3. The Psychology of Magic	- 36 -
4. The Ethics of Magic	- 38 -
5. The Efficacy of Symbols	- 40 -
6. The Magical Theory of Experience	- 43 -
MEDICINE AND MAGIC	- 45 -
MYSTICISM AND MONASTICISM	- 49 -
THE DERVISHES: THEIR CUSTOMS AND BELIEFS	- 56 -
ON SYMBOLISM IN ART	- 60 -
THE POWDER OF SYMPATHY	- 66 -
SUPERSTITIONS CONCERNING BIRDS	- 73 -
THE CAMBRIDGE PLATONISTS	- 80 -
ARCHITECTURAL SYMBOLISM	- 90 -

Forgotten Essays

THE IDEALISTIC POINT OF VIEW	- 95 -
THE HARLEQUINADE	- 104 -
FACTS AND HYPOTHESES IN PSYCHICAL RESEARCH	- 107 -
HINDU MYTHOLOGY	- 111 -
MAGNETIC REPULSION: ITS PRACTICAL SCIENTIFIC	- 115 -
VALUE AND OCCULT PSYCHOLOGICAL SIGNIFICANCE	- 115 -
ROGER BACON: AN APPRECIATION	- 120 -
APHORISMS ON NATURE	- 125 -
IMMANENCE AND CONTINUITY AS OBSTACLES TO THOUGHT	- 128 -
1. Immanence	- 128 -
2. Continuity	- 131 -
UNIVERSAL SYMBOLISM	- 133 -
TRANSCENDENTAL ALCHEMY	- 144 -
OCCULTISM AND THE ATOMIC THEORY	- 148 -
PHILOSOPHY AND TRUTH	- 161 -
THE BOOK OF SECRETS	- 166 -
ALCHEMY AND MODERN SCIENCE	- 171 -
A SUPERNORMAL ADVENTURE	- 177 -
TALISMANIC MAGIC	- 179 -
A DEFENSE OF ALCHEMY	- 186 -
THE SOUL OF THE BEAST	- 202 -
A MASTER OF MAGIC: ALPHONSE LOUIS CONSTANT	- 207 -

H. Stanley Redgrove

HERB-MAGIC	- 214 -
BLAKE AND SWEDENBORG:	- 219 -
A STUDY IN COMPARATIVE MYSTICISM	- 219 -
THE SCIENCE OF SMELLS	- 230 -
EYELESS SIGHT	- 235 -
THE ROSICRUCIAN'S	- 241 -
ARABIAN ALCHEMY	- 248 -
THE LIMITATIONS OF THE LAWS OF NATURE	- 254 -
THE QUEST FOR TRUTH IN ALCHEMY	- 262 -
THE SENSE OF CERTITUDE: SOME NOTES ON INTUITION AND REASON	- 267 -
THE STAR OF PERFECTION	- 272 -
AN ALCHEMICAL BANQUET	- 277 -
THE KABBALAH AND WORD-MAGIC	- 284 -
THE FOUNDATION OF MAGIC	- 288 -
A NEW PLEA FOR MYSTICISM	- 294 -
ABOUT AUTHOR AND MANAGING EDITOR	- 301 -

ON THE INFINITE

THERE is a certain class of people who consider that any postulate (however absurd otherwise) can be stated about that which is infinite with perfect impunity, all argument being met with the statement that our reason being finite, it cannot argue about that which is infinite. Hence the Athanasian doctrine of the Trinity. That we can have some knowledge (be it granted, not perfect) of that which is infinite, is evident from a study of mathematics. Examples can even be given in elementary mathematics; for instance, it can be shown that the more terms of the series

$$\frac{1}{1} + \frac{1}{2} + \frac{1}{4} + \frac{1}{8} + \frac{1}{16} + \frac{1}{32} +$$

be taken the more nearly will the sum approach 2, so that we may say that the sum of an infinite number of terms is 2. Innumerable other series of a similar nature exist, of which recurring decimals afford another example. It should be noticed that the word "infinite" is ambiguous; its clearer and better defined meaning is what may be termed the mathematical one. In this sense, it is an adjective; we should suppose it to convey the attribute of being not-finite, i.e. unlimited, but it does not do so absolutely. Every definition conveys some limit; thus, when we speak of "number" (in the abstract sense) our meaning is limited to a certain general concept. The meaning in intension of the term "infinity" (infinite number) is therefore limited in that it refers to number only, and is therefore limited by the definition of "number," but unlimited in that it refers to a number of unlimited magnitude; whereas finite numbers are limited in this respect as well. This will be further illustrated:

A line is defined mathematically as length without breadth (or thickness). A surface is that which has length and breadth, but no thickness. An infinite line, therefore, although unlimited in length, is still very limited in possessing no breadth or thickness, and is therefore infinitely small as compared with infinite surface, which possesses infinite length and breadth which we can state by saying that infinite surface contains an infinity of infinite lines; similarly, infinite space contains an infinity of infinite surfaces. This brings us to a realization that "infinite" is a relative term, for that which is infinitely great compared with one standard may be infinitely small compared with another. Thus consider the series,

$$x^{-3}, x^{-2}, x^{-1}, x^0, x^1, x^2, x^3$$

The ratio between any term and the next is X. Let X become infinite, then this ratio becomes infinite, so that compared with any term, those to the right are infinitely great, those to the left are infinitely small. Thus, X^2 is infinitely great compared with x^1, but infinitely small compared with X^3 just as infinite surface is infinitely great compared with infinite length, but infinitely small compared with infinite space. It may be argued that this is true so far as mathematical abstractions are concerned, but it is otherwise with actualities. This is wrong, for consider the actual line; it is of (comparatively speaking) small breadth and thickness and greater length. Let it be produced without limit, then we have an infinite line, i.e. that which is of infinite length and small (finite) breadth and thickness; for if it were of infinite breadth and thickness it would cease interesting book Root-Principles, defends the notion of a finite universe against Haeckel and MacCabe. All three authors use the term "infinite" non-mathematically as implying an absolute absence of limit to be a line, and therefore is limited in breadth and thickness by the definition of a line. Its volume is clearly infinite, and yet in the truest sense of the expression, it is not infinite space; for not only can we have that which is of infinite length and breadth and small (finite) thickness, i.e. infinite surface, which is infinitely greater than the infinite line, but also infinite space in the truest sense which has infinite length, breadth and thickness. It might be worthwhile to consider whether actual space is infinite. (see above).

MacCabe would truly remark "the idea of a limit [to the physical universe] is in fact unthinkable," if he only implied the mathematical infinity of space, for otherwise space would end in space, which is nonsense, and Child would be wrong in thinking it easier to imagine a finite than an infinite universe. Space is infinite, but it is still space, and the definition of space implies a necessary limit; for one thing, it is three dimensional, for all we know there may be a fourth, fifth, sixth ... even an infinity of dimensions and to make space the "absolute infinite" is the merest assumption. The same can be postulated of time; it cannot have any beginning or end, i.e. limits in time. This is self-evident, so that time is infinite, but it is even more limited by definition than space, being only one-dimensional. Let us freely allow Haeckel an infinite physical universe, i.e. infinite in so far as space and time are concerned, but limited by the definition of "physical." But let us not assume it to be the "absolute infinite" and deny the existence of the infinite spiritual universe ... may be an infinity of infinite universes.

Space and time are the necessary conditions for physical existence. An interesting hypothesis has been put forward by H. G. Wells in fictional form in his *Time Machine* that space and time are really one, time being the "fourth dimension." In its favor is the fact that the one dimension of time is equally essential as the three spatial dimensions for physical existence. The question arises "Is there a super-space, a super-time?" A *priori* we should answer "Yes"; for if we find it impossible to imagine limits to any of the known dimensions, should we not likewise demand an infinity of dimensions? If the existence of super-space and super-time are postulated a host of otherwise inexplicable phenomena (generally termed "occult" or "spiritualistic" become more readily understood; it seems illogical and moreover unjust to *A priori* label all such phenomena "fraud" or "hallucination," merely because they will not fit in with preconceived notions. This argument for super-space has been dealt with already by other authors; the notion of a super-time has been somewhat neglected. The second use of the word infinite is substantive—"The Absolute Infinite"—That which is All in All, God. The theologian of the past century imagined God up in the sky (so to speak), somewhere entirely out of this world; then He is not Infinite absolutely; a not unsimilar error, fostered by a literal interpretation of the Bible (forgetting that "the letter killeth, but the spirit giveth life", is to imagine creation to have taken place once and for all at some point in time, an assumption involving a change in the Absolute Infinite!

Infinite space is but the finite unit (relatively speaking) of the infinite immensity of the Absolute Infinite, infinite time, but the finite unit of the infinite eternity of the Absolute Infinite. God may be said to be in all space and time, but also, He transcends both, so more truly, should we say space and time are in God. Creation is a continuous causal process extending through all space and time but also transcending both, therefore should we also say space and tune are in creation. What do we mean by such terms as "Personality," "Self-Consciousness"? Whatever may be said in reply, it is admitted that these terms imply the highest products of creation (or, if you prefer it, evolution). Should we therefore deny these attributes to God? Everything that is good and true and not essentially productive of Imitation must be the attributes of God, with this difference, that in Him these attributes will transcend the best of ours. Before concluding, another fallacy must be exploded. The two doctrines, the one of immortality, the other that our existence per se commences at conception, have been held to be mutually exclusive, for it is said that which has a beginning has an end, that which has no end has no beginning, i.e. in any dimension that which has one limit has another. This latter is true, but nevertheless misleading, for it suggests that which has no end never could have had a beginning, which is not true.

To take an illustration from mathematics. Mathematicians agree that the circumference of a circle of infinite radius is a straight line. Take a finite straight line and continually increase it in one direction; so long as it is finite, it has both end and beginning; but if it be increased without limit, it has truly neither end or beginning, being the circumference of a circle, i.e. so long as it has one limit in length it has another yet in the process of its formation it had both beginning and end. Is not this equally true of us? During our formation as perfect spiritual men and women—our earth life—we can point to a beginning and an end in time and to limits in all directions in space. These are not the true limits of the spirit, but are imposed upon it by its close association with our material, space and time-bound body. On our passage to the world of super space and super-time—that is death—we become, as it were, relative to space and time as the line became on production without limit, we are infinite as regards space and time and know no limits of either. Where and when cannot be postulated of spirit. It is, however, necessary that we are subject to that which is to us as spiritual, as were space and time to us as physical. Swedenborg teaches that this appearance of space and time corresponds to states and progression of state.

H. Stanley Redgrove

ON MATTER AND SPIRIT

DURING the past few years, a remarkable change has taken place in the attitude of physical science towards matter. It is no longer regarded as the all in all of the Cosmos and the final explanation of all that is, but as something unsubstantial, a phenomenon itself to be explained. Even from the standpoint of the atomic theory, we see how relatively unsubstantial matter is. What appears so very solid is far from being so; if we could compress a lump of matter of, say, the size of a football until the distances between its constituent atoms vanished, we should have a remarkably small amount left. And now the atoms are regarded no longer as the absolute units, indivisible and eternal gods of nature, but are seen to be themselves capable of disintegration. It is clear, therefore, that the so-called direct evidence of the senses is, in a sense, misleading; the senses inform us of phenomena, not substance, and we are the more inclined to turn to idealism for a solution of the Cosmos.

The change in the attitude of physical science with regard to the ether is equally remarkable and equally significant; admitted tentatively as a probable hypothesis, regarded almost as nothing, so Very unsubstantial was it thought to be, and now—". . . the ether is being found to constitute matter," says Sir Oliver Lodge, and proceeds to point out that the density of the ether must be enormously great; "Yes, far denser—so dense that matter by comparison is like gossamer, or a filmy imperceptible mist, or a milky way. Not unreal or unimportant—a cobweb is not unreal, nor to certain creatures is it unimportant, but it cannot be said to be massive or dense; and matter, even platinum, is not dense when compared with the ether." "... Undoubtedly, the ether belongs to the material or physical universe, but it is not ordinary matter. I should prefer to say it is not 'matter' at all. It may be the substance or substratum or material of which matter is composed, but it would be confusing and inconvenient not to be able to discriminate between matter on the one hand and ether on the other. If you tie a knot in a bit of string, the knot is composed of string, but the string is not composed of knots."

Yet there are "things that are unseen" which are even more substantial than the ether—things of the spirit. What is spirit? What is matter? These are the questions that are at the very basis of philosophy, and if we can only get at the root of them, we may hope for the solution of relatively minor difficulties. It is surprising that in the past, many of those who have believed in the existence of spirit, have, nevertheless, generally regarded spirit as something almost unreal, something unsubstantial, something, in the old sense of the word, ethereal; and this paradoxical position is not unknown today. We see it in the crude materialistic belief of orthodox Christianity, a belief, however, which happily is fast dying out, that at the resurrection it will be necessary for our spirits to be reclothed in our cast-off material bodies. No one seems to have seen the manifest absurdity of this position and to have apprehended the reality and substantiality of spirit better than Swedenborg (though we might also mention such names as Descartes and Berkeley); for him, the spirit was the real man, the material body but the garment; and he argued convincingly for this thesis. And is not this so; for in what does personal identity consist? Not in the material frame, for physiology shows conclusively that our material bodies are continually changing, and that in at least seven years (probably in less time) we each possess an entirely new body. Yet I am still I. It might be argued that personal identity consists in memory.

Now, memory certainly is a manifestation and proof of personal identity, but it cannot be its cause, since if it were, we should have the curious paradox that during those periods which I cannot remember, I was not I; which is manifestly absurd. The only satisfactory solution of personal identity is to be found in spirit. It seems to be generally taken for granted that, whereas we have absolute and direct evidence for the existence of matter, the existence of spirit is rather a matter of inference or belief; in fact, however, the reverse would be somewhat nearer the truth. The evidence for the existence of matter amounts to this: we are aware of sensations (i.e. certain modifications in states of consciousness), and for certain reasons—of which the chief is that, whereas the images of the imagination are almost perfectly under our control, i.e. we can cause a mental image to vary at pleasure or even disappear by mere volition, sensations are only slightly (relatively speaking) under our control—we conclude that sensations are due to an external world, putting forward the hypothesis of matter—"permanent possibility of sensation"—in explanation. We do not know matter in itself, what we do know and experience are changes in states of consciousness. Consequently, we infer from sensation the existence of our own body with the rest of the external world.

Here is the crux of the matter—I infer the existence of my material body, but I know I exist. Introspection at once reveals the fact that I am not my body, otherwise the above process would be impossible. Then what am I? Clearly, therefore, a general term for the ego is required; such a term is "spirit." We do not go to the length of that thorough-going idealism (such as "Christian Science" appears to be) which denies the existence of matter: such a philosophy leads to absurdity. It is quite evident that there is an external world, but it is essential to insist upon the point that we know it only in terms of consciousness. As Professor Huxley wrote: "If the materialist affirms that the universe and all its phenomena are resolvable into matter and motion, Berkeley replies, True; but what you call matter and motion are known to us only as forms of consciousness; their being is to be conceived or known; and the existence of a state of consciousness, apart from a thinking mind, is a contradiction in terms. "I conceive that this reasoning is irrefragable. And, therefore, if I were obliged to choose between absolute materialism and absolute idealism, I should feel compelled to accept the latter alternative." And again, ". . . the most elementary study of sensation justifies Descartes position, that we know more of mind than we do of body; that the immaterial world is a firmer reality than the material. For the sensation, 'muskiness' [for example] is known immediately. So long as it persists, it is a part of what we call our thinking selves, and its existence lies beyond the possibility of doubt. The knowledge of an objective or material cause of the sensation, on the other hand, is mediate; it is a belief as contradistinguished from an intuition; and it is a belief which, in any given instance of sensation, may, by possibility, be devoid of foundation."

It is, therefore, not matter, but spirit that we know, and by this be it understood that I know myself as such, and the external world as an ideal construction in my mind; but do I know that other spirits like to myself exist? That we have evidence for the existence of other spirits through their manifestations on the material plane is apparent; thus, I know my friends John Smith and James Brown in the sense I know matter, that is to say, on account of various sensations infer their existence as material bodies, and from the characteristics manifested by these material bodies, fudging from myself, I conclude John Smith and James Brown to be spirits (spirits manifested on the material plane, that is). The evidence brought forward by mediumistic spiritualism for the existence of spirits other than those manifesting themselves normally on the physical plane is of a similar nature. It is claimed that "discarnate" spirits manifest themselves on the physical plane through the instrumentality of the bodies of "mediums," producing such phenomena as "automatic speaking and writing." Some spiritualists believe that in certain cases, manifestation takes place through a material body manufactured or caused in some way by the spirit for the occasion. The evidence for the former class of these phenomena is, we think, of a convincing nature (too little is known about the latter class of phenomena—materializations, as they are called—to discuss their validity in the present article). But such evidence must in the nature of things be indirect—though not necessarily valueless or illusory—for it is, so to speak, the manifestation of spirit to spirit through the plane of matter. The question naturally arises, "Is there no direct perception of spirit possible to spirit?"

It seems that in telepathy we have some evidence of a partially latent spirit-sense, and in this case the apparently direct nature of telepathic communications is most significant. Telepathy can be regarded from the percipient's point of view as spirit-hearing; and if this is so, may there not be other spirit senses as well? Indeed, does not our own consciousness tell us that there are. We all speak of the "mind's eye" without, it appears, being fully aware of what is thereby implied. Our spiritual sight—our mind's eye—perceives only the objects of our own small spiritual spheres—the ideas comprised within our own minds,—yet it does not seem impossible that the spirit senses might be opened to a wider field of view, and, indeed, this must be the case in that awakening which we call death. It is the claim of the seers (in particular Swedenborg) that their spiritual senses have been opened to their spiritual environment. From what has been said above we shall be the better able to estimate at its full worth such of their claims as can be substantiated by evidence—for here we have direct experiential information of the world of spirit—and we consider such evidence is to be found in the case of the Swedish seer at least. Swedenborg's visions far surpassed those of other seers, both with regard to quantity and quality. They are always clearly and lucidly described, whereas the visions of other seers appear to be so often characterized by haziness and vagueness. We see how well his training in natural science became him as a seer; in his writings we have no emotional rhapsodies but a profound system of rational philosophy. It is also worth noticing that Swedenborg is the one seer for the validity of whose visions there is satisfactory external evidence—we have the testimony of no less an authority than Immanuel Kant.

There is a common tendency to explain away all such experiences by describing them as subjective; in the world of spirit, however, the exact difference between the subjective and the objective is by no means obvious. "The Kingdom of Heaven is within you," it was once truly said. It seems to be generally taken for granted that the objective is real and the subjective, unreal, but from the idealistic point of view this may be questioned. The snakes of *delirium tremens* are quite real to the dipsomaniac, although quite unreal to us. As Professor Huxley wrote"... 'subjective' sensations are as real existences as any others." Indeed, one might say that the real world for each one of us is the world as it exists in each of our minds. In a certain sense, the saying that each one of us makes his own heaven or hell has an application here. However, the objection might be raised that this view would make reality purely relative. This objection is perfectly valid, but, as we hope to make plain in a later essay, the real—the absolutely real—world is the world as it exists in the Mind of the Divine.

To return to the discussion of spiritual perception. It should be noticed that such perception must involve a considerable element of relativity or symbolism. This appears to be the case to some extent in ordinary perception; for example, we do not suppose that a sunset appears the same to the scientist, the artist, and the uneducated man; and this difference has its origin, not in the external reality (whatever it may be) giving rise to the impression of a sunset, not in the physical sense organs of the observers, but in their minds—it is spiritual in origin. The appearance of things in this world depends partly upon the mind of the observer, and it is to be concluded that this factor will be even more prominent in the perception of the spiritual world. In the very nature of things, there must be a difference between a thing and the percept of it—to demand that direct experiential knowledge must imply their identity is to demand an impossibility. Spiritual perception is in a sense direct and in a sense symbolic. Moreover, from what has been said above, we must distinguish between spiritual percepts which inform of true reality—reality which is true for other spirits—such as the visions of Swedenborg, and those subjective sensations whose reality is purely relative.

To summarize the main argument of this essay. We know matter only through and in terms of consciousness, i.e. as an ideal construction. An extreme idealism has sometimes interpreted this as implying the non-existence of the material world, but this view we entirely reject. If there were not some exact ratio or correspondence between our percepts of the external world and the external reality giving rise to them, what may be termed the harmony or unity of experience would be impossible to understand—there would be no such harmony or unity. A less extreme idealism regards matter as non-existent apart from mind, and if by mind is not understood our individual minds but the Divine Mind, then this view is in agreement with the thesis to be maintained in a later essay. As to the reality of spirit, we have absolute evidence in our own consciousness as regards ourselves as individual spirits, and it appears that Swedenborg and perhaps other seers have experienced a direct perception of a wider spiritual universe.

ON THE SELF-EXISTENT

BY "being" we understand anything that exists, and that something does exist, i.e. that being is, is a fact of absolute knowledge. Now the genus "being" can be divided logically into two species, namely, that which is self-existent, i.e. that which requires no antecedent being to explain its existence, and that which is not self-existent, i.e. that which does require some antecedent being to explain its existence. Also, that which does exist must be either one or many. Let us consider these two alternatives. Firstly, suppose only one being to exist, then it must be self-existent, for otherwise the existence of some antecedent being would be postulated, which is contrary to hypothesis. Secondly, suppose more than one being to exist, then at least one must be self-existent, for otherwise, as in the above case, some other being would be necessitated contrary to hypothesis to explain the existence of such. Or, if it could be supposed (which, however, does not appear possible,) that such beings could mutually explain one another's existence, then the complex regarded as a whole would be self-existent being. Consequently, we conclude, as absolutely certain, that self-existent being is.

The next question that arises is whether self-existent being is one or many. There have been in the past, great minds who have been content with a dualistic view of the Cosmos, but the modern tendency is essentially monistic. It may be, indeed, difficult to explain matter and spirit in terms of one substance, still, notwithstanding, it has been felt that this must be possible. To solve the riddle of the universe in terms of two or more self-existent beings does not satisfy the human mind, and appears to be no solution. We can rest satisfied only with Unity. Consequently, we postulate the essential oneness of the self-existent, and term such Being True and Absolute Substance, or more simply, God; and using the term "God" with this wide and perfectly accurate meaning, namely, that of Self-existent Being, we can state, without fear of contradiction, that everyone believes in God. A real atheist is not only unknown, but an impossibility. The so-called atheist merely denies this and that view of God; he cannot deny God.

"Everything has a cause," commences an argument which is often employed to demonstrate the existence of God, "... and therefore there is a First Cause—God." Says the atheist, "If everything has a cause, what caused God?" And he fondly imagines that he has thus disproved God's existence! Is this so? Certainly not. What the atheist has done is to show that the statement "everything has a cause" lands us in a false position, inasmuch as there is that which has no cause—God. And now we come to the great question—What is God the Self-Existent? What is True and Absolute Substance? What is That which requires no explanation for its Being? "Matter," replies Materialism, "the eternal atoms—these are our gods." And we turn to Science and ask, "Is this so?" And Science sighs. "Ah! me," she says, "I, too, used to think that way, the way of Materialism, once, and I used to talk of the indestructibility of matter and the eternal atoms; but deep down in my heart, I always found it hard to believe in sixty or seventy-odd gods, and felt that a monistic explanation must be forthcoming. And once I took an atom in my hand—radium 'tis called—and lo and behold! it exploded into a thousand tiny fragments—some, tiny units of electricity—and then I knew Materialism to be false.

'What is matter?' you ask; that I cannot say for certain, probably the manifestation of electrical forces, probably (if we push the analysis a step further) a singularity in the ether, but the self-existent—certainly not!" And we turn to Philosophy and put the same query, "Does Materialism speak that which is true?" And Philosophy, being in a skeptical mood, laughs. "Matter," she says, "what is matter? What is it but a symbol I create in my mind? I touch, I taste, I see—what? I am conscious, that is the fact I know, and I cadi the varying modes in which I am conscious by different names; some modes of consciousness, those I call by such names as seeing, tasting, touching, I have good reason for believing arise in some way on account of an external world, but what is this external world? Ask me of consciousness, not of matter; I know not matter!" We have seen in the essay "On Matter and Spirit" that from the standpoint of physical science, matter is to be regarded as a phenomenon, and since a phenomenon by definition implies some antecedent being, matter cannot be self-existent. From the standpoint of philosophy, the phenomenal nature of matter is more clearly manifest. For, as has been pointed out in the essay referred to above, it is states of consciousness we experience, and therefore the existence of mind, of spirit which we know, and that of matter which we infer. And since we know matter only through and in terms of consciousness, it is evident that in matter can never be found an intelligible explanation of consciousness, and hence, that spirit or mind can never be reduced to terms of matter. Is God conscious or unconscious? Is it necessary to ask this question—can consciousness be derived from and find its explanation in that which is unconscious? It is matter which is the mystery to be explained, not consciousness. An intelligible explanation of the Cosmos must be expressed in terms of the immediately known—consciousness or spirit; we must attempt, not to explain the Cosmos in terms of matter, for this would result in unintelligibility, but in terms of consciousness, in terms, say, of Will or Love, for will and love are immediately known. God must be not only conscious, but conscious in the highest degree, hence self-conscious. He must Know and Will and Love. He must be the Absolute Infinite. And this is because He is the origin and explanation of the totality of being.

Now, the origin of all being cannot be found in disorder and contradiction, hence it cannot be found in evil; God must be Good. And because He is the Absolute Infinite, therefore, He must be Infinitely Good, Infinitely Wise, Infinitely

H. Stanley Redgrove

Powerful, and Infinitely Loving, all in a most transcendent degree. In what words shall we describe God? Alas! our words express only relatively finite ideas. With what shall we compare God? There is no comparison between the infinite and the finite; yet, when we carefully consider the conclusions we have reached, it seems clear that God is more like to man—and by this is meant like to what is called the spiritual part of man, but what is, in reality, man—considered in the ideal as sinless and perfect, than He is like to that which we call matter—unconscious matter, or that which we call force—blind force. Pantheism and orthodox Christian theology have each realized one-half of a great eternal truth. Pantheism insists on the fact of God's immanence in the physical universe, but makes the mistake of identifying God, either with the totality of matter, as in materialistic pantheism; or with the totality of human souls, as in spiritualistic pantheism. On the other hand, the orthodox Churches teach a belief in the Personality and Transcendency of God—that He is a conscious, loving, willing Being, transcending all else that is—but fails to fully realize His immanence in Nature.

In fact, it has been held that these two doctrines are mutually exclusive, and that God cannot be a transcendent Personality and at the same time immanent in all that is. By his Doctrine of Degrees, however, Swedenborg not only reconciled these two apparently conflicting doctrines, but showed their essential oneness. And is this not so? For must not God as its sole material and efficient cause (using the terms in the Aristotelian sense) be immanent in and yet transcend the whole universe? Sir Oliver Lodge's illustration to help us to understand the probable connection between the ether and matter—a knot in a bit of string—which we have already noted and found useful on another occasion, will help us to understand better, also, the relation existing between God and the physical universe.

The trend of modern physics is towards the view that matter owes its existence to the ether—that it is a phenomenon given rise to by some singularity in the ether, a little bit of ether partitioned off from the rest. Speaking in terms of the above illustration, we might call matter a knot or twist in the ether. In an analogous manner, we regard the physical universe as a sort of "knot" or "twist" in God; God ever creates Nature from the Substance of Himself by defining it and giving it concrete form. Clearly, therefore, where the physical universe is there must be God, for the physical universe is God-made in the truest sense; but the converse proposition—that where God is there must be the realm of the physical extend—by no means follows. And this must be understood in a metaphysical rather than a physical sense, super-spatially and super-temporally rather than spatially and temporally; so that, in other words, God, whilst transcending all Creation—all that proceeds from Him—must yet be necessarily immanent in it all, immanent in all that exists, for in essence the whole of being is God. One of the factors that has helped in the obliteration of this grand dual truth is a non-comprehension of the ambiguous nature of the word "infinite," a non-comprehension of the vast difference between the mathematical use of the term as applied to space or time, and the transcendent meaning of the term as applied to the Absolute—God. As we have had occasion to remark in a former essay, "The theologian of the past century imagined God up in the sky (so to speak) somewhere entirely out of this world; then He is not Infinite absolutely."

"Others have argued that, as space and time are infinite, God must be comprised within these limits; one materialist, indeed, went to the length of denying God's existence since he could not see His brain with a telescope! But in the essay referred to above, it was shown that space and time are infinite only in the mathematical meaning of the term and not absolutely. The very meaning of the term Absolute Infinite demands that God must be in all space and time and must transcend all space and time, for otherwise, the Absolute would be limited by space and time;—in the one case, were God merely transcendent, excluded without these limits; in the other case, were God merely immanent, included within. This being so, it would be more correct to speak of all space and time as being in It has been argued that an immanent God could not be a Personality, and by this term personality we mean a self-conscious being—a being who knows and loves and wills. But from experience, we should conclude precisely the opposite. For are we not ourselves personalities, and are we not immanent in our physical bodies (though in a less true and absolute sense than that in which God is immanent in the physical universe?)

Our immanence is clearly demonstrated by the fact that the unreflective man usually identifies himself with his body (indeed, most of us are guilty of this in unreflective moments), just as the pantheist identifies God with Nature. Our transcendence is clearly shown by the fact that reflection indisputably demonstrates the difference between the ego—the true self—and the physical body. In this connection the ancient mystic doctrine that each man is a replica in small of the whole universe is interesting. For if man can be regarded as the microcosm, the universe as the macrocosm, then, changing the figure, we might speak of the universe as the Grand Man; and the Soul of this Man—the Real Man, of which the physical universe is the manifestation, is God. We see, therefore, that in their affirmative aspects both the pantheistic and transcendental views of God are valid, but they need to be combined one with the other if we would at all realize the truth.

Forgotten Essays

ON CREATION

BY the term "creation" we wish to imply the causal relationship existing between Self-Existent Being and all being which is thence derived—between God and Nature; and we think that this relationship is well expressed by the term, if it is no longer thought of as implying the old erroneous *ex-nihilo* ideas with which it has been long associated. However, before proceeding with the amplification of the doctrine of creation implied in the essay "On the Self-Existent" (and for which we willingly acknowledge our indebtedness to Swedenborg), it will not be out of place to criticize briefly certain ideas regarding the creation process current during the past century; and this is the more necessary since these fallacious views have not altogether been thrown aside.

According to the orthodox theology of the nineteenth century God, at some point in time—and for our present discussion it matters not whether this point be supposed to have been six thousand or six billion (or more) years ago—decided to create the universe. Why, we are not told, unless it was for His own glory. God awoke, so it appears from this theory, from a period of inactivity, spoke the word, and a universe sprang into being out of nothing. Some suppose this to have taken six days. The control of the universe was given over to certain "laws of nature," and God, presumably, retired into a state of inactivity to awake only at rare intervals, when the above "laws" are overcome and a "miracle" results. It is supposed that at some more or less distant date, God will annihilate the universe which He has created.

Could any doctrine be more utterly absurd? It can be compared only with "the fortuitous concourse of the eternal atoms" of the so-called rationalist, who supposes that the order of the Cosmos is explicable in terms of chance! Let us examine its chief errors, since thereby we may hope to come to a right understanding of the creation process, (1) It supposes a change in the Absolute Infinite, and caps its error in this respect by supposing that God will annihilate that which He has brought into being. If at any point in time God has created, then He must have ever created and will forever create—He will not change. (2) It supposes that something could come out of nothing and thence return, an idea so utterly absurd and opposed to thought itself as not to merit discussion. In order to overcome this objection, another theory supposes creation to have been the reducing to order of a chaos. We ask, "Whence the chaos?" To continue.—(3) It misunderstands what is meant by a law of nature. No law of nature can answer the question "Why?" and no scientific man supposes that it can. A law of nature is simply a statement in terms as general as possible of what happens under given circumstances, i.e. the expression of an observed order or uniformity in natural phenomena. In reply to the question "Why does this pen fall when I let go of it?" for example, we might say "Because of the law of gravity," but really and truly this does not explain why at all. The answer simply shows that the falling of the pen is one of a number of phenomena, all of which exhibit a certain sameness, and it is this sameness or uniformity reduced to general terms which we call the law of gravity. And supposing, for the sake of illustration, that Le Sage's gravitation hypothesis was true, this would mean merely that there is a sameness between gravitation phenomena and the phenomena exhibited by colliding bodies in general. It would imply a wider and more fundamental uniformity, and would, in this sense, make the phenomena more easy to understand; but the philosopher would still ask "Why?"—"Why do colliding bodies exhibit these characteristics?" The final "Why?" no law of nature can ever answer.

If we are to get any right understanding of the relation or process we call creation, it is essential that we free our minds from the limitations imposed by the notions of time and space, and think in terms other than these. After all, what are time and space that they should dominate our thought? From the objective point of view, they are merely the conditions for material existence; from the subjective point of view, they are merely "modes of consciousness"—ways we have of regarding things. We all appear to be disposed to think of all things as arranged in either or both of two sequences—the space sequence, and the time sequence—but neither is the absolute order of being. This absolute ontological order is the one of cause and effect. We must no longer think of things as being one antecedent to the other in point of time, or in point of space, but as cause antecedent to effect.

Now, cause and effect may exist at exactly the same time and in exactly the same place, for they are in different planes of being respectively; and in the case of a "material" (or, as we would prefer to put it, "substantial" or "essential") cause this must necessarily be true; for example, the illustration of the string and the knot, or the ether and the knot in the ether—matter. Hence, as we have already pointed out in a former essay, God is in all space and time, but, since He also transcends all space and time, we have seen that it would be more correct to say that space and time are in God. Let us apply this to the creation process. In space and in time, creation has never begun, and it will never end; else the Absolute is variable. Hence, the physical universe fills infinite space; it has existed from infinite time and will exist to infinite time, for it is being ever created. We can speak of a beginning to creation only in reference to the absolute order of being, the end, cause-and-effect sequence. It begins, therefore, with God—the Substance of God's Being is the basis out of which all that exists is created—it proceeds through matter, up through the vegetable and animal kingdoms, and finally man, back to God. Since it begins with God, creation, though in all time and space, transcends all time and space, so that we may speak of time and space as in creation.

H. Stanley Redgrove

Difficulty may be found in realizing creation as a perpetual process—ever present and eternally active—unless we clearly distinguish creation from mere making, and realize that creation is causation proceeding from the Self-Existent. An illustration may help. In terms of the electronic theory of matter, the atom is a system of tiny particles of electricity—the electrons—in rapid motion. Now, this motion is an integral part of the atom. So long as the electrons whirl around, the atom exists; if they were to cease whirling, the atom would vanish from existence. We have already likened the physical universe to a sort of knot or twist in the Substance of God, and the illustration has served its purpose. But it suggests a static rather than a dynamic view—a knot in a bit of string has not to be perpetually made. We must think of the twist as eternally twisting, or take some such analogy as the atom with its whirling electrons. Science eloquently teaches that all Nature is permeated with activity. At the same time, however, there is a difficulty in conceiving motion in the Substance of the Self-Existent as the initial process in creation, since motion implies a certain heterogeneity and differentiation. The tendency of physical science in the past has been to reduce everything to matter and motion, but at the present time, the analysis is being pushed a step further. We have noted already that it appears highly probable that matter is resolvable into the ether; but this is only half of the modem formula of physics; it appears that matter and motion are explicable in terms of ether and stress. Herein, probably, will be found the explanation of the above difficulty.

By means of the doctrine of creation we have striven to make plain herein we believe that the old problem of the synthesis of idealism and materialism may be solved. We do not mean that idealism which denies the existence of the objective world, nor the materialism which teaches that matter is the all in all, and that consciousness is the mere by-product—an epiphenomenon—of material forces. We mean rather that idealism which looks to consciousness, to mind, for ultimate reality and the final explanation of all being; and the materialism such as is necessarily held by the physical scientist—the materialism which believes in the reality of an objective, external world, and that the senses do not altogether delude us.

We have dealt with the relative claims of these systems of thought in a former essay, and it must, we think, be admitted that, if there were no alternative, then we are bound by logic and reason to be pure idealists; but although we know that spirit is, we have good evidence for believing that an external world, that matter exists. Idealism is logical, materialism is practical: is there no synthesis of the two? A synthesis, be it noted, into a monistic system, for a dualism with matter and spirit, as conflicting elements will never satisfy our reason.

We have shown that God and the physical universe are related as cause is to effect, but it seems reasonable to suppose that there is some intermediate factor between the two; indeed, must there not extend a vast ontological series of causes and effects from God to matter, of which each factor is the cause of the succeeding or consequent, and the effect of the preceding or antecedent? We think so; and taking into consideration the characteristics of spirit we conclude that it is such an intermediate factor, related to matter as cause, to God as effect, in a somewhat similar manner to that in which (if these views as to the nature of the atom are correct) the electron may be regarded as related to the atom as cause, to the ether as effect. This must not be taken to mean that I—"my spirit"—am the cause of my body, but that in general spirit is the mediate cause of the totality of matter—the means (first created by and from the Divine Substance) employed by God in the creation or causation of matter; i.e. speaking not with regard to time but with regard to the ontological sequence, God first creates spirit, and thereby creates matter. Both matter and spirit are true and real, but on different planes of being, of which the spiritual is the higher. They are discrete; that is to say, spirit is not a very fine matter, or matter a very gross spirit, but they are related as cause is to effect. This is a point which must be insisted upon, namely that cause and effect are quite distinct and discrete; that, although they correspond, they do not merge one into the other. To take our illustration of the electronic theory again, the electron, according to this view, is the cause of the atom, but atom and electron are quite distinct and discrete, it is not a question of mere size; the atom of hydrogen is not a big electron, or the electron a little atom of hydrogen, they have quite different properties.

If we prefer the language of psychology to that of physics—though this is to a great extent merely a verbal distinction; still, psychology is a science of spirit rather than of matter, and, since spirit is the higher plane, psychology will, perhaps, yield the truer mode of expression—we may quite correctly speak of the physical universe as an idea in the mind of God, but this does not mean that it is in any sense unreal—to be an idea in the Divine Mind is the essence of reality, nought is real save that which is such. And it is because spirit is what it is, because of our likeness (faint though it may be) to God, that this real physical universe is possible to some extent to us as an ideal construction corresponding to the Divine ideal construction. The "external" world we know is the world as it exists in each of our minds, the real "external" world is the world as it exists in the Divine Mind; in so far, then, as our ideal constructions are like to the Divine do we know Reality.

THE THEORY AND PRACTICE OF MAGIC

It is only because of the feebleness of our perceptions and activity that we do not perceive ourselves to be in a fairy world.—Novalis.

1. The Doctrine of Emanations

Magic is usually defined as the (pretended) art of producing marvelous results by the aid of spirits or arcane spiritual forces. It follows, therefore, that those of us who do not hold the simple faith of the materialist must recognize the possibility of a genuine Magic, even though all the magical beliefs of the past be false. The subject of Magic is admittedly interesting as a study of the striving of the human mind after a knowledge of the Cosmos; but how more interesting does it become, if, perchance, within the gross crudities and superstitious absurdities of magical belief, some element of truth lies hidden, perverted and distorted?

In all ages of mankind, is to be found a belief in a spiritual world and attempts to enter into communication with its inhabitants and to utilize its forces; but within the confines of a brief paper such as the following, it would be quite impossible to deal with the history of Magic in any adequate manner. We must content ourselves with a far more restricted program. In the first place, let us briefly consider the doctrine of Emanations, a theory of very great importance in the magical philosophy of the past. According to this theory, all creation is effected by an emanation from the Divine, from which all things derive their various virtues. The divine emanation is supposed to descend step by step (so to speak) through the hierarchies of angels and the stars down to the things of earth, that which is nearer to the Source containing more of the divine nature than that which is relatively distant. As Cornelius Agrippa expresses it—

H. Stanley Redgrove

"For God, in the first place, is the end and beginning of all Virtues; he gives the seal of the Ideas to his servants, the Intelligences; who, as faithful officers, sign all things entrusted to them with an Ideal Virtue; the Heavens and Stars, as instruments, disposing the matter in the meanwhile for the receiving of those forms which reside in Divine Majesty as saith Plato in Timeus) and to be conveyed by Stare; and the Giver of Forms distributes them by the ministry of his Intelligences, which he hath set as Rulers and Controllers over his Works, to whom such a power is entrusted to things committed to them that so all Virtues of Stones, Herbs, Metals, and all other things may come from the Intelligences, the Governors. The Form, therefore, and Virtue of things comes first from the Ideas, then from the ruling and governing Intelligences, then from the aspects of the Heavens disposing, and lastly from the tempers of the Elements disposed, answering the influences of the Heavens, by which the Elements themselves are ordered, or disposed. These kinds of operations, therefore, are performed in these inferior things by express forms, and in the Heavens by disposing virtues, in Intelligences by mediating rules, in the Original Cause by Ideas and exemplary forms, all which must

TABLE OF OCCULT CORRESPONDENCES.*

Arch-angel.	Angel.	Planet.	Day of the Week.	Part of Human Body.	Animal.	Bird.	Precious Stone.	Metal.	Colour.
Raphael	Michael	Sun	Sunday	Heart	Lion	Swan	Carbuncle	Gold	Gold or Yellow
Gabriel	Gabriel	Moon	Monday	Left Foot	Cat	Owl	Crystal	Silver	Silver or White
Camael	Zamael	Mars	Tuesday	Right Hand	Wolf	Vulture	Diamond	Iron	Red
Michael	Raphael	Mercury	Wednesday	Left Hand	Ape	Stork	Agate	Mercury	Mixed Colours or Purple
Zadkiel	Sachiel	Jupiter	Thursday	Head	Stag	Eagle	Sapphire	Tin	Violet or Blue
Haniel	Anael	Venus	Friday	Generative Organs	Goat	Dove	Emerald	Copper	Turquoise or Green
Zaphkiel	Cassiel	Saturn	Saturday	Right Foot	Mole	Hoopo	Onyx	Lead	Black

* Most of these details are from Cornelius Agrippa's *Occult Philosophy*, Book II., Chap. x.

Forgotten Essays

of necessity agree in the execution of the effect and virtue of everything. There is, therefore, a wonderful virtue and operation in every Herb and Stone, but greater in a Star, beyond which, even from the governing Intelligences everything receiveth and obtains many things for itself, especially from the Supreme Cause, with whom all things do mutually and exactly correspond, agreeing in a harmonious consent, as it were in hymns, always praising the highest Maker of all things... There is, therefore, no other cause of the necessity of effects than the connection of all things with the First Cause, and their correspondency with those Divine patterns and eternal Ideas whence everything hath its determinate and particular place in the exemplary world, from whence it lives and receives its original being: And every virtue of herbs, stones, metals, animals, words and speeches, and all things that are of God, is placed here."

The fundamental doctrine of occult philosophy is that of

HENRY CORNELIUS AGRIPPA VON NETTESHEIM.
(1486-1535.)

the unity of the Cosmos; the universe is one vast harmonious whole, and hence, there is some exact analogy, correspondence, or sympathetic relation between its various parts. "What is above is as that which is below, what is below is as that which is above," or as Agrippa puts it: "Through the sympathy of similar, and the antipathy of dissimilar things, all creation hangs together; the things of a particular world

- 33 -

within itself, as well as with the congenial things of another world." All occult arts have been based on these sympathetic relations supposed to exist between things inferior and things superior. Sympathetic Magic, the underlying assumption of which is that by acting on part of a thing or a symbolical representation of it, one acts magically on the whole, or on the thing symbolized, as the case may be, really includes all Magic, for all Magic is based on this assumption. The names of the Divine Being, angels and devils, the planets of the solar system (including sun and moon) and the days of the week, birds and beasts, colors, herbs and precious stones—all, according to old-time occult philosophy, are connected by the sympathetic relation running through all creation, the knowledge of which was essential to the magician; as well, also, the chief portions of the human body, for the old transcendentalists, especially Paracelsus, taught that man is a microcosm; a universe in miniature. In a former contribution, we have already given some of these supposed correspondences: a more complete set are exhibited in the following table, but it must be premised that authorities were by no means always unanimous with regard to all these details, which are, in many cases, based on quite trivial resemblances.

2. Medieval Ceremonial Magic

The ceremonial Magic of the Middle Ages was subdivided into three chief branches—White Magic, Black Magic, and Necromancy. White Magic was concerned with the evocation of angels—spiritual beings supposed to be essentially superior to mankind—and the spirits of the elements— beings which were regarded, apparently, as personifications of the primeval forces of Nature. Goety or Black Magic was concerned with the evocation of demons and devils—spirits supposed to be superior to man in certain powers, but utterly depraved. We may distinguish Sorcery (a term used also to designate Necromancy) from Witchcraft, the sorcerer attempting to command evil spirits by the aid of charms, etc., whereas the witch or wizard was supposed to have made a compact with the Evil One. Necromancy was concerned with the evocation of the spirits of the dead; properly, the term stands for the art of foretelling events by means of such evocations, though it is sometimes loosely employed in a wider sense. It would be unnecessary and tedious to give any detailed account of the methods employed in these magical arts, beyond some general remarks. Those who desire further information on these matters are referred to Mr. A. E. Waite's *Book of Ceremonial Magic*. We propose here to give the reader a very brief account of a magical evocation— Choosing a time when there is a favorable conjunction of the planets, the magician, armed with the implements of magical art, after much prayer and fasting, betakes himself to a suitable spot, alone, or, perhaps, accompanied by two trusty companions. All the articles he intends to employ, the vestments, the magic sword and lamp, the talismans, the book of spirits, etc., have been specially prepared and consecrated. If he is about to invoke a Martial spirit, the magician's vestment will be of a red color, the talismans in virtue of which he may have power over the spirit will be of iron, the day chosen a Tuesday, and the incense and perfumes employed of a nature analogous to Mars. In a similar manner, all the articles employed, and the rites performed must in some way be symbolical of the spirit with which converse is desired. Arriving at the spot, the magician, first of all tracing the magic circle within which, we are told, no evil spirit can enter, commences the magic rite, involving various prayers and conjurations, a medley of meaningless words, and, in the case of the black art, a sacrifice. The spirit summoned then appears (at least, so we are told), and, after granting the magician's requests, is licensed to depart—this latter is said to be most important.

3. The Psychology of Magic

The question naturally arises, What were the results obtained by these magical arts? How far, if at all, was the magician rewarded by the attainment of his desires? Now, with regard to the evocation of the various classes of spirits, one may be forgiven considerable skepticism with regard to the existence of the angels and devils of orthodox faith or of magical belief; and the spirits of the elements need not seriously be taken into account. Devils and angels, other than the spirits of evil and good men, respectively, are difficult to fit in with any philosophical view of the Cosmos, and the belief in their existence appears to depend on no better evidence than some few misunderstood passages in Holy Writ. With regard to Necromancy, it appears that what was aimed at was what is called in the terms of modern Occultism, "a materialization," though we fail to see for what reasons the spirits of the dead should be regarded as particularly well acquainted with future events. Now, the results of scientific psychical research go to show that if the "materialization" of a "discarnate" spirit be a possibility, it is a very rare phenomenon and extremely difficult of production; so that the most that we can say for Necromancy is that it may sometimes have been successful so far as the evocation of "departed" spirits is concerned. But whilst denying, in general, the production of such objective results by the carrying out of magical ritual, we must not forget that there is another side to the question. It cannot be doubted that magical rites must have had a most powerful effect upon the mind, weakened as the magician was by fasting and overpowered by the suffumigations **(The burning of substances to produce fumes as part of some magical rituals.)** employed, and would thereby result in remarkable and powerful subjective phenomena. Undoubtedly many magicians of old time imagined that they held converse with all sorts of spirits, including the Devil himself—non-existent though he be. It is to the powers of the imagination that we must ascribe, in at least the majority of cases, the apparent success, whenever obtained, of these and other magical practices; for it should be carefully noted that a firm faith in the Magic employed and a strong effort of will to bring about the desired result is insisted on in all branches of Magic (at least, by the advanced magician) as essential for success. It is not difficult to understand, therefore, that, under the conditions prescribed by magical doctrine, the imagination should conjure up out of the elements of the memory the apparent specters of "departed" personalities—a view of such phenomena in agreement with that expressed by Eliphas Levi. Indeed, taking into account such facts as those cases of hysterical patients, in which intense and unhealthy pondering of the wounds of Christ has resulted in stigmatization, i.e., the production of marks resembling these wounds on the patient's hands and feet, we would not altogether deny that, in certain other forms of Magic, actual objective results may have been brought about by the powers of the imagination, though we are certainly not prepared to admit all that Paracelsus says of these powers, or even to allow all the claims of modern "faith-healing." Since, however, we have already dealt with the question of the powers of the imagination in the essay "On the Belief in Talismans" before referred to, we shall not further discuss the question herein.

H. Stanley Redgrove

4. The Ethics of Magic

A further question, however, arises. In all magical operations, symbols play an essential part; so much so, indeed, that we may well qualify the definition of Magic already noted, defining Magic as "an attempt to employ the powers of the spiritual world for the production of marvelous results, by the aid of symbols. And we may well ask, Have symbols any real value or efficacy, or are their virtues of a purely imaginary order? This brings us to the definition of Magic (or, at least, of the equivalent Latin term, *magic*) given by Swedenborg, who, it should be noticed, almost invariably employs the word in an evil sense. "Magic," he says, "is nothing but the perversion of order, it is especially the abuse of correspondences." In Swedenborg's doctrines of Influx and Correspondences, we find the basic ideas of the old occult doctrines of Emanation and Sympathies presented in a new

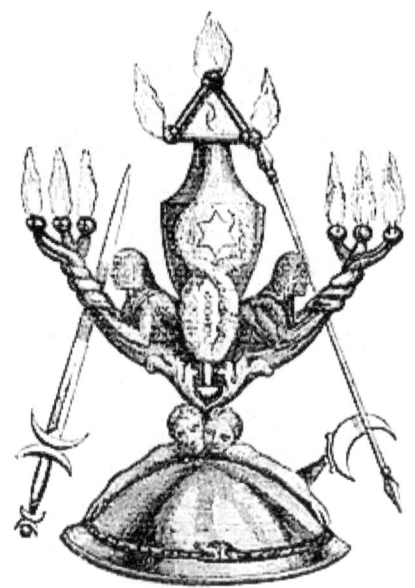

Magical Instruments. Lamp, Rod, Sword, and Dagger.

form, developed to their logical conclusions in such a manner as to appeal, we think, to modern thought. All causation, according to the Swedish philosopher, is spiritual in origin and results from an influx from the divine, though things of the material world may be regarded as "secondary" or instrumental causes. The divine influx descends through successive planes of being which are "discrete" from one another, that is to say, are not connected by continuity, but are related according to the sequence of causes and effects. Each plane of being or "discrete degree" of existence is symbolical of the higher and the prototype of the lower plane. All degrees are related by the grand law of analogy; everything physical has a correspondent on the spiritual plane, everything spiritual a correspondent on the physical plane. Such in brief are the basic ideas of these doctrines in question. Swedenborg uses the term "magic" as denoting a real power in the sense of an actuality, but an unreal power in so far as its results are always of the nature of illusion and fantasy. An examination of the nature of the Magic of the Middle Ages and the following century or two will, we think, show the appropriateness of Swedenborg's definition and the use of the term. The various practices of the past included within the category of Magic were almost entirely the result of evil motives. The distinction, rigid enough in theory, between White and Black, legitimate and illegitimate, Magic was extremely indefinite in practice. As Mr. A. E. Waite justly remarks "Much that passed current in the west as White (i.e. permissible) Magic was only a disguised goeticism, and many of the resplendent angels invoked with divine rites reveal their cloven hoofs. It is not too much to say that a large majority of past psychological experiments were conducted to establish communication with demons, and that for unlawful purposes. The popular conceptions concerning the diabolical spheres, which have been all accredited by magic, may have been gross exaggerations of fact concerning rudimentary and perverse intelligences, but the willful viciousness of the communicants is substantially untouched thereby."

At the same time, however, we propose to employ the term "Magic" in a somewhat different sense. The word itself is derived from Greek; the "wise man of the East", and hence the strict etymological meaning of the term is "the wisdom or science of the magi"; and as an evidence of the validity and ethical value of this true Magic, we must note that the magi were amongst the first to worship the new-born Christ. As a matter of fact, it is clear from a passage in his *Arcana Celestia* that this is Swedenborg's own position with regard to Magic. He says therein that by "magic" is signified "the science of spiritual things," and it is clear that he recognized that there is a genuine Magic, the true wisdom of the magi, and a false Magic, that wisdom perverted—a view of the subject with which our readers will probably agree. We shall, therefore, employ the term "Magic" in its original meaning of the genuine wisdom of the magi, the mystic science of correspondences. In short, we shall use it to stand for the real causal power of the Spirit and the real non-causal efficacy of the symbol.

5. The Efficacy of Symbols

The doctrine, of fundamental importance in Swedenborg's philosophy, that all causation proceeds from the spiritual to the material plane and not reversely, is one with which the spirit of ancient Occultism is thoroughly in accord, as witness, for example, the quotation from Agrippa given above; and we think also, that it is one with which modern transcendentalists will find themselves in agreement. But at first sight it may appear that the phenomenon of sensation stands in contradiction to this doctrine, for here, have we not external material objects causing internal psychical phenomena, as when, for example, the presence of sugar on my tongue gives rise to the sensation of sweetness? The whole question here involved is that of the intercourse of the soul and the body, which is dealt with fully in Swedenborg's little treatise on "Influx." He writes—"... the soul is a spiritual substance, and therefore purer, prior, and interior; but the body is material, and therefore grosser, posterior, and exterior; and it is according to order that the purer should flow into the grosser, the prior into the posterior, the interior into the exterior, thus what is spiritual into what is material, and not the contrary. Consequently, it is according to order for the thinking mind to flow into the sight according to the state induced on the eyes by the objects before them, which state that mind also disposes at its pleasure: and likewise for the perceptive mind to flow into the hearing, according to the state induced upon the ears by speech."

Novalis (Friederich von Hardenberg).
(1772-1801.)

Now, from this standpoint it follows that sensations are caused, not by external material bodies (unless by the term "caused" we imply mere antecedence), but by the powers of the spirit or, to carry the analysis a step further, by God—the origin of all influx. The spirit of man flows into his body (so to speak), this flow being modified by the states of the body, or, perhaps it would be more correct to say, modified by the states of the brain, which are determined by the states of the bodily sense-organs; and hence arise those modifications of states of consciousness which we call "sensations." Now, it should be noticed that the thing sensed and the sense-percept of it are entirely different or "discrete," for whilst the one is material, the other is psychical or spiritual. But it follows from the fact of the harmony of experience that there must be some exact ratio between the two; indeed, we hold that, apart from imperfections either of the sense-organs, etc., or of the percipient mind, there is an exact correspondence between the two—one is symbolical of the other. And since spirit is the prior, and is, indeed, more substantial and real than matter, it would be more correct (though contrary, perhaps, to the common way of regarding things) to describe the object sensed as a symbol of the idea (using the term as including sense-percepts as well as images of the imagination) to which it corresponds, than reversely.

Let us now consider an instance of the intercourse of soul and body. Suppose, to take a trivial yet instructive example, we consider the case of the youngster gazing longingly in the confectioner's window. What do we mean when we say that he is desirous of eating chocolate? What can he who is a psychical or spiritual being want with material chocolate? Would it, therefore, be more correct to say that he desires his bodily organism to eat chocolate? But would his desire be satisfied if this organism ate the chocolate whilst he (the spirit) remained unconscious of the process? Perhaps this would be so in the case of a person who desired the chocolate as nourishment for his body merely, but we know that in the case of the average youngster his desire for chocolate has reference entirely to the pleasant sensations arising when the confection is eaten. Then, consciousness is an essential factor in the satisfaction of his desire, and we cannot avoid the conclusion that what he really desires is the idea of chocolate, or, to speak more precisely, the idea of eating chocolate. True, by the power of his imagination he can conjure up in his mind this desired idea, without the aid of the external world; but the idea thus arising is vague, hazy, ill-defined, and does not bring satisfaction. Let him, however, but place a piece of chocolate on the "taste-buds" of his tongue, and immediately a very vivid taste-idea of chocolate arises in his mind. The objector will argue, perhaps, that these two ideas are very different—the latter is a sense-percept connected with some particular external object, whilst the former is a mere image of the imagination and is not so connected with any external object. True; but in essence the ideas are of a precisely similar nature, considered psychically they are precisely similar modifications of states of consciousness, differing only in intensity. And yet the material chocolate, which indirectly produces this remarkable increase of intensity in the idea, is quite a different thing from the idea which it intensifies—it is material, not psychical or spiritual. But, as we have indicated above, there is an exact correspondence between the two—the material chocolate is a symbol of the idea desired. Here, then, we have the essentials of Magic—the causal power of spirit, and the non-causal efficacy of the symbol; here we have a symbol employed that one may avail himself of a spiritual power. And what we have here demonstrated for but one and that a trivial case of sensation is perfectly general; so much so that we are forced to exclaim with the poet-philosopher Novalis, "*Alie Erfahrung ist Magic, und nur magisch erklárbar,*"—"All experience is Magic, and only magically explicable."

6. The Magical Theory of Experience

It will probably be argued against the standpoint here adopted, that our common experiences of daily life are "natural," whereas Magic has reference to the "supernatural." But what is implied by this word "natural"? The term "natural" is commonly employed as relating to the physical realm, and in this sense, Magic is not natural, since it has reference to psychical processes—not that such are contrary to the order of the physical realm, but that they transcend this order. There is, however, a grand sense in which the term "natural" is sometimes employed as referring to the whole realm of order, and in this sense, genuine Magic is but another aspect of Nature, a profounder insight into her mysteries. Says Cornelius Agrippa, ". . . every day some natural thing is drawn by art, and some divine thing is drawn by Nature, which, the Egyptians, seeing, called Nature a

Magicianess (i.e.), the very Magical power itself, in the attracting of like by like, and of suitable things by suitable."

It may be thought that the position here adopted, namely, that "all experience is Magic, and only magically explicable," is one that is opposed to the spirit of Modern Science: but we do not think that this is so. Physical Science does not pretend to reveal the fundamental underlying Cause of phenomena, does not pretend to answer the final "Why?" This is rather the business of Philosophy, though, in thus distinguishing between Physical Science and Philosophy, we are far from insinuating that Philosophy should be otherwise than scientific. We often hear religious but non-scientific men complain because scientific and perhaps equally as religious men do not in their books ascribe the production of the phenomena with which they are concerned to the Divine Power. But if they were so to do, they would be transcending their business as scientists. In every science, certain simple facts of experience are taken for granted: it is the business of the scientist to reduce other and more complex facts of experience to terms of these data, not to explain these data themselves. Thus, the physicist attempts to reduce other related phenomena of greater complexity to terms of simple force and motion; but, what are force and motion? Why does force produce or result in motion? Are questions which lie beyond the scope of Physics. In order to answer these questions, if, indeed, such be possible, we must first inquire, How and why do these ideas of force and motion arise in our minds? The problem is one for Metaphysics to solve, and Metaphysics lands us at once in the psychical or spiritual world, and the term "Magic" at once acquires a potent meaning. "If," says Thomas Carlyle, "... we ... have led thee into the true Land of Dreams; and ... thou lookest, even for moments, into the region of the Wonderful, and seest and feelest that thy daily life is girt with Wonder, and based on Wonder, and thy very blankets and breeches are Miracles,— then art thou profited beyond money's worth ..."

Forgotten Essays

MEDICINE AND MAGIC

THERE are few tasks at once so instructive and so fascinating as the tracing of the development of the human mind as manifested in the evolution of scientific and philosophical theories. And this is, perhaps, especially true when, as in the case of Medicine, this evolution has followed paths so tortuous, intersected by so many fantastic byways, that one is not infrequently doubtful as to the true road. The history of Medicine is at once the history of human wisdom and the history of human credulity and folly, and the romantic element (to use the expression in its popular acceptation) thus introduced, whilst making the subject the more entertaining, by no means detracts from its importance considered psychologically. Of course, it goes without saying that a work on the history of Medicine, or of any of its branches, could be written so as to prove exceedingly dull and dry, even if scientifically valuable, reading. This criticism, however, can by no means be passed upon a new work by the late Mr. A. C. Wootton on the history of *Pharmacy*, the publication of which is primarily the occasion of these brief remarks on the subject. Mr. Wootton has not only produced a valuable work of reference, in which the history of pharmacy is treated in a very complete and detailed manner, but he has also written a fascinating and, indeed, entertaining book, which any one of moderate scientific tastes will read with interest and pleasure from cover to cover; its value, moreover, is enhanced by a number of excellent illustrations in the text, including portraits of many famous men who have contributed to the building up of Pharmacy. To whom the honor of having first invented medicines is duo is unknown, the origins of Pharmacy being lost in the twilight the authenticity of these works and the identity of Lully the alchemist with the Lully of the Castello story and missionary fame; and (2) the fact that the account of "valency" given in vol. ii. is wholly inadequate to meet the requirements of the general reader. The theories of modern chemistry, perhaps, really lie without the scope of the work, but they should either be omitted or treated in an adequate manner. These, however, are all points of comparatively minor importance.

Of myth. Osiris and Isis, Bacchus, Apollo, father of the famous physician Aesculapius, and Chiron the Centaur, tutor of the latter, are among the many mythological personages who have been accredited with the invention of physic. It is certain that the art of compounding medicines is extraordinarily ancient. Indeed, we are informed that there is a papyrus in the British Museum, containing medical prescriptions (not yet translated) which are supposed to be about 5,600 years old; and the famous Ebers papyrus, which is devoted to medical matters, is reckoned to date from about the year 1552 b.c. It is interesting to note that in the prescriptions given in this latter papyrus, as seems to have been the case throughout the history of medicine, the principle that the efficacy of a medicine is in proportion to its nastiness appears to have been the main idea. Indeed, many old medicines contained ingredients of the most disgusting nature imaginable: a mediaeval remedy, known as oil of puppies, made by cutting up two newly born puppies and boiling them with one pound of live earthworms, may be cited as a comparatively pleasant example of the remedies used in the days when all sorts of excreta were prescribed as medicines. Presumably the oldest theory concerning the causation of disease, is that which attributes all the ills of mankind to the malignant operations of evil spirits: a theory which someone has rather fancifully suggested is not so erroneous after all, if we may be allowed to apply the term "evil spirits" to the microbes of modern bacteriology. Remnants of this theory (which does—shall we say?—conceal a transcendental truth), that is, in its original form, still survive to the present day in various superstitious customs whose absurdity does not need emphasizing; for example, the use of red flannel by old-fashioned folk with which to tie up sore throats; red having once been supposed to be a color very antagonistic to evil spirits, so much so that at one time red cloth hung in the patient's room was much employed as a cure for small-pox! Medicine and Magic have always been closely associated.

Indeed, the greatest name in the history of Pharmacy is also what is probably the greatest name in the history of Magic—the reference, of course, being to Paracelsus. Until Paracelsus, partly by his vigorous invective and partly by his remarkable cures of various diseases, demolished the old school of medicine, no one dared contest the authority of Galen and Avicenna. Galen's theory of disease was largely based upon that of the four humors in man—bile, blood, phlegm, and black bile—which were regarded as related to (but not identical with) the four elements—fire, air, water, and earth,—being supposed to have characters similar to these. Thus, to bile, as to fire, were attributed the properties of hotness and dryness; to blood and air those of hotness and moistness; to phlegm and water those of coldness and moistness; and, finally, black bile, like earth, was said to be cold and dry. Galen supposed that an alteration in the due proportion of these humors gives rise to disease, though he did not consider this to be its only cause; thus, cancer, it was thought, might result from an excess of black bile, and rheumatism from an excess of phlegm. Drugs, Galen argued, are of efficacy in the curing of disease, according as they possess one or more of these so-called fundamental properties, hotness, dryness, coldness and moistness, whereby it was considered that an excess of any humor might be counteracted; moreover, it was further assumed that four degrees of each property exist, and that only those drugs are of use in curing a disease which contain the necessary property or properties in the degree proportionate to that in which the opposite humor or humors are in excess in the patient's system. Paracelsus' views were based upon his theory (undoubtedly true, in a sense) that man is a microcosm, a world in miniature.

Now, all things material taught Paracelsus, contain the three principles termed in alchemist phraseology, salt, sulphur and mercury. This is true, therefore, of man: the healthy body, he argued, is a sort of chemical compound in which these three principles are harmoniously blended (as in the Macrocosm) in due proportion, whilst disease is due to a preponderance of one principle, fevers, for example, being the result of an excess of sulphur (i.e.. the fiery principle), etc. Paracelsus was thus led to seek for chemical remedies, containing these principles in varying proportions; he was not content with medicinal herbs and minerals in their crude state, but attempted to extract their effective essences; indeed, he maintained that the preparation of new and better drugs is the chief business of chemistry. This theory of disease and of the efficacy of drugs was complicated by many fantastic additions; thus, there is the "Archaeus," a sort of benevolent demon supposed by Paracelsus to look after all the unconscious functions of the bodily organism, who has to be taken into account. Paracelsus also held the doctrine of signatures, according to which, the medicinal value of plants and minerals is indicated by their external form, or by some sign impressed upon them by the operation of the stars.

A very old example of this belief is to be found in the use of mandrake (whose roots resemble the human form) by the Hebrews and Greeks as a cure for sterility; or, to give an instance which is still accredited by some, the use of eyebright (a plant with a black pupil-like spot in its corolla) for complaints of the eyes. Allied to this doctrine are such beliefs, once held, as that the lungs of foxes are good for bronchial troubles, or that the heart of a lion will endow one with courage—beliefs which are all of an essentially magical character. It may be thought, perhaps, that. Paracelsus' views were not so great an advance on those of Galen, but whether or not this be the case, his union of chemistry and medicine was of immense benefit to each science, and marked a new era in Pharmacy. Even if his theories were highly fantastic, it was he who freed Medicine from the shackles of traditionalism, and rendered progress in medical science possible. We must not conclude these brief notes without some reference to the magical theory of the medicinal efficacy of words.

The Ebers papyrus already mentioned gives various formulae which must be pronounced when preparing and when administering a drug; and there is a draught used by the Eastern Jews as a cure for bronchial complaints prepared by writing certain words on a plate, washing them off with wine, and adding three grains of a citron which has been used at the Tabernacle festival. But of this, as of other magical beliefs in Medicine, such as the magical virtues of precious stones, the king's touch for scrofula, and Sir Kenelm Digby's sympathetic powder for the cure of wounds, lack of space prevents us from writing further on the present occasion, save to remark that our readers will find much interesting information on these matters, as on the more scientific side of the history of pharmacy, in Mr. Wootton's excellent work.

MYSTICISM AND MONASTICISM

OUR own age is constructive, progressive: that age which is termed "mediaeval" was concerned rather with the appropriation of its intellectual inheritance from the past, from the patristic period and the times of Roman culture and philosophy. Our age looks forward, and asks the many questions it has to ask of Nature herself directly: the Middle Ages looked back, and asked their questions of Augustine and Aristotle; they looked in bygone books and closed their eyes to Nature—her beauty, her truth and her goodness. For these and other reasons the thought and mental outlook of no period in the history of the civilized world is quite so alien to our own as that of the Middle Ages, and it follows, therefore, that for any modern writer of critical acumen to deal with the history of mediaeval thought and emotion sympathetically is an exceptionally difficult task. Yet, it must be admitted that it is only by a sympathetic treatment of the subject that anything of value is to be derived therefrom; only thus is it possible to search out and discover "those human qualities which impelled the strivings of mediaeval men and women, informed their imaginations, and moved them to love and tears and pity." Subject the superstructure of mediaeval thought and emotion to too caustic a criticism from the modem standpoint and it will crumble to pieces before one's eyes. It is the former of these modes of treatment that Mr. H. O. Taylor has very wisely adopted in a recent work upon the subject in question—a very elaborate piece of work, the result of an undoubtedly wide knowledge of his subject. The book constitutes, perhaps, one of the most informing works on the psychological history of mediaeval culture that has been written; and its literary style and sympathetic attitude cannot but commend it to the reader's taste, even if there are times when he is inclined to think that the writer gives his sympathy too free a rein; and although there are some chapters which the average reader may find a trifle dry—as when Mr. Taylor conducts us through the some what arid wastes of Aquinas's dialectic—the book is well leavened by others—such as that dealing with the sad love-history of Helolse and Abelard—in which, though philosophy be not absent, romance is the leading theme.

Mr. Taylor's work, he explains, deals with "the more informed and constructive spirit of the mediaeval time "rather than with" the lower grades of ignorance and superstition abounding in the Middle Ages." Consequently, he is very largely occupied with monastic thought and monastic ideals, for, chivalry excepted, there was very little cultured thought and emotion in these days outside the monastery walls. For the same reason, though Mr. Taylor barely mentions Magic and Witchcraft, he has much to say concerning mystics and Mysticism. And although his definition (or perhaps we should say description) of Mysticism does not bring out the essential rationality of the mystical attitude, and is admittedly limited to a certain phase of Mysticism, it is by no means altogether unsatisfactory.

Like all books that are valuable, Mr. Taylor's *The Mediaval Mind* raises questions in the reader's mind which lie without its immediate scope; and it is on one such question—namely, that of the relation between Mysticism and Monasticism—on which it is proposed to say something in the present place.

Mediaeval theology seems to have been obsessed with a radically erroneous idea of evil—a metaphysical as contradistinguished from an ethical theory,—which placed evil in matter and not in the soul that loves only itself. Sensuality is the root of all sin, it declared, and sensuality is sin not because it is selfish, but because the pleasures that are gained through the senses are essentially evil. Of course, this idea was not so crudely or so explicitly stated as this by orthodox theologians; but it was there, back of the consciousness of mediaeval theology. It was this idea that lay at the root of Monasticism, which declared that the world and the flesh are snares of the devil, and that only in escape therefrom might one hope to attain to eternal blessedness—a view of life in which, perhaps, we may see the inevitable reaction from the sensualism of the days of Rome's decadence. Consequently, mediaeval theology looked with disfavor on human love between man and woman, for even if such love (in the genuine meaning of the term) is love between soul and soul—and that this is true, there have always been true lovers to proclaim—yet its natural outcome is that which is termed passion, its consummation in marriage is an act of bodily joy. It is true that Marriage was declared to be a sacrament, but it stood upon a very different footing to the other sacraments, such as Baptism and the Eucharist. So far from being considered as essential to man's salvation, it was regarded as involving a sort of venial sin, allowed man on account of his frailty; and it was as it still is by the Latin Church) forbidden those who dedicated their lives to God. Mediaeval theology failed to realize that Marriage is a true Sacrament, in all things most holy; and that unchastity and we use the word not as the mediaeval theologian used it as opposed to the state of celibacy, but rather as contradistinguished from the essential chastity of the marriage-state) is evil, not because matter is evil, but rather for a reverse reason, because it is the desecration of the elements of this sacrament.

Indeed, there was a certain tendency in the Middle Ages to look with suspicion on all human love. There were not wanting those who held that soul that truly loves God has no room in it for human love: St. Elizabeth of Hungary so loved the Lord, we read (and may God forgive the blasphemy), that she sent her children away from her, that she might not be distracted from loving Him alone. Not only had mediaeval theology no perception of a human union within a divine, no perception that the soul of man or woman is by itself incomplete, and that it is only by the love-union of a soul with its complement of opposite sex that the complete human being is formed capable of entering into the divine union between God and the Church, i.e. regenerated humanity in the complex; but it also failed to realize in a full and complete manner that to love God is to love one's fellow men—that apart from the love of the neighbor, there is no true love of God. Instead of the pure love of God as Goodness itself and Truth itself, the mediaeval religious mind tended towards a false love of God that was, so to speak, personal and restricted in the bad sense of both these terms. In the Appendix on "The Mystical Interpretation of the Song of Solomon "to his

Christian Mysticism (1899), Mr. Inge has some excellent remarks which may well be quoted in this connection. He says: "The headings to the chapters in the Authorized Version give a sort of authority to the 'mystical' interpretation of Solomon's Song, a poem which was no doubt intended by its author to be simply a romance of true love. According to our translators, the Lover of the story is meant for Christ, and the Maiden for the Church. But the tendency of Catholic Mysticism has been to make the individual soul the bride of Christ, and to treat the Song of Solomon as symbolic of "spiritual nuptials" between Him and the individual 'contemplative.' . . . There is no doubt that the enforced celibacy and virginity of the monks and nuns led them consciously or unconsciously, to transfer to the human person of Christ (and to a much slighter extent, to the Virgin Mary) a measure of those, feelings which could find no vent in their external lives."

The union of the sexes in Marriage is a holy symbol—symbol of the spiritual union between soul and soul, symbol of the most holy union between Goodness and Truth underlying all things that are of God,—else were not Marriage a sacrament; but like all symbols (and because of its holiness, more emphatically so) is it liable to abuse, and was subjected to abuse by those who used it in the erroneous manner Mr. Inge indicates. As he further remarks, "The employment of erotic imagery to express the individual relation between Christ and the soul is always dangerous; but this objection does not apply to the statement that 'the Church is the Bride of Christ'." Of course, it may be argued that a good many of the erotic effusions of a particular type of so-called mediaeval "mystic" (e.g. Mechthild of Magdeburg) are to be understood only spiritually. But as Mr. Taylor writes of this extraordinary personage: "Jesus was a man, Mechthild a woman. Her love not only uses lovers' speech, but actually holds an affinity with a maid's love for her betrothed. If it is the soul's love of God, it is also the woman's love of Him who overhung her from the Cross." The attempt to live according to an unnatural system of morality resulted in an unnatural immorality—it is but another example of the workings of the principle of action and reaction. The subject is nauseating, and we would have welcomed harsher words from Mr. Taylor than those in which he has written of it.

Now it is this, this which we would term the evil side of the monastic spirit, that is so frequently mistaken for Mysticism. And yet we venture to assert that to this spirit is the true spirit of Mysticism altogether opposed: the mere fact of the close association of Mysticism and Monasticism during the Middle Ages proves nothing as to any other than an accidental relationship between them; for all intellectual and moral culture was associated with Monasticism in these days, even chivalry not being exempt from its influence, as we see in the cases of the Templars and Hospitallers. Later, Mysticism emerged from the unhealthy atmosphere of the cloisters into the pure air of God-created Nature, shaking off those monastic accretions which were really contrary to her genuine spirit. The true mystic quests for God, not, as did so frequently the monk, because he fears future torments, but because he is inspired by love—the love of God as Goodness Itself and Truth Itself and the Holy Source of all Existence, not the false "love" of which we have spoken.

He may seek for God within the hidden ground of his own soul, or he may seek for God immanent in Nature's beauties, but if his Mysticism be a right Mysticism, if it be healthy and not deformed, he will engage in both these quests; for in truth, they are but one. And the realization of the immanence of God in all things will save him both from sensuality and from asceticism. He will neither disdain nor abuse God's gifts to man of Nature and sense wherewith to taste of her delights; but use them, treating the things of nature at their true worth, as symbols of spiritual verities, of sacramental efficacy in drawing him towards God. The life of the mystic is the life of human love in every genuine meaning of that expression. It is the life of marriage love, because of the mystical significance of marriage; it is also the life of devotion and sacrifice to the welfare of fellow men and women because to perform such sacrifice is the happiness of him who is a true mystic, the true lover of Christ, of Him Who is Goodness or Love Itself.

Mysticism frequently appears as a revolt against the established and orthodox, when such has become a form without life and love inspiring it from within. But it is not to be expected that Mysticism should have immediately freed itself from the alien shackles of Monasticism and its laudation of the useless life. It is, indeed, no small matter to break utterly away from the spirit of one's age.

We have spoken of the evil aspect of the spirit of Monasticism: it must be understood that we are censuring Monasticism itself rather than those who lived according to its creed. There were bad monks and there were good. There were those of whom it is not for us to speak in praise—it would be presumption to do so. Noble men, loving men—Bernard of Clairvaux, Victor of St. Hugo, Bonaventura—an inventory of their names is hardly needed. They were men of their age, not untouched by the errors of their age—but who is free from all the errors of his age?—and perhaps their sincerity in their errors proves the more strongly the force of their devotion. Such men did love God, truly and with no equivocation; and thus, they have a mighty message for us of this twentieth century, so much concerned with frivolities and useless things that matter nothing. We owe no small debt of gratitude to Mr. Taylor for making known to us their message.

H. Stanley Redgrove

THE DERVISHES: THEIR CUSTOMS AND BELIEFS

SUFISM, the professed religion of the Dervishes, may be briefly defined as Islamic Mysticism. Its birthplace was Persia, but the question as to the nature of its origin is one by no means easy to solve. There is much in the teachings of Sufiism that seems opposed to the spirit of Muhammadism—its universal tolerance, its pantheistic conception of God, its disregard of mere forms and ceremonies, stand in strong contrast to the orthodox teachings of Islam. It has, therefore, been suggested that in Sufiism, we have the reaction of the spirit of an Aryan race against the formalism of a Semitic religion forced upon it from without. On the other hand, it is maintained by Sufi writers that their teachings are in accordance with the true spirit of the Kur'an, and are, indeed, the true esoteric doctrines of the Prophet. Probably there is an element of truth in both of these theories. The possible influence of Neoplatonism, which Sufiism closely resembles in certain respects must also be taken into account. In the beautiful writings of the early Sufi poets, such as Faridu 'd-Din 'Attar (a.d. 1119-1229), Sa'di (a.d. 1184-1291), Jalalu 'd-Din Rumi (a.d. 1207-1273) and Jami (a.d. 1414-1492), is to be found the highest and noblest presentation of Sufi philosophy and ethics. The central doctrine of Sufiism is that of the immanence of God, both in Nature and in the heart and mind of man. Unfortunately, its tendency has been to over-emphasize this fact until the necessary distinction between God and the individual is lost sight of. Thus, an early Sufi, Huseyn ibn Mausur, known as Hallaj (tenth century a.d.), went so far as to declare "I am the Truth"—that is "I am God"—during a condition of religious ecstasy. For this, he was tortured to death by the orthodox followers of the Prophet.

To the Sufi poets, God is Absolute Beauty, the One Only Beloved; and this idea permeates their writings. These are, as might be expected, highly allegorical in form, making large use of sensuous images to give expression to spiritual aspirations and ideas. To the Sufi poets, human love is the symbol of that love which is divine, and in all things beautiful of this earth, they behold only the reflection of the divine beauty. "The Absolute Beauty," writes Jami, "is the Divine Majesty endued with power and bounty. Every beauty and perfection manifested in the theatre of the various grades of beings is a ray of His perfect beauty, reflected therein. It is from these rays that exalted souls have received their impress of beauty and their quality of perfection." To become one with the Divine Beloved is the sole aim of the true Sufi, and in comparison, with this end, he values all else as worthless. "Look not in the world for bliss and fortune," writes Jalcdu 'd-Din Rumi, "since thou wilt not find them; seek bliss in both worlds by serving Him."

It must be confessed, however, that, speaking generally, Sufiism, as represented by the various orders of Dervishes in modern times, has considerably declined from these ancient ideals. As Prof. E. G. Browne remarks, "Many perfect Sufis are to be found amongst the Dervishes, but too often the dervish dress is but a new kind of formalism, even when it be not (as it sometimes is) a cloak for idleness, antinomianism and even libertinism." There are in existence at the present time a very large number of different Dervish orders, of which, perhaps, the Mevlevis (founded by Jalâlu 'd-Din Rûmi) and the Rufa' is (founded by Seyyid Achmet Rufâ in the twelfth century a.d.) are the most important. Their monasteries or Tekkehs are very numerous. That of the Mevlevi Order at Salonica. The central building is known as the "Hall of Celestial Sounds," and it is here that the Dervishes meet for public worship and the performance of their religious dancing. Its interior is marked by extreme simplicity. A new member is only admitted to a Dervish Order after a fairly long probationary period (nearly three years in the case of the Mevlevis). This period is divided into seven stages, through which the neophyte is advanced in accordance with the dreams and visions he experiences. During his probationary period, he is obliged to act as a servant to the other inmates of the Tekkeh, whose precincts he is not generally allowed to leave until he becomes a full member of the Order. His religious exercises consist in repetitions of the attributes of God, prayer and fasting. In the case of certain Orders he has also to become proficient in their religious dancing. Meanwhile, he is instructed in the philosophy and ethics of Sufiism. He is finally received by the Sheykh (or principal of the Tekkeh) and made a full member, each Order having its own ceremony of initiation. The vow of celibacy is not obligatory, and is not, as a matter of fact, very frequently taken. The married dervishes live with their wives, only sleeping at their Tekkeh on certain occasions.

The mode of worship of some of the Orders of Dervishes is of a purely contemplative nature, and the devotions of such are private. But in the case of certain other orders, dancing plays an essential part in their religious services, and the public are admitted to witness such performances. The dance or devr of the Mevlevis (Fig. 3) consists of rapid gyrations continued for about ten or fifteen minutes and generally twice repeated. The younger dervishes are frequently able to perform these gyrations with considerable rapidity; in spite of this, they are said to show no signs of fatigue or giddiness. The performances of the Rufel'is or "Howling Dervishes" are even more remarkable. These dervishes, after having worked themselves to a sufficient pitch of religious frenzy by violent agitations of the body and shoutings of Allah! Allah! and Ya Hoo! ("O Him!"), mutilate themselves with red-hot irons, eagerly plunging them into their flesh or placing them in their mouths. After the performance, their wounds are anointed with the spittle of their Sheykh, and according to Muhammadan witnesses, no trace of any wound or burn remains after twenty-four hours. This testimony may not be altogether erroneous; since it does seem to be a fact—extraordinary and well-nigh inexplicable—that in certain conditions of the mind, the body is capable of withstanding the effects of fire. The chapter on Fire-walking in Mr. Andrew Lang's Magic and Religion (1901) contains a good deal of valuable information bearing on this matter. As might be expected, the dervish Sheykhs whilst alive, and their tombs when dead, are credited with all sorts of magical powers by the more superstitious Muslims. Probably some of the Skeykhs have a practical knowledge of certain of the arcane forces of the mind which modern science is only just beginning to study under the names of hypnotism, telepathy, etc., but undoubtedly most of the marvelous stories related of them have been gradually evolved from the imaginations of successive relators.

The following may, perhaps, be regarded as a case of telepathy. The celebrated Sheykh Seyyid Burhi-nu 'd-Din, had in his younger days been a pupil of Bahau 'd-Din Veled, the father of Jalilu 'd-Din Rumi. On one occasion during a lecture, he suddenly stopped and with tears exclaimed "Alas! my master has passed away from this Tabernacle of Dust to the Abode of Sincerity!" The time of this utterance was noted down, and found, afterwards, to tally exactly with that of the death of Bahau 'd-Din Veled, which had occurred in another town. The story related by Bahau 'd-Din of himself and his spiritual master Sheykh Sa'ed ed Din of Kashgar, if true, is certainly a remarkable case of will power. It is to the effect that these two Sufis, seeing a couple of men wrestling, decided to aid by their wills first one and then the other. The one they aided invariably proved the victor for the time being. We will conclude our remarks with the following amusing legend, comment on which is needless. A certain dervish set out on a pilgrimage riding a donkey given to him by his Sheykh. The donkey died. The dervish, having buried it, announced that the grave was that of a pious companion.

H. Stanley Redgrove

Charitable passersby soon gave him sufficient money to erect a tomb or tomb over the grave, of which he made himself the guardian. In time, the tombs became a noted place of pilgrimage, and many miracles of healing were performed there. The old Sheykh, hearing of its fame, paid it a visit, and recognized his erstwhile disciple. The latter, upon questioning, confessed that it was only the donkey that was buried beneath the turbeh. As the old Sheykh did not appear to be much disconcerted by this confession, the disciple asked who was buried under his master's turbeh: it was the parent of his own ass!

ON SYMBOLISM IN ART

NO art is truly worthy of the name that is not symbolic in form and interpretative in function. Of course, we do not deny a certain value, in some cases, indeed, a high value, to art (so-called) of a purely imitative character; but so long as the artist merely strives accurately to imitate nature (whether by the term "nature" we mean the nature that lies wholly without man, or the nature within him as manifested without) so long, that is, as the artist is merely a mimic, does his work fall short of the true ideal of art. The value of such works, moreover, is not truly artistic but rather scientific; art (if we may so call it) that is purely imitative has no true end or value in itself; it is merely the handmaid of science, and as such is valuable only in so far as it ministers to the end and aim of science; apart from the fact, of course, that it constitutes the necessary technique of true art.

Take, for example, the case of painting. Truly, it is not a worthless task to depict the beauties of nature, thereby bringing to the eyes of those who might otherwise have ever remained blind, the wonderful scenery of nature and the beautiful forms of life. Pictures of this character are useful factors in the curriculum of a true education, which does not overlook aesthetic factors. But so long as they are merely imitative of nature, they must remain inferior to nature. They are of worth only because we are unable to have nature's own beauties continually before our eyes; consequently, they are of value chiefly to the town-dweller, whose spirit would otherwise faint for the symbols of nature. He who lives amidst woodland scenes, with a babbling brook at his feet and the slopes of a rugged mountain overhead, he who is constantly face to face with nature's own picture-language,— he needs not pictures which merely mimic nature.

In the case of music, the worthlessness of a crude realism is very generally recognized—no one, for example, regards what is called "descriptive music" as being of any artistic value or importance. In painting and literature, however, this, unfortunately, is not the case. In modem times, we see manifest in these forms of art a love of false realism exercising its baneful influence. Painters of the purely imitative school rush to put upon their canvases all that is hideous and revolting, and many novelists seem to find pleasure only in describing the like. Pictorial studies of the outward effects of disease (whether physical or moral) are not without interest to the student of physiology or psychology (as the case may be) and the same may be said of novels which are primarily concerned with the inward workings and outward results of vice. But such pictures and novels have no artistic value and the making of such is not art. They are of use merely (shall we say?) as pictorial and graphic adjuncts to pathological science.

The question whether science explains or even attempts to explain nature is one that depends on its reply upon the signification we attach to the word "explain." In the truest meaning of the term, the answer to this question is No! Science does not attempt to explain nature. Her functions are more humble than this. Science is concerned only with facts of experience as such, with phenomena as phenomena, and the problem of the true nature of experience, of the inner meaning of phenomena, she leaves to philosophy. But if it be held that the self-consistent is more easy to understand in virtue of its self-consistency than that which is chaotic and lacking in consistency, then so far may science be said to explain or to strive to explain nature. In a word, science attempts to explain nature in terms of herself; and, although such an explanation (even when as perfect as its essential character permits) can never be thoroughly and finally satisfactory, and must ever leave the eternal Why? Unanswered, still it is one step towards the final solution of the problem of existence and the realization of its true significance.

The aim of true art, however, is to explain nature spiritually. This, also, is the aim of true philosophy. The distinction here lies in the fact that philosophy makes its appeal rather to the head, to the intellect; art to the heart, to the feelings. Art's explanation of life and nature is one that is felt rather than intellectually perceived. It follows that there is (or, at least, should be) no quarrel between art and philosophy; they are complementary one to the other; and it is in their combination that the fullest realization of nature's inner significance is to be found—we mean, not when there is a confusion between the two, but when a man finds his whole spiritual nature responding sympathetically to their dual appeal. A curious device of a modern school of painting may be remarked upon here as an instance of the confusion between art and science. We refer to the device of using only the primary colors, into which all other colors are resolved. Of course, the analysis of color is the business of science; not that of art.

No man can be a true artist who does not realize that all things of life and nature are symbolical and have an inner, spiritual meaning; that the things of this world exist not in and for themselves, but to manifest the ideal in material form.

For it is the high prerogative of true art, in this realization of the symbolism of nature, so to manipulate the symbols with which its various forms are concerned, that their spiritual sense may shine forth and illumine the hearts of men. No man, therefore, can be a true artist who is not, in the genuine sense of the word (not that distorted and depraved meaning assigned to it by modern usage), a mystic. For there is no genuine art without vision—the vision that tells of the true and inner meaning and significance of experience and phenomena. It is the aim of the artist freely to give his vision and its fruits to all those that are able to receive thereof. The artist, indeed, deals with the things of life and experience, for all genuine art is based on such; but he deals with these things at their true worth—as symbols of spiritual verities. It is for him to cause these symbols to yield up their inner meaning to those who have not yet tasted of the vision. Says Emerson, in Nature, "It is not words only that are emblematic; it is things that are emblematic. Every natural fact is a symbol of some spiritual fact. Every appearance in nature corresponds to some state of the mind, and that state of the mind can only be described by presenting that natural appearance as its picture." Here, in a sentence, we have the whole essence of the theory and practice of art. Painting, romance, music and poetry—what is every true work of these but an emblematic picture of the spiritual?

A true work of art is at once realistic, imaginative and symbolical. It is realistic in as much as it is based on nature and experience. It is imaginative in as much as it is not bound down to the limits of a crude realism. And above all it is symbolical, the natural elements of which it is composed being arranged entirely with reference to their spiritual meaning, since the whole aim of the work is that this spiritual meaning may shine forth and be felt and realized in the heart of him who sees or reads or listens. It is here necessary to remark that true symbolism is not the product of idle fancy—the imagination of the true artist is a higher power than this—but is innate in the nature of things. True symbols are the symbols of nature and experience, and they are symbols because of the intimate connection (the ontological relation of cause and effect) between the spiritual and the physical, and because there is nothing in nature or experience which is not spiritual in origin and meaning.

It is true that a lower form of symbolism is recognized, though we doubt the validity of its claim so to be called. At least, the distinction between this lower form and symbolism as we have defined it above will provide us with a criterion whereby, we may differentiate between those works of art which are truly and spiritually symbolical and those which, not being symbolical in this sense, really fall short of the true ideal of art.

An illustration may, perhaps, help to elucidate the point here at issue. It is true of any good modern novel, for example, that it has a meaning which applies beyond the mere incidents (in themselves more or less imaginary) with which it is concerned; but we should not therefore call such a work symbolical in the sense in which the word applies to the Grail legends or any of those old romances founded upon folk-lore which originated in the days when men communed more freely with nature and the spiritual, reading the correspondences between them. These romances, less realistic perhaps than our modern novels, are yet, on the whole, more true; for they deal (not perfectly, we grant) with symbols of spiritual import, and thus contain fragments of a truth which is eternal. Or to take an illustration from music. One might argue that Tschaikowsky's overture "1812" is symbolical, its two main themes being symbols respectively of Russia and France. But it is not symbolical in the sense in which this term applies to the great works of Richard Wagner—the one symbolism is of earth, the other of heaven. In Wagner, perhaps musical symbolism has reached its highest perfection as yet. It is here characterized by a remarkable distinctness and definiteness, as well as a high degree of spirituality. It is true that on account of this distinctness and definiteness of his symbolism, Wagner has been so much criticized; but, on the other hand, it is to these characteristics that his greatness and popularity are due. No one can fail to understand and interpret his music aright; hence, he fulfils the aim of his art. In the overture to Tannhduser, for example, no one could mistake the meanings of the symbols of the "Pilgrim's Chorus" and "Venusberg Music." The libretto—in itself a fine, symbolic work of art—is, really, not needed to interpret the music, which itself tells us so clearly of the battle of the passions, and of the final victory of those that are noble. Similar remarks, also, apply in the case of poetry—that art in some respects noblest of all. We must be careful not to confuse poetry with verse; for, although verse is the dress in which poetry generally bedecks herself as more becoming to her nature, sometimes she adopts the less charming garb of prose; whilst, on the other hand, she who would often be taken for poetry is some servant arrayed in her mistress's robes. There is some verse in reading which we feel a disharmony between content and form, the form irritating us if we wish to attend to the content, tending to distract our attention therefrom. Such is not true poetry. In reading true poetry we feel an aesthetic satisfaction arising on account of the perfect agreement between content and form, we feel that the thoughts embodied in such poetry would be unfittingly clothed in any other form of language—we feel, in a word, the power and charm of true spiritual symbolism.

In view of the fantastic theories and productions of certain modern schools of painting it is very necessary to insist on the value of the true symbols of spiritual verity which nature offers to this art,—in landscape, in seascape, and especially in the human form, which of all forms is most divine, and beautiful, and replete with meaning. It is not by distorting nature or by departing from her ways that the art of painting will fulfil its true end, but by rightly utilizing nature's symbols. An element of realism, as we have pointed out above, is essential to true art. True art is not crudely realistic, nor does it employ fantastic pseudo-symbols. True art takes the true symbols of nature and experience, and makes manifesting their spiritual message.

THE POWDER OF SYMPATHY

THE study of bygone superstitions is both useful and interesting because of the valuable insight it gives into the history of the development of the human mind. For it was out of the superstitions of the past that the science of the present gradually evolved. In the Middle Ages, what by courtesy we may term medical science, was little better than a heterogeneous collection of superstitions, and although various reforms were instituted with the passing of time, superstition still continued for long to play a prominent part in medical practice. One of the most curious of these old medical (or, perhaps we should say, surgical) superstitions was that relating to the Powder of Sympathy; a remedy chiefly remembered in connection with the name of Sir Kenelm Digby (1603-1665), though he was probably not the first to employ it. The Powder itself, which was used as a cure for wounds, was in fact nothing else than common vitriol, though an improved and more elegant form (if one may so describe it) was composed of vitriol desiccated by the sun's rays, mixed with gum tragacanth. It was in the application of the Powder that the remedy was peculiar. It was not, as one might expect, applied to the wound itself, but any article that might have the blood from the wound upon it was either sprinkled with the Powder or else placed in a basin of water in which the Powder had been dissolved, and maintained at a temperate heat. Meanwhile, the wound was kept clean and cool.

Sir Kenelm Digby appears to have delivered a discourse dealing with the famous Powder before a learned assembly at Montpellier in France; at least, a work purporting to be a translation of such a discourse was published in 1658, and further editions appeared in 1660 and 1664. Kenelm was a son of Sir Everard Digby who was executed for his share in the Gunpowder Plot. In spite of this fact, however, James I., appears to have regarded him with favor. He appears to have been a man of a romantic temperament, possessed of charming manners, considerable learning and even greater credulity. His contemporaries appear to have differed in their opinions concerning him. Evelyn, the diarist, after inspecting his chemical laboratory, rather harshly speaks of him as "an errant mountebank." Elsewhere, he well refers to him as "a teller of strange things"—this on the occasion of Digby's telling a story of a lady who had such an aversion to roses that one laid on her cheek produced a blister! To return to the Late Discourse: after some preliminary remarks, Sir Kenelm records a cure which he claimed to have effected by means of the Powder. It appears that James Howell (afterwards historiographer royal to Charles II) had, in the attempt to separate two friends engaged in a duel, received two serious wounds in the hand. To proceed with the writer's own words—"It was my chance to be lodged hard by him; and four or five days after, as I was making myself ready, he [Mr. Howell] came to my house, and prayed for me to view his wounds; for I understand, said he, that you have extraordinary remedies upon such occasions, and my surgeons apprehend some fear that it may grow to a Gangrene, and so the hand must be cut off...." "I asked him then for anything that had the blood upon it; so, he presently sent for his Garter, wherewith his hand was first bound: and having called for a Bason of water, as if I would wash my hands, I took a handful of powder of Vitriol, which I had in my

Study, and presently dissolved it. As soon as the bloody Garter had brought me, I put it within the Bason, observing in the interim what Mr. Howel did, who stood talking with a Gentlemen in the corner of my Chamber, not regarding at all what I was doing; but he started suddenly, as if he had found some strange alteration in himself. I asked him what he ailed? I know not what ails me, but I find that I feel no more pain; me thinks that a pleasing kind of freshness, as it were a wet cold napkin did spread over my hand, which hath taken away the inflammation that tormented me before. I replied, since that you feel already so good an effect of my Medicament, I advise you to cast away all your Plaisters, onely keep the wound clean, and in a moderate temperature 'twixt heat and cold. This was presently reported to the Duke of Buckingham, and a little after to the King [James I], who were both very curious to know the issue of the business, which was, that after dinner I took the Garter out of the water, and put it to dry before a great fire; it was scarce dry. but Mr. Howell's servant came running and told me, that his Master felt as much burning as ever he had done, if not more, for the heat was such, as if his hand were 'twixt coals of fire. I answered, that although that had happened at present, yet he should find ease in a short time; for I knew the reason of this new accident, and I would provide accordingly, for his Master should be free from that inflammation it may be before he could possibly return unto him: but in case he found no ease, I wished him to come presently back again, otherwise he might forbear coming. Thereupon he went, and at the instant I did put again the Garter into the water: thereupon he found his Master without any pain at all. To be brief, there was no sense of pain afterward; but within five or six days the wounds were cicatrized, and entirely healed."

Sir Kenelm proceeds, in this discourse, to relate that he obtained the secret of the Powder from a Carmelite who had learnt it in the East. Sir Kenelm says that he told it only to King James and the celebrated physician, Sir Theodore

Mayerne. The latter disclosed it to the Duke of Mayerne, whose surgeon sold the secret to various people, until ultimately, as Sir Kenelm remarks, it became known to every country barber. However, Digby's real connection with the Powder has been questioned. In an appendix to Dr. Nathaniel Highmore's *The History of Generation*, published in 1651, entitled *A Discourse of the Cure of Wounds by Sympathy*, the Power is referred to as Sir Gilbert Talbot's Powder; and it was Sir Gilbert Talbot (1553-1616) who brought the claims of the sympathetic Powder before the notice of the then recently formed Royal Society, although Digby was a by no means inactive member of the Society. Highmore, however, in the Appendix to the work referred to above, does refer to Digby's reputed cure of Howell's wounds already mentioned; and after the publication of Digby's Discourse, the powder became generally known as Sir Kenelm Digby's Sympathetic Powder. As such, it is referred to in an advertisement appended *to Wit and Drollery* (1661) by the bookseller, Nathaniel Brookes.

The belief in cure by sympathy, however, is much older than Digby's or Talbot's Sympathetic Powder. Paracelsus (1493—1541) described an ointment consisting essentially of the moss on a man who had died a violent death, combined with boar's and bear's fat, burnt worms, dried boar's brain, red sandalwood and mummy, which was used to cure wounds in a similar manner, being applied to the weapon with which the hurt had been inflicted. Physicians in Paracelsus' day and for long afterwards seemed to regard the efficacy of a medicine as being directly proportional to the absurdity of its ingredients; as witness the above prescription. With reference to this ointment, readers will probably recall the passage in Scott's *Lay of the Last Minstrel* (canto 3, stanza 23) respecting the magical cure of William of Deloraine's wound by the Ladye of Branksome:

> "She drew the splinter from the wound
> And with a charm she stanch'd the blood:

> She bade the gash be cleans'd and bound:
> No longer by his couch she stood;
> But she had ta'en the broken lance,
> And washed it from the clotted gore
> And salved the splinter o'er and o'er.
> William of Deloraine, in trance,
> Whene'er she turned it round and round.
> Twisted as if she gall'd his wound.
> Then to her maidens she did say
> That he should be whole man and sound
> Within the course of a night and day.
> Full long she toil'd; for she did rue
> Mishap to friend so stout and true."

Francis Bacon writes of sympathetic cures as follows:

"It is constantly Received, and Avouched, that the Anointing of the Weapon, that maketh the Wound, wil heale the Wound it selfe. In this Experiment, upon the Relation of Men of Credit, (though my selfe, as yet, am not fully inclined to believe it,) you shal note the Points following; First, the Ointment . . . is made of Divers ingredients; whereof the Strangest and Hardest to come by, arc the Moss upon the Skull of a dead Man, Vnburied; And the Fats of a Boare, and a Beare, killed in the Act of Generation. These Two last I could easily suspect to be prescribed as a Starting Hole; That if the Experiment proved not, it mought be pretended that the Beasts were not killed in due time; For as for the Mosse, it is certain there is great Quantity of it in Ireland, upon Slain Bodies, laid on Heaps, Vnburied. The other Ingredients are, the Bloud-Stone in Powder, and some other Things; which seeme to have a Vertue to Stanch Bloud; As also the Mosse hath. . . . Secondly, the same kind of Ointment, applied to the Hurt it selfe, worketh not the Effect, but onely applied to the Weapon. . . . Fourthly, it may be applied to the Weapon, though the Party Hurt be at a great Distance. Fifthly, it seemeth the Imagination of the Party to be Cured, is not needfull to Concurre; For it may be done without the knowledge of the Party Wounded; And thus, much hath been tried, that the Ointment (for Experiments sake,) hath been wiped off the Weapon, without the knowledge of the Party Hurt, and presently the Party Hurt, hath been in great Rage of Paine, till the Weapon was Rean-nointed. Sixthly, it is affirmed, that if you cannot get the Weapon, yet if you put an Instrument of Iron, or Wood, resembling the Weapon, into the Wound, whereby it bleedeth, the Annointing of that Instrument will serve, and work the Effect. This I doubt should be a Device, to keep this strange Forme of Cure, in Request, and Use Because many times you cannot come by the Weapon it solve. Seventhly, the Wound be at first Washed clean with White Wine or the Parties own Water; And then bound up close in Fine Linen and no more Dressing renewed till it be whole."

Owing to the demand for making this ointment, quite a considerable trade was done in skulls from Ireland, upon which moss had grown owing to their exposure to the atmosphere, high prices being obtained for fine specimens.

The idea underlying the belief in the efficacy of sympathetic remedies, namely, that by acting on part of a thing or on a symbol of it, one thereby acts magically on the whole or the thing symbolized, is the root-idea of all magic, and is of extreme antiquity. The idea does, we believe, enshrine a real transcendental truth, but that the use of the Sympathetic Powder is thereby justified would not be a valid inference. Digby and others, however, tried to give a natural explanation to the supposed efficacy of the powder. They argued that particles of the blood would ascend from the bloody cloth or weapon, only coming to rest when they had reached their natural home in the wound from which they had originally issued. These particles would carry with them the more volatile part of the vitriol, which would effect a cure more readily than when combined with the grosser part of the vitriol. In the days when there was hardly any knowledge of chemistry and physics, this theory no doubt bore every semblance of truth. In passing, however, it is interesting to note that Digby's Discourse called forth a reply from J. F. Helvetius, physician to the Prince of Orange, who afterwards became celebrated as an alchemist who had achieved the magnum opus.

Writing of the Sympathetic Powder, Prof. De Morgan wittily argues that it must have been quite efficacious. He says, "The directions were to keep the wound clean and cool, and to take care of diet, rubbing the salve on the knife or sword. If we remember the dreadful notions upon drugs which prevailed, both as to quality and quantity, we shall readily see that any way of not dressing the wound would have been useful. If the physicians had taken the hint, had been careful of diet, etc., and had poured the little barrels of medicine down the throat of a practicable doll, they would have had their magical cures as well as the surgeons." As Dr. Pettigrew has pointed out, Nature exhibits very remarkable powers in effecting the healing of wounds by adhesion, when her processes are not impeded. In fact, many cases have been recorded in which noses, ears and fingers severed from the body have been re-joined thereto, merely by washing the parts, placing them in close continuity and allowing the natural powers of the body to effect the healing. Moreover, in spite of Bacon's remarks on this point, we must take into account the effect of the imagination of the patient, who usually was not ignorant that a sympathetic cure was to be attempted; for without going to the excesses of "Christian Science" in this respect, we must recognize the fact that the state of the mind exercises a powerful effect on the natural forces of the body, and a firm faith is undoubtedly helpful in effecting the cure of any sort of ill.

SUPERSTITIONS CONCERNING BIRDS

AMONGST the most remarkable of natural occurrences, must be included many of the phenomena connected with the behavior of birds. Undoubtedly, numerous species of birds are susceptible to atmospheric changes (of an electrical and barometric nature) too slight to be observed by man's unaided senses; thus, only is to be explained the phenomenon of migration and also the many other peculiarities in the behavior of birds whereby approaching changes in the weather may be foretold. Probably, also, this fact has much to do with the extraordinary homing instinct of pigeons. But, of course, in the days when meteorological science had yet to be born, no such explanation as this could be known. The ancients observed that birds by their migrations or by other peculiarities in their behavior prognosticated coming changes in the seasons of the year and other changes connected with the weather (such as storms, etc.); they saw, too, in the homing instincts of pigeons, an apparent exhibition of intelligence exceeding that of man. What is more natural, then, for them to attribute foresight to birds, and to suppose that all sorts of coming events (other than those of an atmospheric nature) might be foretold by careful observation of their flight and song?

Augury, that is, the art of divination by observing the behavior of birds, was extensively cultivated by the Etrurians and Romans. It is still used; we are informed, by the natives of Samoa. The Romans had an official college of augurs, the members of which were originally three patricians. About 300 b.c. the number of patrician augurs was increased by one and five plebeian augurs were added. Later, the number was again increased to fifteen. The object of augury was not so much to foretell the future as to indicate what line of action should be followed, in any given circumstances, by the nation. The augurs were consulted on all matters of importance, and the position of augur was thus one of great consequence.

Auguries, however, were also obtained from other animals and from celestial phenomena (e.g. lightning), etc. In what appears to be the oldest method, the augur, arrayed in a special costume, and carrying a staff with which to mark out the visible heavens into houses, proceeded to an elevated piece of ground, where a sacrifice was made and a prayer repeated. Then, gazing towards the sky, he waited until a bird appeared. The point in the heavens where it first made its appearance was carefully noted, also the manner and direction of its flight and the point where it was lost sight of. From these particulars an augury was derived, but, in order to be of effect, it had to be confirmed by a further augury. Auguries were also drawn from the notes of birds, birds being divided by the augurs into two classes—(i) oscines: "those which give omens by their note," and (ii) alites: "those which afford presages by their flight." Another method of augury was performed by the feeding of chickens specially kept for this purpose. This was done just before sunrise by the pullarius or feeder, strict silence being observed. If the birds manifested no desire for their food, the omen was of a most direful nature. On the other hand, if from the greediness of the chickens the grain fell from their beaks and rebounded from the ground, the augury was most favorable. This latter augury was known as *tripudium solistimum*.

"Any fraud practiced by the pullarius," writes the Rev. Ed. Smedley, "reverted to his own head. Of this we have a memorable instance in the great battle between Papirius Cursor and the Samnites in the year of Rome 459. So anxious were the troops for battle, that the pullarius dared to announce to the consul a *tripudium solistimum*, although the chickens refused to eat. Papirius unhesitatingly gave the signal for a fight, when his son, having discovered the false augury, hastened to communicate it to his father. 'Do thy part well,' was his reply, 'and let the deceit of the augur fall on himself. The tripudium has been announced to me, and no omen could be better for the Roman army and people.' As the troops advanced, a javelin thrown at random struck the pullarius dead. 'The hand of heaven is in the battle,' cried Papirius, 'the guilty is punished I' and he advanced and conquered."

A coincidence of this sort, if it really occurred, would very greatly strengthen the popular belief in auguries.

The cock has always been reckoned by a bird possessed of magic power. At its crowing, we are told, all unquiet spirits who roam the earth depart to their dismal abodes, and the orgies of the Witches Sabbath terminate. A cock is the favorite sacrifice offered to evil spirits in Ceylon and elsewhere. Alectromancy was an ancient and peculiarly senseless method of divination (so-called) in which a cock was employed. The bird must be young and quite white. Its feet are cut off and crammed down its throat with a piece of parchment on which must be written certain Hebrew words. The cock, after the repetition of a prayer by the operator, is placed in a circle divided into parts corresponding to the letters of the alphabet, in each of which a grain of wheat is placed. A certain psalm is recited, and then the letters are noted from which the cock picks the grains, a fresh grain being put down for each one picked up. These letters, properly arranged, will give the answer to the inquiry for which divination is made.

The owl was reckoned a bird of evil omen by the Romans, who derived this opinion from the Etrurians, along with much else of their so-called science of augury. It was particularly dreaded if seen in a city, or, indeed, anywhere in the day. Pliny informs us that on one occasion "a homed owl entered the very sanctuary of the Capitol; ... in consequence of which, Rome was purified on the nones of March in that year."

The folklore of the British Isles abounds with quaint beliefs and stories concerning birds. There is a charming Welsh legend concerning the robin, which the Rev. T. F. T. Dyer quotes from *Notts and Queries.*

"Far, far away, is a land of woe, darkness, spirits of evil, and fire. Day by day, does this little bird bear in his bill a drop of water to quench the flame? So near the burning stream does he fly, that his dear little feathers are scorched; and hence he is named Brou-rhuddyn (Breast-burnt). To serve little children, the robin dares approach the infernal pit. No good child will hurt the devoted benefactor of man. The robin returns from the land of fire, and therefore he feels the cold of winter far more than his brother birds. He shivers in the brumal blast; hungry, he chirp« before your door."

Another legend accounts for the robin's red breast by his having attempted to pluck a thorn from the crown encircling the brow of the crucified Christ in order to alleviate His sufferings. No doubt it is on account of these legends that it is considered a crime, which will be punished with great misfortune, to kill a robin. In some places, the same prohibition extends to the wren, which is popularly believed to be the wife of the robin.

In other parts, however, the wren is (or at least was) cruelly hunted on certain days. In the Isle of Man, the wren-hunt took place on Christmas Eve and St. Stephen's Day, and is accounted for by a legend concerning an evil fairy who lured many men to destruction, but had to assume the form of a wren to escape punishment at the hands of an ingenious knight-errant.

For several centuries there was prevalent over the whole of civilized Europe a most extraordinary superstition concerning the small Arctic bird, resembling, but not so large as, the common wild goose, known as the Barnacle or

Bernicle Goose. Max Muller has suggested that this word was really derived from Hibemicula, the name thus meaning Irish goose; but common opinion associated the barnacle goose with the shellfish known as the barnacle (which is found on timber exposed to the sea), supposing that the former was generated out of the latter. Thus, in one old medical writer, we find:

There are founde in the north parts of Scotland, and the Hands adjacent, called Orchades [Orkney Islands], certain trees, whereon doe growe certaine shell fishes, of a white color tending to russet; wherein are conteined little liuing creatures: which shells in time of maturitie doe open, and out of them grow those little living things; which falling into the water, doe become foules, whom we call Bamakles ... but the other that do fall vpon the land, perish and come to nothing: this much by the writings of others, and also from the mouths of people of those parts...

The writer, however, who was a well-known surgeon and botanist of his day, adds that he had personally examined certain shell-fish from other parts, and on opening the shells had observed within birds in various stages of development. No doubt he was deceived by some purely superficial resemblances—for example, the feet of the barnacle fish resemble somewhat the feathers of a bird. He gives an imaginative illustration of the barnacle fowl escaping from its shell, which we here reproduce.

Turning, now, from superstitions concerning actual birds, to legends of those that are purely mythical, passing reference must be made to the roc, a bird existing in Arabian legend, which we meet in the Arabian Nights, and which is chiefly remarkable for its size and strength.

The phoenix, perhaps, is of more interest. Of "that famous bird of Arabia," Pliny writes as fellows, prefixing his description of it with the cautious remark, "I am not quite sure that its existence is not all a fable."

H. Stanley Redgrove

"It is said that there is only one in existence in the whole world, and that one has not been seen very often. We are told that this bird is of the size of an eagle, and has a brilliant golden plumage around the neck, while the rest of the body is of a purple color; except the tail, which is azure, with long feathers intermingled with a roseate hue; the throat is adorned with a crest, and the head with a tuft of feathers. The first Roman who described this bird . . . . was the senator Manilius. . . . He tells us that no person has ever seen this bird eat, that in Arabia it is looked upon as sacred to the sun, that it lives five hundred and forty years, that when it becomes old, it builds a nest of cassia and sprigs of incense, which it fills with perfumes, and then lays its body down upon them to die; that from its bones and marrow there springs at first a sort of small worm, which in time changes into a little bird; that the first thing it does is to perform the obsequies of its predecessor, and to carry the nest entire to the city of the Sun near Panchaia, and there to deposit it upon the altar of that divinity.

"The same Manilius states also, that the revolution of the great year is completed with the life of this bird, and that then a new cycle comes round again with the same characteristics as the former one, in the seasons and the appearance of the stars. . . . This bird was brought to Rome under the censorship of the Emperor Claudius . . . and was exposed to public view. . . . This fact is attested by the public Annals, but there is no one that doubts that it was a fictitious phoenix only."

The description of the plumage, etc., of this bird applies fairly well, as Cuvier has pointed out, to the golden pheasant, and & specimen of the latter may have been the "fictitious phoenix" referred to above. That this bird should have been credited with the extraordinary and wholly fabulous properties related to Pliny and others is not, however, easy to understand. The phoenix was frequently used to illustrate the doctrine of the immortality of the soul (e.g. in Clement's First Epistle to the Corinthians), and it is not impossible that originally it was nothing more than a symbol of immortality, which in time became to be believed in as a really existing bird. The fact, however, that there was supposed to be only one phoenix and also that the length of each of its lives coincided with what the ancients termed a "great year" may indicate that the phoenix was a symbol of cosmological periodicity. On the other hand, some ancient writers (e.g. Tacitus) explicitly refer to the phoenix as a symbol of the sun, and in the minds of the ancients the sun was closely connected with the idea of immortality. Certainly, the accounts of the gorgeous colors of the plumage of the phoenix might well be descriptions of the rising sun. It appears, moreover, that the Egyptian hieroglyphic *benu* which is a figure of a heron or crane (and thus akin to the phoenix), was employed to designate the rising sun.

There are some curious Jewish legends to account for the supposed immortality of the phoenix. According to one, it was the sole animal that refused to eat the forbidden tree when tempted by Eve. According to another, its immortality was conferred on it by Noah because of its considerate behavior on the Ark, the phoenix not clamoring for food like the other animals.

There is a celebrated bird in Chinese tradition, the Fung Hwang, which some sinologues identify with the phoenix of the West. According to a commentator on the 'Rh Ya, this "felicitous and perfect bird has a cock's head, a snake's neck, a swallow's beak, a tortoise's back, is of five different colors and more than six feet high." Another account (that in the Lun Yu Tsch Shwai Sking) tells us that "its head resembles heaven, its eye the sun, its back the moon, its wings the wind, its foot the ground, and its tail the woof." Furthermore," its mouth contains commands, its heart is conformable to regulations, its ear is thoroughly acute in hearing, its tongue utters sincerity, its color is luminous, its comb resembles uprightness, its spur is sharp and curved, its voice is sonorous, and its belly is the treasure of literature." Like the dragon, tortoise and unicorn, it was considered to be a spiritual creature; but unlike the Western phoenix, we read of it in the plural. The birds were not always to be seen, but according to Chinese records, they made their appearance during the reigns of certain sovereigns. The Fung Hwang is regarded by the Chinese as an omen of great happiness and prosperity, and its likeness is embroidered on the robes of empresses to ensure success. Probably, if the bird is not to be regarded as purely mythological and symbolic in origin, we have in the stories of it no more than exaggerated accounts of some species of pheasant. Japanese literature contains similar stories.

THE CAMBRIDGE PLATONISTS

THERE is an opinion, unfortunately, very common, that religious mysticism is a product of the emotional temperament, and is diametrically opposed to the spirit of rationalism. No doubt this opinion is not without some element of justification, and one could quote the works of not a few religious mystics to the effect that self-surrender to God implies, not merely a giving up of will, but also of reason. But that this teaching is not an essential element in mysticism, that it is, indeed, rather its perversion, there is adequate evidence to demonstrate. Swedenborg is, I suppose, the outstanding instance of an intellectual mystic; but the essential unity of mysticism and rationalism is almost as forcibly made evident in the case of the Cambridge Platonists. That little band of "Latitude men," as their contemporaries called them, constitute one of the finest schools of philosophy that England has produced; yet their works are rarely read, I am afraid, save by specialists. Possibly, however, if it were more commonly known what a wealth of sound philosophy and true spiritual teaching they contain, the case would be otherwise.

The Cambridge Platonists—Benjamin Whichcote, John Smith, Nathanael Culverwel, Ralph Cudworth and Henry More, are the more outstanding names—were educated as Puritans; but they clearly realized the fundamental error of Puritanism, which tended to make a man's eternal salvation depend upon the accuracy and extent of his beliefs; nor could they approve of the exaggerated import given by the High Church party to matters of Church polity. The term "Cambridge Platonists" is, perhaps, less appropriate than that of "Latitudinarians," which the latter name emphasizes their broad-mindedness (even if it carries with it something of disapproval). For although they owed much to Plato and, perhaps, more to Plotinus, they were Christians first and Platonists afterwards, and they took nothing from these philosophers which was not conformable to the Scriptures—with the possible exception of More.

Benjamin Whichcote was born in 1609, at Whichcote Hall, in the parish of Stoke, Shropshire. In 1626 he entered Emmanuel College, Cambridge, then regarded as the chief Puritan college of the University. Here, his college tutor was Anthony Tuckney, a man of rare character, combining learning, wit and piety.

Between Whichcote and Tuckney there grew up a firm friendship, founded on mutual affection and esteem. But Tuckney was unable to agree with all Whichcote's broad-minded views concerning reason and authority; and in later years this gave rise to a controversy between them, in which Tuckney sought to controvert Whichcote's opinions: it was, however, carried on without acrimony and did not destroy their friendship.

H. Stanley Redgrove

Whichcote became M.A. and was elected a fellow of his college, in 1633, having obtained his B.A. four years previously. He was ordained by John Williams in 1636, and received the important appointment of Sunday afternoon lecturer at Trinity Church. His lectures, which he gave with the object of turning men's minds from polemics to the great moral and spiritual realities at the basis of the Christian religion, from mere formal discussions to a true searching into the reason of things, were well attended and highly

appreciated; and he held the appointment for twenty years. In 1634, he became a college tutor at Emmanuel. He possessed all the characteristics that go to make up an efficient and well-beloved tutor, and his personal influence was such as to inspire all his pupils, amongst whom were both John Smith and Nathanael Culverwel, who considerably amplified his philosophical and religious doctrines. In 1640 he became B.D. and nine years after was created D.D. The college living of North Cadbury in Somerset was presented to him in 1643, and shortly afterwards, he married. In the next year, however, he was recalled to Cambridge, and installed as

Provost of King's College in place of the rejected Dr. Samuel Collins. But it was greatly against his wish that he received the appointment, and he only consented to do so on the condition that part of his stipend should be paid to Collins—an act which gives us a good insight into the character of the man. In 1650, he resigned from North Cadbury, and the living was presented to Cudworth (see below), and during the end of this year and the beginning of the next, he was Vice-Chancellor of the University in succession to Tuckney. It was during his Vice-Chancellorship that he preached the sermon that gave rise to the controversy with the latter. About this time, also he was presented with the living of Milton in Cambridgeshire. At the Restoration he was ejected from the Provostship, but having complied with the Act of Uniformity, he was, in 1662, appointed to the cure of St. Anne's, Blackfriars. This church being destroyed in the Great Fire, Whichcote retired to Milton, where he showed great kindness to the poor. But some years later he returned to London, having received the vicarage of St. Lawrence Jewry. His friends at Cambridge, however, still saw him on occasional visits, and it was on one such visit to Cudworth, in 1683, that he caught the cold which caused his death.

John Smith was born at Achurch near Oundle in 1618. He entered Emmanuel College in 1636, became B.A. in 1640, and proceeded to M.A. in 1644, in which year he was appointed a fellow of Queen's College. Here he lectured on Arithmetic with considerable success. He was noted for his great learning, especially in theology and Oriental languages, as well as for his justness, uprightness and humility. He died of consumption in 1652.

Nathanael Culverwel was probably born about the same year as Smith. He entered Emmanuel College in 1633, gained his B.A. in 1636, became M.A. in 1640. Soon afterwards, he was elected a fellow of his college. He died about 1651. Beyond these scant details, nothing is known of his life. He

H. Stanley Redgrove

was a man of very great erudition, as his posthumous treatise on The Light of Nature makes evident.

Henry More was born in Grantham in 1614. From his earliest days, he was interested in theological problems, and his precociousness in this respect appears to have brought down upon him the wrath of an uncle. His early education was conducted at Eton. In 1631 he entered Christ's College, Cambridge, graduated B.A. in 1635, and received his M.A. in 1639. In the latter year, he was elected a fellow of Christ's and received Holy Orders. He lived a very retired life, refusing all preferment, though many valuable and honorable appointments were offered to him. Indeed, he rarely left Christ's, except to visit his "heroine pupil," Lady Conway, whose country seat, Ragley, was in Warwickshire. Lady Conway appears to be only remembered for the fact that, dying whilst her husband was away, her physician, F. M. van Helmont (son of the famous alchemist, J. B. van Helmont), preserved her body in spirits of wine, so that he could have the pleasure of beholding it on his return. She seems to have been a woman of considerable learning, though not free from fantastic ideas. Her ultimate conversion to Quakerism was a severe blow to More, who, whilst admiring the holy lives of the Quakers, regarded them as enthusiasts. More died in 1687.

More's earliest works were in verse, and exhibit fine feeling. The following lines, quoted from a poem on "Charitie and Humilitie," are full of charm, and well exhibit More's character:

"Farre have I clambred in my mind
But nought so great as love I find:
Deep-searching wit, mount-moving might.
Are nought compar'd to that great spright.
Life of Delight and soul of blisse!
Sure source of lasting happinesse!
Higher than Heaven! Lower than hell!

> What is thy tent? Where maist thou dwell?
> My mansion hight humilitie,
> Heaven's vastest capabilitie
> The further it doth downward tend
> The higher up it doth ascend;
> If it go down to utmost nought
> It shall return with that it sought."

Later he took to prose, and it must be confessed that he wrote too much and frequently descended to polemics (for example, his controversy with the alchemist Thomas Vaughan, in which both combatants freely used abuse).

Although in his main views More is thoroughly characteristic of the school to which he belonged, many of his less important opinions are more or less peculiar to himself.

The relation between More's and Descartes' theories as to the nature of spirit are interesting. When More first read Descartes' works, he was very favorably impressed with his views, though without entirely agreeing with him on all points; but later the differences became accentuated. Descartes regarded extension as the chief characteristic of matter, and asserted that spirit was extra-spatial. To More, this seemed like denying the existence of spirit, which he regarded as extended, and he postulated divisibility and impenetrability as the chief characteristics of matter. In order, however, to get over some of the inherent difficulties of this view, he put forward the suggestion that spirit is extended in four dimensions: thus, its apparent (i.e., three dimensional) extension could change, whilst its true (i.e., four dimensional) extension remained constant; just as the surface of a piece of metal can be increased by hammering it out, without increasing the volume of the metal. Here, I think, we have a not wholly inadequate symbol of the truth: but it remained for Berkeley to show the essential validity of Descartes' position, by demonstrating that, since space and extension are perceptions of the mind and thus exist only in the mind as ideas, space exists in spirit: not spirit in space.

More was a keen believer in witchcraft, and eagerly investigated all cases of these and like marvels that came under his notice. In this he was largely influenced by Joseph Glanvil, whose book on witchcraft, the well-known *Saducismus Triumphatus*, More largely contributed to and probably edited. More was wholly unsuited for psychical research; free from guile himself, he was too inclined to judge others to be of this nature also. But his common-sense and critical attitude towards enthusiasm saved him, no doubt, from many falls into the mire of fantasy.

As Principal Tulloch has pointed out, whilst More is the most interesting personality amongst the Cambridge Platonists, his works are the least interesting of those of his school. They are dull and scholastic, and More's retired existence prevented him from grasping in their fullness some of the more acute problems of life. His attempt to harmonize catastrophes with Providence, on the ground that the evil of certain parts may be necessary for the good of the whole, just as dark colors, as well as bright, are essential to the beauty of a picture—a theory which is practically the same as that of Modern Absolutism—is a case in point. No doubt this harmony may be accomplished, but in another key.

Ralph Cudworth was born at Aller in Somersetshire, in 1617. He entered Emmanuel College in 1632, three years afterwards gained his B.A., and became M.A. in 1639. In the latter year, he was elected a fellow of his college. Later, he obtained the B.D. degree. In 1645 he was appointed Master of Clare Hall in place of the ejected Dr. Pashe, and was elected Regius Professor of Hebrew. On March 31, 1047, he preached a sermon of remarkable eloquence and power before the House of Commons, which admirably expresses the attitude of his school as concerns the nature of true religion. I shall refer to it again later. In 1650, Cudworth was presented with the college living of North Cadbury, which Whichcote had resigned, and was made D.D. in the following year. In 1654, he was elected Master of Christ's College, with an improvement in his financial position, there having been some difficulty in obtaining his stipend at Clare Hall. In this year, he married. In 1662, Bishop Sheldon presented him with the rectory of Ashwell in Hertfordshire. He died in 1688. He was a pious man of fine intellect; but his character was marred by a certain suspiciousness which caused him wrongfully to accuse More in 1665 of attempting to forestall him in writing a work on Ethics, which should demonstrate that the principles of Christian Morality are not based on any arbitrary decrees of God, but are inherent in the nature and reason of things. Cudworth's great work—or, at least, the first part, which alone was completed—The Intellectual System of the World, appeared. In it Cudworth deals with Atheism on the ground of reason, demonstrating its irrationality. The book is remarkable for the fairness and fullness with which Cudworth states the argument of Atheism.

So much for the lives and individual characteristics of the Cambridge Platonists: what were the great principles that animated both their lives and their philosophy? These, I think, were two. Firstly, the essential unity of religion and morality; secondly, the essential unity of revelation and reason. With clearer perception of ethical truth than either Puritan or High Churchman, the Cambridge Platonists saw that true Christianity is neither a matter of mere belief, nor consists of the mere performance of good works; but is rather a matter of character. To them, Christianity connoted regeneration. "Religion," says Whichcote, "is a good mind, and a good life," and again "Heaven is first a Temper, and then a Place." To the man of heavenly temper, they taught, the performance of good works would be no irksome matter imposed merely by a sense of duty, but would be done spontaneously as a delight. To drudge in religion may very well be necessary as an initial stage, but it is not its perfection.

H. Stanley Redgrove

In his sermon before the House of Commons, Cudworth well exposes the error of those who made the mere holding of certain beliefs the essential element in Christianity. There are many passages I should like to quote from this eloquent discourse, but the following must suffice—

"We must not judge of our knowing of Christ, by our skill in Books and Papers, but by our keeping of his Commandments. . . . He is the best Christian, whose heart beats with the truest pulse towards heaven. Not he whose head spinneth out the finest cobwebs. He that endeavors really to mortifie his lusts, and to comply with that truth in his life, which his Conscience is convinced of; is-nearer a Christian, though he never heard of Christ; then he that believes all the vulgar Articles of the Christian aith, and plainly denyeth Christ in his life. . . . The great Mysterie of the Gospel, it doth not lie only in Christ wilhonl ns, (though we must know also what he hath done for us) but the very Pith and Kernal of it. Consists of Christ inwardly formed in our hearts. Nothing is truly Ours, but what lives in our Spirits. Salvation itself cannot save us, as long as it is only without us; no more than Health can cure us, and make us sound, when it is not within us. But somewhere at a distance from us; no more than Arts and Sciences, whilst they lie only in Books and Papers without us; can make us learned."

The Cambridge Platonists were not ascetics: their moral doctrine was one of temperance. Their sound wisdom on this point is well evident in the following passage from Whichcote: "What can be alleged for Intemperance; since Nature is content with very few' things? Why should anyone overdo in this kind? A man is better in Health and Strength, if he be temperate. We enjoy ourselves more in a sober and temperate Use of ourselves.'"

The other great principle of animating their philosophy was, as I have said, the essential unity of reason and revelation. To those who argued that self-surrender implied a giving-up of reason, they replied that "To go against Reason, is to go against God: it is the selfsame thing, to do that w'hich the Reason of the Case doth require; and that w'hich God Himself doth appoint: Reason is the Divine Governor of Man's Life; it is the very Voice of God." Reason, Conscience and the Scriptures, these, taught the Cambridge Platonists, testify of one another and are the true guides which alone a man should follow. All other authority they repudiated. But true reason is not merely sensuous, and the only way whereby it may be gained is by the purification of the self from the desires that draw it away from the Source of all Reason. "Holiness," says More, "is the best way to knowledge"; and again, "God reserves His choicest secrets for the purest minds." Or as Smith, who speaks of "a Good life as the Prolepsis and Fundamental principle of Divine Science," puts it, "... if ... Knowledge be not attended with Humility and a deep sense of self-penury and self-emptiness, we may easily fall short of that True Knowledge of God which we seem to aspire after." Right Reason, however, they taught, is the product of the sight of the soul, the true mystic vision.

In what respects, it may be asked in conclusion, is the philosophy of the Cambridge Platonists open to criticism? They lacked, perhaps, a sufficiently clear concept of the Church as a unity, and although they clearly realized that Nature is a symbol which it is the function of reason to interpret spiritually, they failed, I think, to appreciate the value of symbols. Thus, they have little to teach with respect to the Sacraments; and whilst admiring his morality, they criticized Boehme as an enthusiast. But, although he spoke in a very different language, spiritually he had much in common with them. Compared with what is of positive value in their philosophy, however, the defects of the Cambridge Platonists are but comparatively slight. I commend their works to all lovers of spiritual wisdom.

H. Stanley Redgrove

ARCHITECTURAL SYMBOLISM

IN an essay "On Symbolism in Art," published in 1912, I suggested that "a true work of art is at once realistic, imaginative and symbolical," and that its aim is to make manifest the spiritual significance of the natural objects dealt with. If these suggestions are accepted, then a criterion for distinguishing between art and craft is at once available; for we may say that, whilst craft aims at producing works which are physically useful, art aims at producing works which are spiritually useful. Architecture, from this point of view, is a combination of craft and art. It may, indeed, be said that the modem architecture which creates our dwelling houses, factories, and even to a large extent our places of worship, is pure craft unmixed with art. On the other hand, it might be argued that such works of architecture are not always devoid of decoration, and that "decorative art," even though the "decorative artist" is unconscious of this fact, is based upon rules and employs symbols which have a deep significance. The truly artistic element in architecture, however, is more clearly manifested if we turn our gaze to the past. One thinks at once, of course, of the pyramids and sphinx of Egypt, and the rich and varied symbolism of design and decoration of antique structures to be found in Persia and elsewhere in the East. It is highly probable that the Egyptian pyramids were employed for astronomical purposes and thus subserved physical utility, but it seems no less likely that their shape was suggested by a belief in some system of geometrical symbolism, and was intended to embody certain of their philosophical or religious doctrines.

The mediaeval cathedrals and churches of Europe admirably exhibit this combination of art with craft. Craft was needed to design and construct permanent buildings to protect worshippers from the inclemency of the weather; art was employed, not only to decorate such buildings, but it dictated to craft many points in connection with their design.

The builders of the mediaeval churches endeavored so to construct their works that these might, as a whole and in their various parts, embody the truths of the Christian religion. Thus, the cruciform shape of churches, their orientation, etc. The practical value of symbolism in church architecture is obvious. As Mr. F. E. Hulme remarks:

"The sculptured fonts or stained-glass windows in the churches of the Middle Ages were full of teaching to a congregation of whom the greater part could not read, to whom therefore one great avenue of knowledge was closed. The ignorant are especially impressed by pictorial teaching, and grasp the meaning far more readily than they can follow a written description or a spoken discourse."

The subject of symbolism in church architecture is an extensive one, involving many side issues. I intend, in this essay, to touch only upon one aspect of it, namely, the symbolic use of animal forms in English church architecture. A volume on the subject has recently appeared by Mr. A. H. Collins. It does not deal with the matter exhaustively, nor very philosophically, but it contains materials for such a study. In a word, it is a book of data rather than a book of interpretation; and as a book of data ought to prove of great value to students.

As Mr. Collins points out, the great sources of animal symbolism were the natural history books of the Middle Ages (generally called Bestiaries) and the Bible, mystically understood. The modern tendency is somewhat unsympathetic towards any attempt to interpret the Bible symbolically, and certainly some of the interpretations that have been forced upon it in the name of symbolism are crude and fantastic enough. But the belief of the mystics, culminating in the elaborate system of correspondences, of Swedenborg, that every natural object, every event in the history of the human race and every word of the Bible, has a symbolic and spiritual significance is, I suggest, fundamentally true. We must, however, distinguish between true and forced symbolism. The early Christians employed the fish as a symbol of Christ, because the Greek word for fish,—Jesus Christ, the Son of God, our Savior. Of course, the obvious use of such a symbol was its entire unintelligibility to those who had not yet been instructed in the mysteries of the Christian faith, since in the days of persecution some degree of secrecy was necessary. But the symbol only has significance in the Greek language, and that of an entirely arbitrary nature. There is nothing in the nature of the fish, apart from its name in Greek, which renders it suitable to be used as a symbol of Christ. Contrast this pseudo-symbol, however, with that of the Good Shepherd, the Lamb of God, or the Lion of Judah. Here we have what I regard as true symbols, something of whose meanings are clear to the smallest degree of spiritual sight, though the second of them has frequently been misinterpreted.

It was a belief in the spiritual or moral significance of nature, similar to that of the mystical expositors of the Bible, that inspired the medieval naturalists. The Bestiaries always conclude the account of each animal with the moral that might be drawn from its behavior. The interpretations are frequently very far-fetched, and as the writers were more interested in the morals than in the facts of natural history themselves, the supposed facts from which they drew their morals were frequently very far from being of the nature of facts. Sometimes the product of this inaccuracy is grotesque, as shown by the following quotation—

"The elephants are in an absurd way typical of Adam and Eve, who ate of the forbidden fruit, and also have the dragon for their enemy. It was supposed that the elephant used to sleep by leaning against a tree. The hunters would come by night, and cut the trunk through. Down he would come roaring helplessly. None of his friends would be able to help him, until a small elephant should come and lever him up with his trunk. This small elephant was symbolic of Jesus Christ, Who came in great humility to rescue the human race which had fallen through a tree."

I do not think this absurd legend found its way from the Bestiaries into church architecture.

In some cases, though the symbolism is based upon quite erroneous notions concerning natural history, and is so far fantastic, it is not devoid of charm. The use of the pelican to symbolize the Savior is a case in point. Legend tells us that when other food is unobtainable, the pelican thrusts its bill into its breast (whence the red color of the bill) and feeds its young with its life's blood. Were this only a fact, the symbol would be most appropriate. There is another and far less charming form of the legend, given by Mr. Collins, according to which the pelican uses its blood to revive its young, after having slain them through anger aroused by the great provocation which the young are supposed to give it.

Mention must also be made of the purely fabulous animals of the Bestiaries, such as the basilisk, centaur, dragon, griffin, hydra, mantichora, unicorn, phoenix, etc. The centaur was a beast, half-man, half-horse. It typified the flesh or carnal mind of man, and the legend of the perpetual war between the centaur and a certain tribe of simple savages who were said to live in trees in India, symbolized the combat between the flesh and the spirit. Concerning the griffin, we read that—

"The griffin is a fabulous bird which lives in the deserts of India, where it can find nothing to eat. To obtain sustenance for its young it will go off to other regions, and it is so strong that it can fly away with a live ox. The griffin signifies the devil, who is ready to carry away our souls to the deserts of hell."

H. Stanley Redgrove

The mantichora is described by Pliny, on the authority of Ctesias, as having—

"A triple row of teeth, which fit into each other like those of a comb, the face and ears of a man, and azure eyes, is of the color of blood, has the body of the lion, and a tail ending in a sting, like that of the scorpion. Its voice resembles the union of the sound of the flute and the trumpet; it is of excessive swiftness, and is particularly fond of human flesh."

The unicorn is described by the Bestiaries as "a small animal with the body of a horse, the head of a stag, the feet of an elephant; and it has one long straight horn four feet in length." Its horn preserves one against poisoning. To capture the animal a chaste virgin bedecked with ornaments is set in the middle of a forest. As soon as the unicorn sees her, it comes and places its head in her lap and may then be easily captured. For this reason, it was supposed to symbolize the Incarnation, the virgin typifying Mary, the unicorn's horn the unity of the Godhead, and the smallness of the animal the great condescension and humility of Christ; though the symbols are crude and inappropriate enough. The belief in the existence of these fabulous beasts may very probably have been due to the materializing of what were originally nothing more than mere arbitrary symbols, as I have already suggested of the phoenix in a former contribution. Thus, the account of the mantichora may, as Bostock has suggested, very well be a description of certain hieroglyphic figures, examples of which are still to be found in the ruins of Assyrian and Persian cities. This explanation seems, on the whole, more likely than the alternative hypothesis that such beliefs were due to mal-observation; though that, no doubt, helped in their formation.

It may be questioned, however, whether the architects and preachers of the Middle Ages altogether believed in the strange fables of the Bestiaries. As Mr. Collins says in reply to this question, "Probably they were credulous enough. But, on the whole, we may say that the truth of the story was just what they did not trouble about, any more than some clergymen arc particular about the absolute truth of the stories they tell children from the pulpit. The application, the lesson, is the thing!" With their desire to interpret Nature spiritually, we ought, I think, to sympathize. But there was one truth they had yet to learn, viz., that in order to interpret Nature spiritually, it is necessary first to understand her aright in her literal sense.

THE IDEALISTIC POINT OF VIEW

ALL experience is subjective. But in spite of the self-evident nature of this fact, its significance does not seem always to be fully recognized; otherwise, materialistic theories of the Cosmos would be propounded with a less degree of assurance than is actually the case.

I shall here attempt a brief analytical examination of experience in general. Firstly, I may distinguish between what are termed respectively "sense-impressions," and "mental images" or "images of the imagination." The feelings or emotions arising on account of these sense-impressions and mental images may be grouped together as a third element of experience;—with such, however, I am not concerned on the present occasion. In popular opinion and according to the terms of materialistic philosophy, sense-impressions and mental images differ from each other inasmuch as sense-impressions arise on account of a material world external to us, with which they are immediately connected; whilst mental images do not so arise, and have no immediate connection with this material world. A moment's consideration, however, shows us that this is not a statement of the differences between sense-impressions and mental images as experienced,—the differences, that is to say, in virtue of which we are entitled to divide our experiences into two categories, and in virtue of which we can determine to which category each of our experiences belongs,—but a hypothesis to explain such differences assumed to be existent. It may be a valid hypothesis; on the other hand, it may not. I shall, however, attempt a statement of these differences without involving myself in any hypothesis whatever.

An examination of one's own experiences reveals two differences between those forms of experiences termed respectively "sense impressions" and "mental-images." In the first place, sense impressions are generally very vivid as compared with mental images. This difference, however, is a purely relative one. Sense impressions which are not attended to and barely penetrate the fringe of consciousness can hardly be called vivid; whilst in dreams, on the other hand, whatever may be the cause, the dramatic images of our imaginations take on an apparent vividness comparable only with the sense-impressions of waking life.

The second and more fundamental distinction between sense impressions and images of the imagination is to be found in the degree of control we have over them. If I desire to do so, merely by an effort of will I can conjure up in my mind a complete mental image of an orange, that is to say, not merely a visual image of an orange, but a representation of all the sense-impressions connoted by the term. But in order to experience the corresponding sense-impressions, I must first of all experience other sense impressions—such complex series of sense-impressions I call "going to the fruiterer's and buying an orange" or "instructing a servant to procure me an orange," etc.,—and it is quite possible in certain circumstances that I may not be able to obtain the desired sense-impression, however much I may strive so to do. Sense-impressions always occur in certain groups and follow a definite and fixed order. Thus, the characteristic gustatory and odoriferous sensations connoted by the term "orange" are always accompanied by such sensations as those of roundness, smoothness, yellowness, etc. Or to take another example: the complex series of sense-impressions called "putting one's hand in the fire" is invariably followed by an intense sensation of pain. This order in the grouping and sequence of sense-impressions constitute what are called the "laws of nature," and our control of our sense-impressions is strictly limited thereby. It is quite easy to call up in the mind representations of all the sense-impressions connoted by the term "orange," substituting, however, an idea of pinkness in place of yellowness, or squareness in place of roundness; but similar groupings of sense-impressions themselves have never been experienced. Or to take another example: it is quite easy to picture in one's mind the process of putting one's hand in the fire without at all proceeding to conjure up a representation of the very painful sensations which inevitably follow the corresponding sequence of sense-impressions.

Now, it is of the very utmost importance to notice that these two differences are the only differences between sense-impressions and mental images of which we have any consciousness, and it is wholly in virtue of these that we divide our experiences into the two groups we call respectively "sense-impressions" and "mental images," and decide to which group any particular state of consciousness is to be assigned. In everyday life, we have, as a rule, no difficulty in deciding this question; for, usually, our sense-impressions are very vivid, the images of our imaginations very vague, compared one with the other. And in any case of doubt, the method adopted to decide the question always depends, in the last analysis, on the difference in our power of control over these two forms of experience.

As I have already indicated, the usual explanation of the differences between those forms of experience called respectively "sense-impressions" and "mental images" is that the former arise on account of an objective world of matter external to us, whereas mental images bear no direct relation to this world. I must here distinguish between two different uses of the word "matter," however. By the idealist, the term, if used at all, is employed merely to denote the fact that certain sense-impressions are invariably grouped together. This is the strictly scientific use of the term, since science being concerned only with facts of experience as such, for science "matter" can imply nothing more than certain facts of experience, or the relations they bear one to another. In this sense of the term, there can be no question as to the existence and reality of "matter"; the only point that may be raised is whether it is advisable to use the term in this manner, since it is so frequently employed as implying much more than merely this.

This brings me to the second use of the word. By the materialistic philosophers and in popular phraseology, the term "matter" is employed not merely to denote the fact that sense-impressions always occur in definite groups, but as supplying an explanation of this fact. Matter is supposed to be a thing-in-itself, something existing outside of all conscious beings, independent, in a sense, of all phenomena and all experience. The thorough-going materialist asserts more even than this. He denies the existence, in any real sense, of aught else save matter. This hypothetical matter is supposed to be possessed of certain properties or attributes, each of which is responsible for a definite sense-impression. Thus, we find certain sense-impressions, such as roundness, yellowness, smoothness, juiciness and a characteristic taste and smell, grouped together, and this we call an orange. According to the materialistic theory, each one of these sense-impressions is dependent upon a certain property of matter; we find them always grouped together in this way, because the properties of matter on which they depend are always grouped together in the same portion of matter—the real, material orange. We can experience a mental image of a pink orange or a cubical orange; but we cannot experience the corresponding sense-impressions, because a real pink material orange or a real cubical material orange does not exist. But even according to the materialistic theory itself, it is evident that we can know nothing of matter beyond its properties, nothing of matter in itself. Divest an orange of all its properties and what remains? If the above theory were true, we should have pure matter, matter in itself; but, in point of fact, so far as we are concerned, we have absolutely nothing. It seems, therefore, rather absurd to limit the application of the term "real" to the hypothetical material orange—using the term "material" as the materialists employ it, as denoting not merely a phenomenon, but a self-existent "thing-in-itself."

To such an extent has our language become impregnated by materialistic ideas that the term "imaginary" has come to mean something the reverse of real: the assumption underlying this use of the word, of course, is that all reality is connoted by the term "matter." It is abundantly evident, however, that a mental image—an "imaginary" thing—has a perfectly real existence in the individual mind. The comparative unimportance of mental images as compared with sense-impressions arises, not because mental images are unreal, but because they are almost entirely under our control. If I experience those sense impressions I call "putting my hand in the fire," then, inevitably, I shall also experience a very vivid sensation of pain, and not only this, but it may very probably happen that the possibility of my experiencing certain other sensations may become for ever inhibited—in ordinary phraseology, my hand may be permanently destroyed. It is highly important, therefore, that I do not experience those sense-impressions I call "putting my hand in the fire." But the corresponding play of images in the imagination implies no such unpleasant consequences. I can mentally reproduce or imagine the series of sense-impressions of "putting my hand in the fire" and then banish the ideas from my mind. When this power of control over mental images is lost or inhibited, as in dreams, hysteria, and madness generally, they are no longer distinguished from sense-impressions. We see, therefore, that we call sensations "real," and mental images "unreal," not because they are thus distinguished, for clearly both forms of experience are real as such, but because the latter are in every sense our own, originating and existing only in our individual minds; whereas our sense-impressions are determined according to an order imposed on us from without and in virtue of which our control of them is strictly limited. Of course, in a manner, our individual sense-impressions are real for each one of us alone. As sensations, they exist in the minds of each one of us and for each one of us alone. But in another manner, our sense-impressions are, to a large extent, universally valid. It is not, however, altogether easy to make plain exactly in what way this statement is true without involving the hypothesis of an external world; and from this fact may be concluded the validity of such a hypothesis, divested, however, of the untenable assumption that matter is anything more than the sum of its properties, anything more than itself a phenomenon. We must, on the other hand, beware of overstating the facts. We are not justified in saying that the world as it exists in one individual mind is the same as it exists in the mind of some other. Indeed, we cannot even say that, for any two individuals, sensations are identical, which are denoted by the same term, for we have no means of directly comparing sensations existing in different individual minds. All we can state is the principle of relativity; though, indeed, this is of immense importance.

Our individual sense-impressions, said to be one in origin, may or may not be different; but the relations between them, we know, are identical. The distance I call one inch may appear longer to me than to you, but for both of us, the distance called two inches is twice that called one inch. In other words, our individual sense impressions are all subject to the same laws of order and sequence, laws of experience, or "laws of nature," as they are called. It is not merely true for me that the series of sense-impressions I call "putting my hand in the fire" is followed by an intense sensation of pain, this and all other determinations in the order and sequence of sense-impressions which lie beyond man's control are true for every individual. A teacher is lecturing at the blackboard to an attentive class: if one of the students experiences at some moment a mental image of the blackboard falling over, it certainly by no means follows that any other or others of the students present will experience a like mental image. On the other hand, however, if one of the students experiences the corresponding sense-impressions, each one of the students present will, in general, experience corresponding sense-impressions. This latter fact is expressed by saying that the hypothetical material blackboard giving rise to the sense-impressions of a blackboard in the mind of each student has actually fallen over; though we really know nothing beyond the fact that all the individuals present experienced corresponding sense-impressions.

Moreover, defining the "laws of nature" as certain observed orders and sequences in sense-impressions, we find that it is not always necessary for the fulfilment of the law, for the necessary sequence of sense-impressions to be restricted to one mind. Indeed, we often experience the results of laws which have, so to speak, worked apart from the individual mind altogether, and we are compelled to postulate a Divine or Universal Mind. We cannot, in truth, restrict the universe to the concept of it in the individual mind. The possibilities of sense-impressions far transcend the experience of any individual, or even the experiences of all individuals. Processes take place which no man has ever experienced and which, therefore, do not exist in the individual mind, processes which we know must take place because the results of them do come within the experience of the individual.

We cannot believe, for example, that the flowers and the trees, the stones and rivers of some hitherto unexplored and uninhabited country, spring into existence the moment they begin to exist in the mind of the explorer. We must at least admit the perennial possibility of their existence as sense-impressions in any and every individual mind. In other words, we must admit the existence of a world outside of us, existing for us as a permanent possibility of sensation. This world may be referred to as an objective, material world; using the term "material" in a sense intermediate between the purely idealistic and the purely materialistic meanings, as connoting this permanent possibility of sensation, but in no way affording an ultimate explanation of the fact, and in no way implying any transcendency of the world of phenomena. The laws of nature, we see, are universally true; whence the fallacy of any system of thought, such as Christian Science in its philosophical aspect, which holds that the world of sensuous experience is an illusion of the mortal mind. The same laws of nature, i.e., the same orderly sequences in our sense-impressions, hold good for every one of us whether we know of them or not: the result is always that given by such laws whether expected or not.

Thus, to take an illustration I have used elsewhere, the student obtains a red coloration by the addition of a solution of litmus to an acid, though he may know nothing of chemistry, or may even expect a green color. Surely, here is no delusion. True Idealism does not teach that there is. True Idealism asserts the reality of sense-impressions when rightly understood. We see that, whilst the reality of the images of our imaginations is purely individual or subjective—"imaginary" money, for example, is quite as good as so-called "real" money so far as he who imagines is concerned; but it will not satisfy his creditors—sense-impressions are, in a manner, universally true; they do, to some extent, inform us of objective truth. Hence, we may postulate the existence of an objective or material world, in the sense defined above. But, since all experience and knowledge is necessarily subjective, absolute objectivity is unthinkable. With the postulation of the Divine Mind, however, this difficulty is overcome; and we realize that what we, in our ignorance, call "objective" is really subjective—subjective to the Divine Mind. Hence, it is real in a manner that the images of our imaginations are not real; and we may re-define "the objective" as that which is universally true or real, in contradistinction to "the subjective,"—that which is true or real for the individual mind alone. Here also is to be found the answer to the objection that to make reality subjective is to make reality relative. As I have elsewhere remarked, "we may quite correctly speak of the physical universe as an idea in the mind of God; but this does not mean that it is in any sense unreal—to be an idea in the Divine Mind is the essence of reality; nothing else is truly real save that which is such. And it is because spirit is what it is, because of our likeness (faint though it may be) to God, that this real physical universe is possible to some extent to us as an ideal construction corresponding to the Divine ideal construction. The external world we know is the world as it exists in each of our minds; the real world is the world as it exists in the Divine Mind; in so far, then, as our ideal constructions are like to the Divine do we know Reality—reality, that is, which is not merely individual, but universal. All science, every endeavor so to interpret and coordinate sense-impressions as to eliminate the errors of the individual, and arrive at truths universally valid, is an attempt rightly to read the thoughts of God, rightly to understand His Will.

H. Stanley Redgrove

THE HARLEQUINADE

MUCH of what passes for music, nowadays, may be not inaptly described as futile; and, indeed, with all deference due to contemporary composers, it may be said that even the most valuable of modern musical compositions fall far short of the different standards of perfection attained by Bach, Mozart, Beethoven and Wagner. Similar remarks apply in the case of most of the other arts; the products of the twentieth century cannot seriously compete with those of the past. There are no modern poets to compare with Shakespeare, Wordsworth or Blake, to single out three very different examples of the highest merit; and although this age is not destitute of great painters, it may be doubted whether there is one to equal Tintoretto, not to mention other names glorious in the annals of painting. As for modern architecture—the least said the better.

I doubt, however, whether a similar criticism could be justly made of modern dramatic art; and I venture to suggest that if the present period be remembered at all for the production of artistic works, it will be for those of its play-writers. Of course, if one wishes so to do, one can still witness melodramas with the conventional characters, which are crude without being genuinely realistic and sentimental without being genuinely romantic. On the other hand, however, it is the present age which has produced the genuinely realistic works of Bennett, Houghton and Galsworthy, in which, as it were, particular instances culled from life are used to symbolize some aspect of the modern spirit; the genuinely imaginative idealism of Maeterlinck, Rostand and Barrie, and the extraordinary sui generis genius of Shaw.

Amongst the names of those who have written idealistic or mystical plays of the highest artistic value, must now be included that of Dion Clayton Calthrop. He had, before the production of *The Harlequinade*, achieved considerable fame as an essayist of very great merit. The collection of his essays published under the title of *The Harlequin Set* is one of the most delightful books I know. In it (a sketch of the history of the Harlequinade forms the first essay) one can trace the seed out of which the play has arisen; and it is the same spirit which animates both—the spirit of belief in the magic of nature and love, and of revolt against the futility of modern life with its money-grabbing, soul-destroying, meanly commercial aims. To read the book or to see the play makes one long for the simple—yet truly so wonderfully complex and magical—delights of nature—the smell of the country air at five o'clock on a summer's morning, of the flowers and the grass; and a glass of home-brewed ale at a country inn; ... and the love of a good woman.

Mr. Calthrop, like Maeterlinck in The Blue Bird, and Barrie in Peter Pan, makes use of symbols which children love. And, indeed, one is inclined to query whether the folly of childhood is not wiser than the common sense of old age. "Do you think they understood it?" asks Alice of her Uncle Edward, referring to the audience. (Uncle Edward, I should explain, is the make belief producer of The Harlequinade; whilst the charming Alice acts the part of a prologue and interpreter.) "Why, a child could understand it," says Uncle Edward. Alice doubts, "But then they're not children."

The Harlequinade is a fantasy set in a sort of historical dress. It all commenced at Olympus. Mercury, Charon and Momus the demi-god set out to search for Psyche, who had wandered from the celestial regions, leaving Hipponax, the philosopher who proved that the gods did not exist, to row departed souls over the Styx. It is thus the story of the soul's self-realization, of its return to the dwelling of the gods, which, as we learn as the story progresses, is only achieved in the self-forgetfulness, the self-sacrifice, of love. But with the progress of time, the belief in the gods grew faint in people's minds; and so the gods became actors that by their art they could still keep alive the belief in the great realities of life. And so in the second scene, an Italian pantomime of the sixteenth century, Mercury has become transformed into Harlequin, Psyche into Columbine ("dear little dove"), and Charon and Momus into Clown and Pantaloon. Columbine is wedded to a deadly dull young man, who is immersed in his books and ignores the red rose—symbol of her love—which she gives him. The rose, however, is secured by the "man of the world," and the soul would have been lost, seduced by the lust of the world, had it not been for Harlequin. His ingenuity saves the situation, and the curtain falls on the embrace of Columbine and her husband, who has awakened to the knowledge that red roses are of more worth than books.

Coming to the eighteenth century, we find, in the third (and finest) scene, that the gods have become servants; for, as Alice explains to us, in those days, people thought that religion and love were at their beck and call. It is the same story—only different. The hero, symbol of mankind, is not now immersed in bookish learning, but in himself—yet not even in his true self, but in a mere image of himself created by the conventions of his day. To him, however, the gods come, though it be in the guise of valet and chambermaid. At the sound of Psyche's singing, he is unable to read his epigrams—witty, but utterly superficial—on love, but orders them to be cast into the fire. A new force has entered into his life, though as yet he realizes it not. Cheated of his wealth, yet willing to be cheated for honor's sake, cheated of his bride—false, unloving and unloved—he takes a pistol in his hand and fires at his forehead. But the bullet only shatters his image in the mirror—his false self. He has attained self-realization, and the little chambermaid (Psyche, Columbine) has taught him love. The fourth scene is a caustic criticism of the modem commercial spirit. It shows us the "theatre" of the future, controlled by a great American syndicate, which gives the public machine-made plays—in which gramophones take the place of actors—whether they want them or not. Yet the gods are not quite dead. They plead for one more opportunity, and with a shout of "Here we are again," the Clown and his fellow-actors usurp the platform and tear down the symbols of commercialism. Finally, in the fifth scene, the gods return to Olympus. But, as Alice tells us, this is only to round off the play. In reality they never return. They are immortal and are ever with us. They may, to use her term, no longer perform "magicky magic," yet their true magic is never dead, but lives forever in the joys of nature, in love, in kindliness and sympathy, and in that foolishness which is of the highest wisdom. I can only say in conclusion that The Harlequinade is one of the most delightful, inspiring and deeply mystical plays I have seen. The acting is good, and I would especially mention the grace and naïveté of Miss Kathleen Nesbitt, who plays the part of Alice.

FACTS AND HYPOTHESES IN PSYCHICAL RESEARCH

THE business of science is not merely that of collecting and substantiating facts. That is only the preliminary work. The business of science proper is the correlation of facts, their explanation, not in ultimate terms, but in accordance with the law or concept of nature's uniformity. As far as psychical research is concerned, not much has been done beyond this preliminary work as yet: the chief questions that have been asked are: Are the phenomena genuine, and, if so, do they indicate the survival of personality after bodily death? But, as Mr. Hereward Carrington points out in his latest book, it is only when these questions shall have been answered that the scientific investigation of psychic phenomena will begin. Suppose, for a moment, that certain of the phenomena are genuine and are produced, in some manner, by a discarnate intelligence, the question still remains: In what manner? And not this question alone, but a hundred others require answering concerning the *modus operandi*, concerning the relation between the psychical and the physical, concerning the forces in play, concerning the limitations and difficulties encountered by the active intelligence, concerning the necessity and functions of the medium....

Science progresses by the formulation of hypotheses. A hypothesis is just a guess, not made at random, but under the influence of an array of facts. A good hypothesis should adequately "explain" the facts dealt with, i.e., bring them within some larger unity; it should involve the minimum of assumption, and it should indicate certain conclusions capable of experimental verification. A verified hypothesis is a theory. Science progresses by clinging to her theories and discarding her bad guesses, that is, those of her hypotheses, which are not verifiable. But it must be remembered that no theory bears the stamp of absolute truth nor carries a warrant of validity greater than that derived from experience.

Mr. Carrington is of the opinion, in agreement, I think, with every savant who has really investigated the question, that a certain number of the so-called "spiritualistic" phenomena are genuine, and he is inclined to the belief, also in common with many other learned researchers, that in certain cases they are produced by the agency of discarnate personalities. He considers that the time has now come when something may be done beyond the "preliminary work" referred to, and some hypotheses attempted in reply to the many questions arising therefrom. In his book, already referred to, therefore, he does not content himself with accounts of psychic phenomena, observed both by himself and by others, but devotes himself largely to discussing various explanations that have been put forward, adding his own quota thereto. The result is a very interesting and suggestive volume.

Mr. Carrington is most at home in the domain of the physical phenomena of "spiritualism." Certainly, these phenomena are, in a sense, more definite than those of automatic writing or speaking. There are so many subtle factors to be taken into account when dealing with the latter class of phenomena—questions of subconscious knowledge, telepathy, etc.—which do not affect the former. Moreover, in dealing with physical manifestations, we have phenomena which can be recorded and measured by means of instruments, so that the human factor—which is always the difficult one to allow for—may be to this extent eliminated.

The discussion of the physical phenomena of "spiritualism" raises the world-old question of the relation between soul and body. The theory, due independently, I think, to Hibbert and Lodge, that the soul exercises directive control over the body, utilizing, but not adding to, its energy, is a very attractive one. But how is this directive control exercised? Even if it be explained with Bergson on the analogy of the hair-trigger action of a rifle, still the fact remains that a certain quantity of energy (though small indeed) is needed to release even a hair-trigger, so that the suggested explanation brings us face to face with a contradiction to the law of the conservation of energy—one of the best established laws of physical science. Mr. Carrington inclines to the theory of inter-actionism. Arguing from the physical phenomena of "spiritualism," he maintains that the will is itself a definite energy, physical in a sense, but endowed with intelligence and transcending the law of conservation. Personally, I am doubtful if these facts are sufficient to necessitate the hypothesis. Let us suppose that the will, as does indeed appear to be the case, is capable of moving objects quite apart from the body, does that prove anything more concerning the will than is evident from the movements of the body itself? In each case, we observe a physical movement occasioned by physical force flowing from a psychic source. All that the former class of phenomena indicate is the existence of some new force—akin perhaps to that of electric or magnetic attraction,—but there is no evidence that it is any more psychic than the force which moves the pen with which I am writing these words.

In the last analysis, however, is not all force psychic, is not will the only force we know? I believe that finally the mind is forced to accept what Mr. Carrington calls "psychical monism," and rejects in his book, or what I should call "epistemological idealism." It is the world of ideas which is the real world, and it is there that causality exists. The atoms, forces, energies, etc., of science are only conceptual tools, created by the imagination to enable us to deal the more easily with our sensations.

But I would say nothing against the use of such tools, without which thinking would be well-nigh impossible; and it is from this standpoint that Mr. Carrington's hypothesis concerning the will is rightly to be valued. I suggest that it might be possible to approach the question from the mathematical point of view, making use of the mental tool whose nature I have attempted to explain in *A Mathematical Theory of Spirit* I do not intend, however, to follow out further this line of thought on the present occasion, beyond making the suggestion that there may exist a psychical correlate to physical energy, capable of giving rise to forces operative in the physical realm. Mr. Carrington has a valuable chapter on the analysis of mind, in which he well indicates the value of "confession." Hysteria, with all its distressing symptoms, is frequently the result of the suppression of a feared idea: once the idea has been discovered by psychoanalysis or otherwise and boldly faced by the patients, health is regained. Mr. Carrington's book also contains very many other matters of interest: there is a discussion of the value as well as the danger of hypnotism, there are suggestive studies of the facts underlying witchcraft and fairy stories (though I think the latter are myths embodying mystical truths, rather than exaggerated accounts of psychical phenomena), as well as a word of warning to unqualified dabblers in psychical research.

HINDU MYTHOLOGY

IT was not so very long ago that the European regarded all Asiatics as unlettered heathens. For some time past, however, we have come to realize that, if the Asiatic has much to learn of us, we have also something to learn of him. The recent formation in London of an "East and West Union," through the efforts of Mr. Das Gupta and Miss Clarissa Miles (whose names, no doubt, are well known), in order to bring about a better understanding and relationship between the inhabitants of the two Continents, is one evidence out of many of our changed attitude towards the East.

The mistake is sometimes made of attempting to maintain that Eastern and Western systems of thought and religion are essentially the same. Similarities in the moral teachings of Gautama and Jesus are insisted upon and comparisons instituted between the Krishna legends and the life of the latter. No doubt there are certain elements common to all systems of morality, and there are certain doctrines (that of "The Trinity" is a case in point, to which I shall refer later) which curiously enough confront us in otherwise disparate religions. But the Indian outlook on life, nature, and God is almost totally different from that of the European. Jesus, the Christ, came, He declared, to reveal the Divine Father of all mankind, and that men "might have life, and that they might have it more abundantly." In Buddhism, on the other hand, there is no Absolute Being, thus no God; and

Gautama, the Buddha, came, he declared, to teach men the way of liberation from existence.

The concept of Vishnu as of a God who becomes incarnate in man, at times when humanity is threatened with some dire calamity, and who is especially to be worshipped by love (bhakti), does, however, resemble that of the Christian doctrine of the Logos; especially as Vishnu is a member of a Triad, expressed by the mysterious word Aum, of which one God, Brahma, the Demiurge, is essentially a transcendent God, whilst the other, Siva, is essentially a God immanent in Nature. I have, however, dealt with the question of the Hindu Triad elsewhere, and have traced out the analogy between it and the Christian Trinity as far as this is possible.

If we are to understand and appreciate the thought and literature of the East aright, we must begin, I think, by studying the essential differences between the Eastern and Western outlooks. In India, to coniine our attention to this one great division of the East, the uneducated masses are given over to the rankest superstition, and the popular myths contain incidents concerning the gods of the grossest character. Not merely polytheism, but idolatry and devil-worship are rife. But superstition is by no means dead in Europe, and the state of many of this continent's inhabitants can only be described as that of intellectual darkness. India, moreover, we must remember, has produced not only two great world-religions, several systems of speculative philosophy, and its own scheme of physical science, but a magnificent literature which will endure comparison with that of any other nation. If we have to teach India much in the way of the practical utilization of Nature's forces, if we have to make plain to her the joy of living and that merit, or rather true virtue, is not to be gained by the mere mortification of the body, still India, with its wonderful and fantastic mythology, has important lessons to teach us. As writes the Kev. E. Osborn Martin in a recent work on the subject, [Hindu

Mythology] constantly emphasizes the superiority of the spiritual over the intensely material conceptions of our present-day Western life. Plutocracy will not feel flattered by the Hindu conception of the 'god of wealth' as a demon of a most unpleasant type, or the god of prosperity, Ganesa, who has a most repulsive appearance, and who is depicted as lord of an inferior type of goblins. Then, again, how marvelously these multitudinous deities cover every possible activity and every phase of human life. The contribution the Hindu will ultimately make to the religious consciousness of the world will be no slight one, for Hindu mythology and the practice of Hinduism teach us that to the Hindu, religion is taken into the very core and center of daily life. For our Western externalism in religion, the Hindu has uncompromising disdain; and instead of a faith which is in so many instances fading from the horizon of the West, the Hindu offers a real ardor of faith... Though it may not be a faith which appeals to our Western reason, or to our sense of helpful religion, no one... would question the reality of such a faith. Hindu mythology, even today, is instinct with this wondrous faith, nay, is often transfigured by it, for it bears the mark of a supreme and very real religious consciousness."

In the Vedas, India's oldest Scriptures, we find a pantheistic view of Nature, in which her various facts and forces, the sun, the moon, the heavens, the earth, the refreshing and vivifying rain, and the Soma plant which yields intoxicating liquor, are personified. A philosophical insight is also betrayed which is very remarkable in works of such an early date. In the Yajur-Veda, Yaruna, first-the open sky and then the omniscient God of the Universe, instructs Bhrigu, one of the Divine Rishis, to seek in meditation Brahma, the Supreme Spirit, "whence all beings are produced; by which they live when born, towards which they tend, and unto which they pass." After food (or matter), breath, and thought are suggested as solutions to the problem and rejected by Bhrigu or Varuna, we read that, "He

H. Stanley Redgrove

[Bhrigu] thought deeply and then he knew 'ananda' (or felicity) to be Brahma: for all things are indeed produced from desire; when born they live by joy; they tend towards happiness; they pass into felicity."

With the gradual increase in power of the Brahminical school, other gods came into prominence and took the lead of the Hindu pantheon—gods which may be described as the personifications, not of mere natural facts or forces, but of underlying principles—especially Vishnu, the Preserver, who is worshipped in his various avatars or incarnations—the noble hero, Kama; the amorous Krishna (already mentioned); Buddha (who came, say the Hindus, to bring false teaching); Kalki (who has yet to come); etc., and Siva, the Destroyer The symbol of Siva, as the reproductive as well as the destructive force of Nature, of whose eternal round of births and deaths he is the personification, is the lingam.

Brahminism aimed at coordinating the various disparate strands of earlier Hindu mythology and of interpreting its legends philosophically. But in view of the introduction by Brahminism of the caste-system and of animal sacrifices, the result was hardly beneficial, and there have been many revolts from it, in addition to Buddhism. Brahminism is essentially electic, and any god is welcomed into its pantheon and explained as an avatara of Vishnu. This multitudinous nature of its divine beings, this collecting into a loosely-knit whole of many disparate beliefs and legends, makes the study of the subject especially difficult. But it is well worth undertaking. The Rev. E. O. Martin's book, to which I have already referred, should prove an excellent and comprehensive introduction for the intending student, and will be found of much interest also by the general reader.

MAGNETIC REPULSION: ITS PRACTICAL SCIENTIFIC

VALUE AND OCCULT PSYCHOLOGICAL SIGNIFICANCE

THERE is an old saying that "seeing is believing." For most of us, however, it would, perhaps, be more true to say that "feeling is believing." Our concept of reality is closely bound up with that of solidity, and our concept of solidity is the product of tactual and muscular sensations. It is not until we have learnt to associate visual sensations with those of a tactual and muscular nature that we see things as solid. Perhaps this fact explains why many people, though entertaining no doubts as to the reality of matter, are very skeptical as to the existence of the ether; because, although the existence of the ether is involved in every act of vision, it does not, usually, appeal to the sense of touch. But, as a matter of fact, both matter and ether are, so to speak, in the same boat on the waters of reality. They are both constructions of the scientific imagination, built so that the mind may more easily deal with its sensations, and are both equally real or unreal, whichever way one likes to look at it.

In certain electrical and magnetic phenomena, however, the ether is made apparent to our muscular sense, and in no way more strikingly than in the phenomenon of magnetic repulsion—a phenomenon by no means as well-known as that of magnetic attraction.

It was a stream of thought much like the foregoing that ran through my mind a few days ago when I visited the laboratory of M. Bachelet, the French savant concerning whose extraordinary invention—the levitated railway—one has been hearing so much nowadays—mostly inaccurate information, by the way.

H. Stanley Redgrove

There was an ordinary electro-magnet, through which an alternating current was passing at a pressure of 3,000 volts. I placed my hand on top and could feel nothing, but an aluminum disc placed on the back of my hand was immediately shot off. It was in vain that I tried to force an aluminum cup on to the magnet by pressure perpendicular to it: an invisible stress in the ether defied all my efforts. When an aluminum disc was placed over the magnet and restrained from flying off at a tangent by a piece of wire through the center, it remained suspended in the air (or, rather, in the ether) a couple of inches or more above the magnet. If two discs were used, one of aluminum, the other of iron, both were forced up; if the iron was uppermost, the aluminum screening it, as it were, from the action of the magnet. When, however, a direct current was used, the iron was attracted and forced the aluminum down. When the iron disc was placed underneath, the alternating current being used, it was strongly attracted to the magnet, whilst the aluminum was repelled.

Forgotten Essays

It would be futile to pretend that modern science has completely solved all the theoretical problems of magnetism; but the theories advanced by Ampère and Weber will help us very greatly to understand these facts.

According to Ampère, magnetism is nothing more or less

M. Bachelet, the Inventor of the Levitated Railway.

than a whirl of electricity. What is electricity? There is the problem. But let us say, waiving any attempt at a complete explanation, that it is a strain, or some sort of singularity, in the ether. So far as that statement goes, it is certainly correct. Ampère's theory is borne out by the fact that an ordinary solenoid i.e., a coil of wire through which a current is passing) behaves like a magnet. But Ampère's currents are not currents through matter in bulk, not currents from atom to atom, but within the atom itself. Ordinary currents stop, because they meet with resistance in passing from atom to atom. But Ampère's theory asserts that a current within an atom meets with no resistance, and continues forever. This explains the permanent magnetization of iron.

When a piece of iron, or other magnetizable body, is placed in a magnetic field (i.e., near a magnet), it becomes a magnet itself. Why is that? At first, we might suppose that it derives some sort of energy from the magnetic field. But experiment shows that this is not the case, because a magnet used to magnetize bars of iron, etc., becomes in no way weakened by the continued process.

The iron becomes a magnet because, as Swedenborg first divined, every particle of the iron is already a magnet. The magnetic field drills these particles into order, or polarizes them (as we say), so that their magnetism becomes apparent, whereas formerly the magnetic field of one particle neutralized that of another.

The result of this is that the iron, now become a magnet, is attracted by the original magnet. But the magnetic field has another effect also. Any conductor placed in an electric field has generated in it (by "induction" as it is called) a current opposing that of the original current. This current almost immediately dies away, because of resistance. But in the case of atomic currents, there is, according to Ampere's theory, no resistance. Hence, as Weber has pointed out, the current in each of the atoms of iron will be weakened, through the generation in them of an opposing current, and each atom will be actually a weaker magnet than before.

Now, if a body is used whose atoms are either neutral or diamagnetic (that is, have currents in them opposite to that in the iron atom), it is obvious that a current will be generated in these atoms (or intensified if already present) opposing that of the magnet. The result is that the body will be repelled. This phenomenon (called "diamagnetism") is, however, very slight in effect. But if an alternating current is used, a whirl of electricity (eddy current) in the body of the material will be continually induced (each time the direction of the original

Forgotten Essays

current changes) as fast as it dies away through resistance. This produces the strong repulsion in the experiments described.

The question may be asked: If this is the true explanation of magnetic repulsion as exhibited by aluminum, copper and other neutral and diamagnetic bodies, why is not a similar phenomenon exhibited by the human body? The solution of the difficulty lies, no doubt, as pointed out by M. Bachelet, in the fact that these metals have a very much greater molecular density than that of flesh and bone. Their particles are small and closely packed, whereas the much larger molecules which make up the human body are comparatively few and far apart.

The phenomenon of magnetic repulsion has been known for long, but it appears to have been little studied with a view to its practical utilization. To M. Bachelet belongs the honor of bending this natural force to man's use. In his railway, the moving carriage is, essentially, an iron cylinder, with an aluminum foot running its whole length. Throughout the whole length of the line electro-magnets are placed at short intervals, which, acting on the aluminum, raise the carriage in the air (it is kept in position by guides), thus destroying its weight and all friction save that of the air. The carriage is drawn along by solenoid magnets, placed at intervals along the route, through which the carriage passes. These solenoid magnets act on the iron-core of the carriage, drawing it forwards. Immediately the carriage reaches any solenoid, the current is cut off in that solenoid, the momentum of the carriage carrying it forward until it reaches the sphere of attraction of the next solenoid.

M. Bachelet claims that he can by this means attain a speed of 300 miles per hour, and that the cost of construction and running is comparatively small. Whether the invention will be found suitable for the transit of passengers is a moot question. Devices which work admirably on a small scale not infrequently fail on a larger scale; and statements in certain of the daily papers, that we shall soon all be travelling to Brighton in a quarter of an hour, must be taken *cum grano salis* **(take something with a grain of salt)**. What M. Bachelet proposes to do immediately, however, is to apply his invention to the rapid transit of mail matter, for which it seems admirably suited, and I believe that an offer respecting this was received from the Russian Government prior to the European war.

ROGER BACON: AN APPRECIATION

IT has been said that "a prophet is not without honor, save in his own country." Thereto might be added "and in his own time"; for, whilst there is continuity in time, there is also evolution, and England of today, for instance, is not the same country as England of the Middle Ages. In his own day, Roger Bacon was accounted a magician, whose heretical views called for suppression by the Church. And for many a long day afterwards was he mainly remembered as a co-worker in the black art with Friar Bungay, who together with him constructed, by the aid of the devil and diabolical rites, a brazen head which should possess the power of speech—the experiment only failing through the negligence of an assistant. Such was Roger Bacon in the memory of the latter Middle Ages and many succeeding years; he was the typical alchemist, where that term carries with it the depth of disrepute, though indeed alchemy was for him but one, and that not the greatest, of many interests.

It was not until the publication, by Dr. Samuel Jebb, in 1733, of the greater part of Bacon's *opus majus*, nearly four and a half centuries after his death (which occurred circa 1294), that anything like his rightful position in the history of philosophy began to be assigned to him. But let his spirit be no longer troubled, if it were ever troubled by neglect or slander, for the world, and first and foremost his own country, has paid him due honor. His septcentenary (he was probably born in 1214) has been duly celebrated this year at his alma mater, Oxford, his statue has there been raised as a memorial to his greatness, and savants have meted out praise to him in no grudging tones. Indeed, a voice has here and there been heard depreciating his better-known namesake Francis, so that the later luminary should not, standing in the way, obscure the light of the earlier; though for my part I would suggest that one need not be so one-eyed as to fail to see both lights at once.

To those who like to observe coincidences, it may be of interest that the septcentenary of the discoverer of gunpowder should coincide with the greatest war under which the world has yet groaned, even though gunpowder is no longer employed as a military propellant.

Bacon's reference to gunpowder occurs in his *Epistola dc Secretis Operibus Artis et Naturas et de Nullitate Magics*, a little tract written against magic, in which Bacon endeavors to show, and succeeds very well in the first eight chapters, that nature and art can perform far more extraordinary feats than are claimed by the workers in the black art. The last three chapters are written in an alchemical jargon of which even one versed in the symbolic language of alchemy can make no sense. They are evidently cryptogrammic and probably deal with the preparation and purification of saltpeter, which had only recently been discovered as a distinct body. In chapter xi, there is reference to an explosive body, which can only be gunpowder—by means of it, says Bacon, you may, "if you know the trick, produce a bright flash and a thundering noise." He mentions two of the ingredients, saltpeter and sulphur, but conceals the third (i.e. charcoal) under an anagram. Claims have, indeed, been put forth for the Greek, Arab, Hindu and Chinese origins of gunpowder, but a close examination of the original ancient accounts purporting to contain references to gunpowder, show that only incendiary and not explosive bodies are really dealt with. But whilst Roger Bacon knew of the explosive property of a mixture in the right proportions of sulphur, charcoal and pure saltpeter (which he no doubt accidentally hit upon whilst experimenting with the latter body), he was unaware of its projective power. That discovery was, in all probability, due to Schwarz.

Roger Bacon has been credited with many other discoveries. In the work already referred to he allows his imagination freely to speculate as to the wonders that might be accomplished by a scientific utilization of nature's forces—marvelous things with lenses, in bringing distant objects near and so forth, carriages propelled by mechanical means, flying machines. . . but in no case is the word "discovery" in any sense applicable, for not even in the case of the telescope does Bacon describe means by which his speculations might be realized. Roger Bacon's greatness does not lie in the fact that he discovered gunpowder, nor in the further fact that his speculations have been validated by other men. His greatness lies in his secure grip of scientific method as a combination of mathematical reasoning and experiment. Men before him had experimented, but none seemed to have realized the importance of the experimental method. Nor was he, of course, by any means the first mathematician—there were a long line of Greek and Arabian mathematicians behind him, men whose knowledge of the science was in many cases much greater than his,—or the most learned mathematician of his day; but none realized the importance of mathematics as an organon of scientific research as he did; and he was assuredly the priest who joined mathematics to experiment in the bonds of sacred matrimony. We must not, indeed, look for precise rules of inductive reasoning in the words of this pioneer writer on scientific method. Nor shall we find these even in the works of Francis Bacon. Moreover, the latter despised mathematics, and it was not until quite recent years that the scientific world came to realize that Roger's method is the more fruitful—witness the modern revolution in chemistry produced by the adoption of mathematical methods.

Roger Bacon, it may be said, was many centuries in advance of his time; but it is equally true that he was the child of his time: this may account for his defects judged by modem standards. He owed not a little to his contemporaries, for his knowledge and high estimate of philosophy he was largely indebted to his Oxford master Grosseteste, whilst Peter Peregrinus, his friend at Paris, fostered his love of experiment, and the Arab mathematicians, whose works he knew, inclined his mind to mathematical studies. He was violently opposed to the scholastic views current in Paris at his time and attacked great thinkers like Thomas Aquinas and Albertus Magnus, as well as obscurantists, such as Alexander of Hales. But he, himself, was a scholastic philosopher, though of no servile type, taking part in scholastic arguments. If he declared that he would have all the works of Aristotle burned, it was not because he hated the Peripatetic's philosophy—though he could criticize as well as appreciate at times—but because of the rottenness of the translations that were used. It seems commonplace now, but it was a truly wonderful thing then. Roger Bacon believed in accuracy, and was by no means destitute of literary ethics. He believed in correct translation, correct quotation, and the acknowledgment of the sources of one's quotations—unheard-of things, almost, in those days. But even he was not free from all the vices of his age: in spite of his insistence upon experimental verification of the conclusions of deductive reasoning, in one place at least he adopts a view concerning lenses from another writer, of which the simplest attempt at such verification could have revealed the falsity. For such lapses, however, we can make allowances.

Another and undeniable claim to greatness rests in Roger Bacon's broad-mindedness. He could actually value at their true worth the moral philosophy of non-Christian writers—Seneca and Al-Ghazali, for instance. But if he was catholic in the original meaning of that term, he was also catholic in its restricted sense. He was no heretic, and the Pope for him was the Vicar of God, whom he would wish to see reign over the whole world, not by force of arms, but by the assimilation of all that was worthy in that world. To his mind—and here he was certainly a child of his age, in its best sense, perhaps,—all other sciences were handmaidens to theology, queen of them all. All were to be subservient to her aims: the Church he called Catholic was to embrace in her arms all that was worthy in the works of "profane" writers—true prophets of God in so far as writing worthily they unconsciously bore testimony to the truth of Christianity—and all that nature might yield by patient experiment and speculation guided by mathematics. Some minds see in this a defect in his system, limiting its aims and outlook; others see it as the unifying principle giving coherence to the whole. At any rate, the Church regarded his views as dangerous, and restrained his pen for the greater portion of his life, keeping him in confinement some part of this period.

Roger Bacon may seem egotistic in argument, but his mind was humble to learn. He was not superstitious; but he would listen to common folk who worked with their hands, to astrologers and even magicians, denying nothing which seemed to him to have some evidence in experience—if he denied much of magical belief, it was because he found it lacking in such evidence. He often went astray in his views, he sometimes failed to apply his own method, and that method was in any case primitive and crude. But it was the right method, in embryo at least, and Roger Bacon, in spite of tremendous opposition, greater than that under which any man of science may now suffer, persisted in that method to the end, calling upon his contemporaries to adopt it as the only one which resulted in right knowledge. Across the centuries, let us salute this noble and great spirit.

APHORISMS ON NATURE

Do not let us be deceived by words. "Principle" is a great offender. What do those mean who speak of gravity, for instance, as "a principle"? Are they confusing the word with "principal," and postulating some guardian-demon to watch over and direct the motions of bodies? Modem science, at least, should beware of the errors of her parent, and not commit that of the phlogistonists over again.

* * * * *

Gravity is not a "cause"; it is simply a general term used to cover many facts. So also, no law of nature has anything to do with the metaphysical concept of causation. A law of nature is simply a statement of generalized facts of experience.

Note that a natural law is a statement. Hence, were it more correct to speak of man inventing rather than discovering this or that natural law. The laws of nature axe tools man devises for dealing with his experiences, not the causes of those experiences.

* * * * *

There is thus a closer analogy between the laws of nature and the laws of a country than some think. True in the first case corresponds to good in the second. But a false law of nature, i.e., one which doesn't work, is reckoned no law and is discarded. This is, unfortunately, not always the case with a bad law where under the people groan.

* * * * *

The only cause known to man is his will. He has read his own volition into nature, and tried to make this adequate to explain his own life and actions. But a child cannot conceive and bring forth its own mother.

* * * * *

Man may be sure that there is another Will beside his own, since nature resists his operations and follows her own orders and sequences.

* * * * *

The attempt to explain sensation as the result of the action on man of an objective world external to him, and consequently outside of his understanding, is an attempt to explain the known by means of the unknown.

* * * * *

The attempt to explain some sensations as the result of the action of one man (or mind) on another is a reasonable and successful attempt. Why not for all sensations? Is it less reasonable if infinity has to be postulated of the Man (or Mind) who acts?

* * * * *

Modern science has doubtless rendered animism impossible—and materialism for the same reason. For she shows nature to us as a harmoniously working unity, whilst the atoms, forces and "principles" of materialism are as much disparate demons as those of animism. But science has not banished will from nature: only she bids us postulate One Will instead of many.

* * * * *

Nevertheless, this One Will may have many servants and, perhaps, some enemies.

* * * * *

Now that matter has been dissolved into a prior element, the new materialists speak of this element, the ether, as "uncreate and self-existent." So did the old materialists speak of matter. Thus, history repeats itself, and the errors of one age are committed in the next.

* * * * *

Behold! the ether is a creation of the scientific imagination, as was also matter. It is a finer, better tool, more adjusted to the needs of advancing experience. Sensation, thought, will, love—all that pertains to spirit—these alone are the elements of reality—empirical reality.

* * * * *

Space and time, as Kant proved, are merely forms of thought, mental categories. They exist only in mind. But there is another category, a more profound manner of arranging and beholding phenomena—the category of causation.

* * * * *

"Creation" is the theologian's term for that which the metaphysician calls "causation." But how often is it misused to describe processes which occur in and occupy both time and space.

* * * * *

If the language of mathematics is used, then causation may be described as perpendicular to both space and time. In a sense, however, it includes both these and the dimension perpendicular to them as well. Thus, it both cuts across and includes, as less within greater, both space and time. It is an ever-active process, beginning neither here nor there, neither then nor now, transcending the categories of space and time.

* * * * *

H. Stanley Redgrove

He, who like Swedenborg and many another seer, can get his eye in line with this dimension, shall see out of time and space into the spiritual realm, until something of the splendor of God shall become visible to him.

*****

Every natural object, or (to speak more correctly) phenomenon, is the product and symbol of a spiritual process and reality. And every true poet is a spiritual seer.

IMMANENCE AND CONTINUITY AS OBSTACLES TO THOUGHT

1. Immanence

> Flower in the crannied wall,
> I pluck you out of the crannies,
> I hold you here, root and all, in my hand.
> Little flower—but if I could understand
> What you are, root and all, and all in all,
> I should know what God and man is.

SO wrote Tennyson. Deeply conscious of the immanence of the infinite in the finite, of God in nature, he realized that if one could only grasp in its entirety the meaning of one of nature's least products, then would the whole significance of nature and of That which lies behind it burst upon one's intellectual sight. But the truth which he so well perceived has, like all truths, a reverse as well as an obverse side. Blake opens his "Auguries of Innocence" with the words—

> To see a World in a grain of sand.
> And a Heaven in a wild flower.
> Hold Infinity in the palm of your hand.
> And Eternity in an hour.

To some, as to Blake and all true mystics, it is given to see something of heaven in every wild flower; but the whole? That escapes even the longest-sighted, and hence the whole significance of the flower is never grasped. If complete knowledge of any so-called finite natural object yields knowledge of the whole infinite Cosmos, then only a being capable of infinite knowledge can completely know any such object. The finite mind is incapable of this, for we must never confuse knowledge of or about the infinite, which is certainly posable to man, and infinite knowledge, which is as certainly impossible. No man can see a world, hence no man can see a grain of sand; no man can see Heaven in its entirety, hence no man can see, in its entirety, a single flower. Tennyson did well in underlining his "if": the condition is an unattainable one.

In the early days of Science, man conceived nature to be a very simple affair: a few general principles (perhaps, indeed, one would suffice), a few simple laws—why, the thing was almost done already, hardly anything remained to be discovered or explained. And then men of science realized that their simple laws were only first approximations, that nature was complex, highly complex, infinitely complex in fact. As measurement became more exact, laws, which hitherto had sufficed to correlate these measurements, were found insufficient and inaccurate, and new and more complicated laws had to be devised. The behavior of gases under pressure and temperature is a case in point, which may be mentioned in illustration. In the early part of the nineteenth century, it seemed that the law followed was extremely simple, and could be expressed by the formula—

$$PV = RT$$

—where P is the pressure, V the volume, of the gas, T its temperature in degrees centigrade plus 273, and R a constant for all gases. But as refinements were effected in the methods of measuring gaseous volumes, pressures and temperatures, the law broke down as other than a rough approximation.

Another, and more complicated law was proposed by van der Waal, in which certain other factors were allowed for, as under—

$$\left(P + \frac{a}{V}\right)(V - b) = RT$$

But although this agrees with nature more accurately than the simpler statement, it by no means does so with absolute accuracy. Everywhere in the recent history of science the same gradual increase in complexity may be observed—only one of the old, simple laws still holds sway, namely that of gravity, and no doubt the time will come when that, too, will have to be given up.

Truly, there may be one fundamental principle in nature, one fundamental law, which, if we could grasp it, would give us the key to the whole of her behavior; but if so, it is infinitely complex, and thus we shall never grasp it. This being the case, there is no single one of nature's phenomena that we can grasp in its entirety, for this infinitely complex principle is immanent within every such phenomenon. As our investigation becomes more precise, so do the phenomena become more complex. Water, to the naked eye, looks a very simple body—under the microscope it is seen to present a thousand problems, and the chemist in his study of it finds a thousand more. And when these are solved, new problems will present themselves in increasing numbers. Thus, from the seemingly simple are we enticed into the endless pursuit of the infinite; thus, always does the immanent infinite baulk us of finality.

The same is true if we turn to philosophy. When we are young, the world seems so simple—such a simple philosophy suffices to make it, so we think, completely intelligible. But its simplicity soon fades, and we find ourselves surrounded by endless problems. The simplest object becomes a mystery. The mystery of substance, the mystery of thought, from these two we can never escape. And there are thousands more. The simplest matter, we find, involves innumerable metaphysical problems, which we must solve, if we would understand the subject aright. But we cannot solve them, not because there comes a point from which our reason refuses to advance, but because reason can forever advance without reaching its end. And we are obliged to be content and to act upon a partial understanding, an approximate solution.

Yet we should never despair at this insuperable obstacle that the infinite, immanent in the finite, presents to our thought; for it is, as I have said, an obstacle to finality, not an obstacle to progress. Indeed, the very infinitude of the problems that confront us promises us what is better than finality—infinite progress. And for thought not to progress is for thought to cease to be. Happy alone is he who has new worlds to conquer. Thought has infinite worlds.

2. Continuity

Yet another obstacle confronts thought in its conquest of nature. There comes a time when we find language inadequate to our needs; and how to think without language? We endeavor to make our language more precise, only to find that much of nature's behavior slips between our words. We widen their significations, and then they begin to mean nothing at all, for a word only has meaning in virtue of differentiation from other words. Are materialism and idealism really distinct philosophies? we are sometimes tempted to ask. "Contraries meet," says an old proverb: is it perhaps true in a deeper sense than one usually attributes to proverbial philosophy? I believe in God, I say, you believe in Matter. Do we indeed differ, other than verbally?

When this stage has been reached and an affirmative reply is contemplated, thought becomes completely stultified. Anything means anything, or everything, or nothing. We seek precision of language again. But how definite our words, save in words—themselves needing definition?

Bergson, better perhaps than any other philosopher, has revealed the nature of the obstacle to thought herein involved; and it may be summed up in the word "continuity." Language, if it is to be precise and mean anything at all, must be made up of signs standing for distinct ideas; but nature does not consist of distinct things. Everything in nature merges, into everything else—there are no sharp boundaries either in space or time. The intellect, according to Bergson, is incapable of dealing with this continuity of phenomena. It acts, therefore, like a cinematograph, taking a series of snapshots of what is a continuous event, and then attempts to picture the event as a whole by synthesizing these elements. But how great—infinitely great indeed—is that which is thereby lost sight of compared with that which is seen! Indeed, as Bergson says, the chief function of the intellect is not to receive but to shut out from the mind the multitudinous voices of reality.

How is the difficulty to be overcome? How deal with reality as a continuous whole—how think reality thus? To the former part of this query, Bergson replies that instinct, not thought, is equal to the task. To the latter he answers, Impossible: life, which is reality, can only be lived, not made intelligible to thought. But I feel more optimistic. At first sight that the solution should be found in mathematics seems highly absurd, for is not mathematics, as the science of number, essentially concerned with discrete quantities? But mathematics is more than the science of number. It is a system of symbology of universal application. It fills in the gaps—the infinite gaps—between discrete numbers, with what are termed "irrational quantities"—happily chosen name, as if to signify a transcendence of intellect, though in truth it signals intellect's enlargement—and expands the line of numbers into a surface by means of so-called "imaginary quantities." Here, then, is an organon of thought superior to language, not bound to discontinuity as language is. But how apply it? Ah! that is the task.

UNIVERSAL SYMBOLISM

THERE are few beliefs so widespread, in point of both time and place, as that of the spiritual significance of nature, so tersely expressed by Paul in his Letter to the Christians at Rome: "... The invisible things of [God] since the creation of the world are clearly seen, being perceived through the things that are made, even his everlasting power and divinity." "The nature of this Universe is in all things alike," we read in the so-called *Golden Verses* attributed to Pythagoras, and commenting upon this, Hierocles writing in the fifth or sixth century, remarks that "Nature, in forming this Universe after the Divine Measure and Proportion made it in all things conformable and like to itself analogically and in different manners. Of all the different species diffused throughout the whole, it made, as it were, an Image of the Divine Beauty, imparting variously to the copy the perfections of the Original." This belief that Nature is symbolical of deity, of spirit, persisted throughout the line of Greek philosophy, which extended from Pythagoras through Plato to Plotinus, Porphyry and Iamblichus, becoming especially prominent in the case of the Neo-Platonists. We find it, too, playing a most important part in the Kabalah, that curious body of teaching at once embodying the ancient esoteric doctrines of Jewry and owing so much to Neo-Platonism. But the Kabalah did not, I think, owe this belief to that source, for the conviction in the spiritual significance of nature is as much native to Israel as to Greece. The Psalmist gives expression to it with no uncertain voice, when he sings,—

"The heavens declare the glory of God;
And the firmament sheweth his handiwork.

H. Stanley Redgrove

> Day unto day uttereth speech.
> And night unto night sheweth knowledge."

But, in fact, as I have already said, the belief in question is the exclusive possession of no race and no time, and is to be found playing a part in most religions systems and many philosophies. If I mention some instances of it and not others, this is because it is obviously impossible for me to write an entire history of human thought, for almost that would be necessary, if a complete catalogue of the forms and instances of this belief were required.

The early nature-philosophers, who laid the basis of mediaeval alchemy, naturally adopted the doctrine of symbolism in their attempt to solve nature's riddles. The three alchemical principles, salt, sulphur and mercury, are, as I have shown elsewhere, nothing but physical analogues to the body, soul and spirit in man, assumed by the alchemists to exist in the metals, because these were regarded by them as symbols of man in the various stages of his spiritual development. It was this belief in the principle of analogy which led them also to postulate the existence of the Philosopher's Stone, which would transmute all base metals into silver or gold—obviously an assumed metallic analogue to the Savior of mankind—and gave rise to the whole of their fantastic theories. It might be urged that, inasmuch as these theories are fantastic, the concept of nature as a glass wherein spiritual verities are mirrored, is not a safe one for philosophic speculation and, in fact, is erroneous. On the other hand, it should not be forgotten that a priori reasoning is always precarious, even when it starts from a major premise of undeniable validity, for everything then depends on the minor premises. The alchemists knew far too little, both as concerns man and as concerns metals, to put their theory of analogy to a fair and detailed test, such as they essayed. But even in such circumstances, they did make many useful discoveries, and it seems that the fantastic garb in which their doctrines are clothed not infrequently covers a real and extraordinary insight into nature's secrets. In any case, the alchemical interpretation of nature is certainly not the only interpretation possible in terms of spiritual significance, and I mention it merely as an instance and not as affording any proof or disproof of the doctrine of nature's symbolism.

The poets and artists, in so far as they are poets and artists, invariably make use of nature's spiritual significance, albeit oft-times unconsciously. The true artist (and the word maybe used as inclusive of "poet") perceives a meaning in nature and human emotion that escapes the ordinary sight. It is this perception of nature's deeper meaning that constitutes his inspiration, and art may be said to be an endeavor to give adequate expression to this vision. But, indeed, all language is symbolic; for what is a word, written or spoken, but a natural phenomenon expressive of an idea or desire, that is, a spiritual fact? The characteristic of art may be said, then, to lie, not in the mere fact of its symbolism, but in the depth of its spiritual meaning and the universality of its appeal.

To those whose perception of the interior import of nature takes a religious form, the term "nature mystics" has been applied. The word "mysticism" has suffered much from hard usage, but in its best and truest sense it may be said to involve this perception that nature is a vast system of symbols whereby God converses with men, as, perhaps, its most essential element. But if this be so, is not the title "mystic" applicable, in varying degree, to every truly religious man—to every religious man whose religion is not merely a hypocritical outward show, or a belief in some artificial method of escaping the supposed wrath of God? The performance of every religious rite is a recognition of the symbolism of nature—that certain bodily acts are conformable to and expressive of spiritual states. Some religious communities have, indeed, reduced such rites to a minimum, because of the danger of unspiritual minds imagining that the mere rite is enough, that it is of value in itself and not only as a vehicle of a right spiritual state. But there are none that can wholly dispense with ritual.

In one of his letters Kingsley wrote—"The great Mysticism is the belief which is becoming every day stronger with me that all symmetrical natural objects, aye, and perhaps all forms, colors, and scents which show organization or arrangement, are types of some spiritual truth or existence of a grade between the symbolic type and the mystic type. When I walk the fields I am oppressed every now and then with an innate feeling that everything I see has a meaning, if I could but understand it. And this feeling of being surrounded with truths which I cannot grasp, amounts to an indescribable awe sometimes! Everything seems to be full of God's reflex, if we could but see it: Oh, how I have prayed to have the mystery unfolded, at least hereafter. To see, if but for a moment, the whole harmony of the system! To hear once the music which the whole universe makes as it performs His bidding!" I think that a feeling and belief like these of Kingsley's come to many minds, and with some the belief becomes deepened into certitude. Not only the great Christian mystics, but many others of the world's greatest thinkers, have experienced this and testified to it in their books. The names of Emerson and Carlyle will, of course, occur to every reader, because of the wide popularity of the works of these great men; but they are merely two out of a host. That everything natural has an inner meaning, that one is ever surrounded with the symbols of spiritual verities, that everything is full of God's reflex, that the whole Cosmos is pervaded throughout with harmonious music—the discords man makes being resolved by the Master Musician—such is their unanimous testimony. And I would add that the true mystic is he who values natural objects primarily on account of the spiritual lessons they teach, and who, fixing his sight upon their symbolic meaning, uses them at all times in accordance with their spiritual worth. To him is all history a parable, and, as concerns the mystics of Christendom, especially is this true of the sacred histories of the Scriptures. The Bible, Christian mysticism with one voice asserts, has an inner meaning of far more moment than that of the letter—the life of Jesus as recorded in the Gospels is, of course, by no means unimportant considered as a matter of historic truth, but it is, Christian mysticism teaches, of still greater import considered as a parable of what must be accomplished in the mind and heart of every man who would walk in the way of the regenerate life.

According to the Doctrine of Degrees enunciated by the Swedish philosopher Swedenborg, there are to be found two entirely distinct kinds of degrees in all things that exist. On the one hand, there are what he calls "continuous degrees." These are such as merge one into the other: for instance, degrees of light and shade, of color, of lightness and heaviness, of cold and heat, etc. They permit of no sharp lines of demarcation being drawn, but they are never coexistent. On the other hand, "discrete degrees," as he calls them, do not merge one into the other, but are related as end, cause and effect, and are at once coexistent and capable of being sharply distinguished from each other. This doctrine, to my mind, throws a very considerable amount of light on the subject of universal symbolism, converting what is vague in many respects into a precise organon of philosophical thought. Let us ask why it is that the things of nature are significant of and symbolize spiritual truth and divine verities. If nature be regarded as a product of super-nature, then from the standpoint of the Doctrine of Degrees the answer is obvious. Nature symbolizes Spirit, and shows to the seeing eye the glories of God, because God, Spirit and Nature form a trine of discrete degrees. The spiritual significance of nature exists in virtue of the fact that natural phenomena and spiritual activity are related as effect is to cause. To this relation, Swedenborg gives the name "Correspondence," the term being used to distinguish that symbolism that is inherent in the nature of things from a mere likeness or analogy. As Tulk, one of Swedenborg's exponents, well put it, "In the views of Swedenborg, correspondency is the relationship between a cause in the mind and an effect which is presented to the senses." Swedenborg's Law of Correspondences may be stated thus: Every natural object exists as the correspondent of an idea or emotion. It is his sharply-drawn line of demarcation between correspondence on the one hand and mere analogy or likeness on the other, which gives the law its practical value as an organon of thought, though its utility has yet to gain general recognition. As has been pointed out, long before Swedenborg's day, men had perceived the truth of the old Hermetic axiom, "What is below is as that which is above, what is above is as that which is below, to accomplish the miracles of The One Thing," and had used it in a vague and groping way. Some, such as Bruno, Francis Bacon, and the alchemist who wrote the Sethon-Sendivogius treatises, grasped it, perhaps, in a more philosophical manner; but, until the Doctrine of Degrees had been formulated and a basis thus provided, the felt fact of the correspondence between the natural and the spiritual could not become a law or organon sufficiently definite for the purposes of philosophical thought. Of some laws, such as this, it is truer to say that they have gradually evolved in the consciousness of man, than that they were discovered. But, as Emerson remarks in his essay on Swedenborg; or the Mystic, "Swedenborg first put the fact of correspondence into a detached and scientific statement"; and if precision and accuracy are the marks of a scientific law, then the "Law of Correspondences" may be rightly denominated Swedenborg's.

We are very apt to disregard the immense part symbolism plays in our thought and action. It may be truly said that the whole of the natural world, as depicted by Science, is a symbolic structure. Atoms and ether, forces and energy, are all constructions of the scientific imagination, scaffoldings erected by it to get at and utilize new facts, or, rather, machines for transmuting experience, coordinating its elements, and predicting its outcome. And in so far as these tools efficiently perform their intended work, may we regard them as genuine symbols. One school of metaphysicians looks upon "matter" as a thing-in itself, existing outside of mind. But in so doing they deny the existence of matter at the same time as they assert it, for a thing existing outside of mind, obviously, cannot be thought of or known. This, however, is not the truly scientific view. Science is not rightly concerned with metaphysical problems; hence, to it, "matter" can be no more than a convenient hypothesis, a mind-created symbol, for dealing with experience. That such a tool is not perfectly adapted to the needs of growing scientific experience is shown by the recent resolution of matter into the ether. Materialists speak of the ether as though it were merely another sort of matter: which, indeed, it is, though in a sense opposed to thief's, since it is a new creation of the scientific imagination, a new symbol, a finer and more delicate tool for coordinating and predicting facts of experience. But there are some who make the mistake of regarding the ether as a thing in-itself, whilst strenuously denying that matter is anything more than a phenomenon. They are committing the fundamental error of materialism, though seemingly unaware of the fact.

Why is it that a man's words and actions are significant to his fellows? What is a word, a sentence, a discourse, a book, but a series of sounds or a series of black marks on a white surface? What confers on them their meaning? Have they not meaning only because they are effects flowing from the man's will as end or purpose, operating through his intelligence as cause, and because effects correspond to causes and ends? This, indeed, is the essence of the law of correspondences, that what is true of this trine of discrete degrees is true of every such trine, that effect always corresponds to cause, and cause and effect to end. But, in as much as this relation between a spiritual cause and a natural effect is not an empirically determinable one, it may be asked, firstly, How are any specific correspondences to be determined? and secondly, Of what practical utility to thought would such be if and when determined? Swedenborg has one answer to both these questions, namely, that the relationship of correspondence results in similarity of use. He says: "The Lord's kingdom is a kingdom of ends which are uses; or, what is the same thing, it is a kingdom of uses which are ends. On this account, the universe has been created and formed by the Divine Being that uses may everywhere be clothed with such forms as will present them in act or effect, first in heaven and afterwards in the world; and thus by successive degrees down to the grossest substances of nature. It is therefore evident that the correspondence of natural things with spiritual or of the world with heaven is effected by uses and that uses unite them; and that the forms with which uses are clothed are correspondences and are the means of union so far as they are forms of the uses. In nature and its three kingdoms, all things which exist according to order are forms of uses, or effects formed from use for the sake of use; and that is why the things in nature are correspondences."

If it be admitted that Nature, as I hold, is the outcome of Purpose, then the soundness of Swedenborg's argument will not be questioned. Just as the continuity and oneness of the laws of Nature's behavior evince the oneness of this Purpose, so does the fact that she is capable of analysis into innumerable objects indicate that this Purpose is analyzable into innumerable strands. Now, the purpose of a thing is manifest only in what we call its "function" or "use." Hence, the products on the three planes of being of any single strand of the Divine Purpose will be alike—in other words, will correspond—in respect of their "functions" or "uses." They will, in fact, just because they are separated by a discrete degree, be alike in no other respect. As Sir William Barrett has well put it, borrowing a word from the science of biology: "...

Correspondence is more than an analogy, more than a mere likeness without a deeper bond of union. It is rather a homology, a correspondence of structure, but a homology on different planes of existence." "In Biology," he adds, "organs are said to be homologous where they are constructed on the same plan and develop from corresponding embryonic parts, as in the case of the arms of a man and the wings of a bird or the human hand and the paddle of a porpoise, bone corresponding to bone. In biology, this conformity to type is strongly suggestive of a true relationship of inheritance from a common ancestor. I have ventured to apply this term, homologous, to spiritual law in the natural world."

Thus, the heart and the lungs, according to Swedenborg, correspond to the will and intelligence in man, because they perform uses for his body similar to those effected by his affections and intelligence for his soul, or true self. Indeed, the heart and the lungs, with their ramifications, may be said to constitute the body, just as the will and intelligence, with all they contain, or are made up of, may be said to constitute the man. Again, consider the correspondence, asserted to exist by Swedenborg, between the heat and the light of the sun, and the love and the wisdom of God. Does not the heat of the sun perform a function for the earth similar to that effected by the divine love in the spiritual world, that is, in the heart of man—nourishing it with its energy and calling it forth into life? Light alone—as in the winter—is unable to do this, just as truth without affection fails to quicken the moribund heart. But light enlightens the bodily eyes, enabling them to see, just as wisdom or truth enlightens the eyes of the spirit, enabling the intelligence to perform its analogous function. Or again, consider the correspondence said to obtain between man's affections and the members of the animal kingdom. Is not this relation recognized in such expressions as, "A man of lion heart," "Wise as serpents and harmless as doves," "Gentle as a lamb," and so on? Do we not, in the use of such expressions, realize that a man's character (the result of his affections and activity) may be well described by the symbolic use of animals? Indeed, just as the generation of man's body in his mother's womb epitomizes the process of the evolution of man, showing that man, as it were, sums up, in a physiological sense, the animal kingdom, so is his soul a synthesis of spiritual activities, of which the members of this kingdom are the manifested effects in the realm of nature.

We find the fact of correspondence recognized in many other expressions, such as the invariable use of "the heart" to designate the affectional side of men. It may, however, be here objected that I am basing my argument on mere forms of speech. But what are "forms of speech," and why should they be designated "mere"? There are certain forms of speech which are common to practically every race, certain symbols which are universally admitted to be appropriate; and this universal agreement should convince us that such symbolism is not arbitrary, but inherent in the nature of things. Such forms of speech originated with language itself, in those ancient days when, living nearer to nature, man, perhaps, enjoyed an instinctive perception of something of her meaning, which he has now to a large extent lost. Bergson's philosophy, with its insistence that life can only be grasped by instinct or intuition and not made completely intelligible to thought, is full of suggestion in this connection.

It may, perhaps, be thought that in making the principle of correspondence between nature and spirit exact, Swedenborg destroyed its poetic nature, and rendered it ineffective for the purposes of artistic creation. But that I think would be a mistake, for although his Law of Correspondences is, as I have intimated, certainly precise, it is by no means formal or scholastic. The criterion of use endows it with considerable flexibility. The products of man's technical skill, indeed, have in many cases each but a single specific use; but one of the characteristics of the objects of nature and of the first things derived therefrom by primitive man is the multiplicity of their uses. I remember reading an essay, at once humorous and profound—I forget who was the author—in which the stick and the umbrella were contrasted from this point of view. The stick can be used to assist one in walking, jumping, climbing, to defend one in case of attack, to poke the fire, etc., etc., whereas the umbrella has but one use—to protect one from rain. In general, then, it may be said that every natural object has various uses, these being determined by other natural objects with which it is brought into relation, and consequently every natural object is correspondentially related to as many forms of spiritual activity. The strands of the Divine Purpose interweave with one another, and nothing is produced but by the cooperation of many such strands.

The fact of Correspondence—of Universal Symbolism—is the cement which binds the elements of the Universe together, which makes the whole, indeed, a Universe. Deprive thought of this tool and the Universe seems not a universe, but a collocation of unrelated planes of experience, and the mind is forced into dualism, or can adopt a monistic view of the Cosmos only by disregarding one-half of experience. If the concept of discrete degrees—of the fundamental distinction between matter and spirit, between desire and thought and action—enables the mind to analyze the Universe into a number of disparate planes, that of Correspondences—of the inherent symbolism of Nature, according to which thought symbolizes desire, and action thought—enables it to synthesize the Universe from these elements, making of it an ordered Unity.

H. Stanley Redgrove

TRANSCENDENTAL ALCHEMY

WELL, has it been said that "the proper study of mankind is man," and the study of man means first and foremost, I suggest, the study of man's ideals and aspirations, his convictions and beliefs, the ever-persistent struggle of his intellect with experience—its victories and its defeats. On that ground alone I have based, and continue to base, an appeal for the more systematic study, in a spirit at once sympathetic and critical, of the whole curious heritage of thought that the past has bequeathed to the present under the title of "Occult Philosophy." But there are other reasons, and I would add a few further words concerning these, more especially in their application to that branch of occult philosophy termed "Alchemy." The mind seems always to be fascinated by mystery, and I do not think there is any subject surrounded by mystery quite so completely as Alchemy. Its very nature—its subject-matter and the object it had in view—is a controverted question. Its texts are written in hieroglyphics, and their authors are for the most part mysterious personages, elusive shadows which loom large, but escape the grasp of the would-be biographer. But I do not tender this attractiveness as a reason for study, because it would seem to me to be a somewhat superficial one. The reasons which count, with me, over and above the one already stated, are two. In the first place, we have the fact, as fact I deem it to be, that modern research has demonstrated that, in spite of all their follies and mistakes (which I do not want to gloss over), the alchemical philosophers did grasp—in a strange intuitive way, and certainly not in the precise manner of modern science—certain primary concepts concerning the universe of the greatest value and importance. And in the second place, we have in alchemical literature certain flashes (shall I say) of a light which transcends the light of nature, certain intimations—vague, indefinite, it may be—of an experiment and an experience not of the world of minerals and metals, but of the soul.

This is an intellectually-intolerant age. We too rashly assume that there is only one engine of thought, only one conceptual structure—though it is a modern philosopher who has proved otherwise—that will enable us effectively to explore the world of experience; and we are in consequence, too apt to label as "mere superstition" whatever does not concur with current conviction. I wonder, sometimes, how many of our present most dearly cherished convictions the twenty-first century will denominate "superstition." I am certainly not a reactionary. I do not want thought to go back, but ever to travel onwards. But no earnest seeker after truth can afford to neglect any opportunity or to pass by any intimation. The world may have gained much in, say, the last hundred or two hundred years—it may have lost only a little. But even this little is worth rescuing.

I have referred to the fact that there is a difference of opinion concerning the very nature of Alchemy itself. There are those who regard it as having been a foolish and fantastic effort for material wealth, whilst, on the other hand, there is a school which puts forward and defends the view that Alchemy had nothing whatever to do with metals, but was a spiritual science or art concerned only with the soul of man. Both are partial and hence erroneous views; and it is only when we see in Alchemy an attempted philosophy which took the whole universe for its province that we can begin to understand it aright. The one thing that is not mysterious in Alchemy is its first principle—the belief that is its *raison d'etre*. Thomas Vaughan, the Welsh alchemist who wrote under the pseudonym of "Eugenius Philalethes," I put it in these words:—"When I seriously consider the system or fabric of this world I find it to be a certain series, a link or chain which is extended from unconditioned to unconditioned, from that which is beneath all apprehension to that which is above all apprehension." The emerald Tablet attributed to Hermes Trismegistos has it more plainly: "What is below is like that which is above, and what is above is like that which is below, to accomplish the miracle of The One Thing." This was the belief fundamental to Alchemy—its working-hypothesis as we should now say—which led to a system of deductive physics, in which the chemical reactions of metals and other bodies were sought to be explained by analogies drawn from the realm of theology, and speculations indulged in concerning chemical possibilities (such as the transmutation of metals) derived from the same source.

But we should hardly expect every alchemist to entertain exactly the same ideas concerning his subject or to view it from the same standpoint. There are to be found in the history of Alchemy, alchemists of all sorts there were charlatans and there were fools; there were men who knew nothing of the high origins of alchemical philosophy, but saw in it (to their own detriment) an easy method of acquiring wealth. There were, on the other hand, included in the ranks of the alchemists some of the best minds of the past, Roger Bacon for example—and I would name Paracelsus also, in spite of those who deny his title to greatness—earnest men, seekers after truth. There were alchemists more concerned with the purely physical side of their subject, men who in some cases made useful chemical discoveries (Glauber is a good example); others whose main interest was metaphysical or speculative. I call these latter transcendental alchemists.

Now it is obvious that if the theories and technical terms of Alchemy arose out of an attempt to explain nature's phenomena by analogy with supemature, these theories and technical terms might in their turn be utilized as a means whereby to discuss psychological processes occurring in the soul of man. To show that they were so utilized one has only to turn to the works of Jacob Boehme. Vaughan, whom I have already mentioned, must also be reckoned an alchemist after this transcendental order. It is true that he attempted—in a rather haphazard manner, if one may judge from his MS. notes—to apply his metaphysical theories occasionally to the problem of metallic transmutation; and it is recorded that he met with his death as the result of an accident occurring during one such experiment. But it was the metaphysical—the transcendental—side of the subject which always interested him most, and it is this which forms the greater portion of the subject matter of his writings. In one place, indeed, he goes so far as to write, "For Alchemy—in the common acceptation, and as it is a torture of metals—I did never believe: much less did I study it." This, perhaps, is an exaggeration: but it indicates the bent of his mind. Nor is that which follows devoid of truth: "On this point, my books—being perused—will give thee evidence; for there I refer thee to a subject that is universal, that is the foundation of all Nature, that is the matter whereof all things are made, and wherewith being made are nourished." The reader who wishes to probe the secret of metallic transmutation will not, I think, find much to his purpose in Vaughan, but he who is in search of those intimations which I have referred to above may meet with a different reward. Vaughan's works are not such as "he who runs may read"; but that is not to say they are not worth the trouble of reading. Indeed, to those who are not of that company which considers Mysticism foolishness, I would almost write of Vaughan as an indispensable author.

Apart from the other difficulties inherent in the study of alchemical philosophy to the modern student, there is the difficulty of obtaining the texts. The originals are, in all cases, extremely rare. Vaughan is no exception to this rule, but during the last twenty years or so, something has been done to make his works accessible. In 1888 Mr. A. E. Waite edited four of his treatises under the title of The Magical Writings of Thomas Vaughan, and more recently (1910) has edited his *Lumen de Lumine*, whilst Euphrates was included in the "*Collectanea Hermética*," edited by Dr. W. Wynn Westcott, and was published in 1896. All these volumes, I believe, are now out of print, so that a collected edition of his works, which has just been issued under the editorship of Mr. Waite, is especially welcome. I do not know how students of occult and mystical philosophy would fare at all were it not for Mr. Waite's indefatigable labors. Their debt to him, as measured by the number of essential reprints for which he is responsible, is a large one; and they have not only to thank him for this, but for guidance as well. The present volume, in addition to a Biographical Preface and Introduction by Mr. Waite, contains a very large number of annotations in the form of footnotes, which are particularly useful. It is good that those who have gone before should guide with their lamp of learning those who come behind. Only thus will the labyrinth of Alchemy be traversed and the discovery of his heart of truth be achieved.

OCCULTISM AND THE ATOMIC THEORY

THE theory that all material bodies are made up of small particles or atoms is an extremely old one. It played an important part in the Epicurean philosophy of ancient Greece, and almost certainly Epicurus derived it from some still more ancient source. The atomic theory of modern science is, however, a very different thing from the atomic theory of Greek philosophy, being the outcome of an endeavor to correlate a large number of definite facts—to express them, as it were, in the simplest possible formula—whereas the atomic theory of Epicurus and Leucippus was merely a hazy speculation. There has been much discussion in recent days concerning the ultimate truth of the atomic theory, and the theory itself has undergone important modifications as the result of investigations in a field of facts not hitherto cognized by science, to which further reference will be made later. It must be remembered, however, that science is not concerned with ultimate truth, and that so far as, but no farther than, the atomic theory is found useful as a formula coordinating the various classes of facts it was devised to coordinate, so far is it true.

It would, of course, be impossible here to essay any detailed account of the origin of the atomic theory of modern science, especially as the subject is very involved and technical. Certain salient features may, however, be pointed out. The modem atomic theory may be said to be the product of two distinct lines of investigation and thought. On the one hand, the study of the ratios by weight in which bodies chemically combine with one another revealed certain remarkable regularities, which, as Dalton saw, could be very easily explained by a revival of Epicurus' theory in a modified and exact form. As a result, he put forward, in the early days of the nineteenth century, his atomic theory, according to which, in its original form, the chemical elements—that is to say, bodies incapable of being broken down by analytical methods—are made up of small indivisible particles or atoms, which for any one element are all alike in their chemical properties, and are characterized by a definite weight; whilst the atoms, or smallest particles, of compound bodies are formed by the juxtaposition of atoms of different elements, every different combination of elements forming a different compound, with properties (in many cases) quite unlike those of the elements constituting it. The atoms of elements Dalton called atoms of the first order; those of compounds atoms of the second, third, fourth, etc., orders, according to the number of elementary atoms which each contained.

The other line of investigation which led to the same conclusion was that of the physical properties of gases. In the first place, Robert Boyle, in the seventeenth century, had found that the volume of any gas at constant temperature is inversely proportional to its pressure. Next, Dalton found that all gases at constant pressure have the same co-efficient of expansion under heat, the actual value being 1/173 per 1º C. The significance of these two remarkable laws did not escape notice, and it was seen by Gay-Lussac that they could be explained by the assumption of an atomic structure for all gaseous bodies. Moreover, he had himself discovered the remarkable law that the volume-ratios in which gases chemically combine with one another are always expressible by means of simple numbers, and that the contraction in volume which usually follows as the result of such combination is always some simple fraction of the total volume. It seemed, at first sight, only necessary to adopt Dalton's atomic theory and to make the further assumption that the effective volumes of the particles or atoms of all gases (under the same conditions of pressure and temperature) are the same, for all these laws to fall in line. But when the attempt was made to work out the actual contraction-ratios on this assumption, glaring contradictions at once emerged and a controversy ensued between Dalton and Gay-Lussac.

In a few years, however, the whole matter so far was cleared up by Avogadro, though his views did not gain full recognition until many years later. The great point made clear by Avogadro was that the particles demanded by the weight-ratios in which chemical bodies combine are distinct from the particles demanded by the pressure-temperature-volume relations of gases; in other words that the chemical "atoms" and the physical "atoms" are not the same. The latter are now termed "molecules" to avoid confusion, though Avogadro used a different nomenclature. The molecule is (except in the cases of the recently discovered rare gases of the atmosphere and a few other bodies, such as mercury vapor) composed of more than one atom. The exact number of atoms in one molecule of any body is a hypothetical number, but in order to reconcile Dalton's and Gay-Lussac's theories, all that it is necessary to assume is that in the case of a compound the molecule is identical with what Dalton called an atom of the second, third, fourth or higher order, as the case may be, whilst in the case of an element the molecule consists, in many cases, of two atoms.

But although all the known relevant facts were thus harmonized and correlated, men of science almost at once began to speculate as to whether the end of the quest had been reached, and many attempts were made to resolve the sixty-odd different, sorts of atoms postulated by Dalton's theory into one primal entity. The actual weights of the various sorts of atoms were, of course, unknown; but comparatively simple chemical methods were devised for determining these weights relative to one another. Since the atom of hydrogen was found to be the lightest, its weight was chosen as the arbitrary standard, and the other weights were expressed in terms of this as unity. It was found that when this was done a very large proportion of the atomic weights came out as whole numbers, or very nearly so, and the theory was put forward that all other atoms were built up by the conglomeration of hydrogen atoms. This theory, however, failed to be substantiated, and it may be said that nothing effectual was achieved towards the unification of matter until it was definitely established, in recent years and mainly by the researches of Professor Sir J. J. Thomson, that when electricity is forced through a highly rarefied gas, it is conveyed by (or rather, in the form of) minute negatively-charged particles, much smaller than the smallest known atom, that of hydrogen. Since the nature of these particles—first called "corpuscles," but now known as "electrons"—was found to be independent of the gas used, it was not unreasonably concluded that here perhaps was the unity behind the multiplicity of atoms for which so long search had been made. This conclusion was much strengthened by the discovery of radium and other strongly radio-active elements, whose atoms were found to be unstable, decomposing spontaneously into atoms of other elements with the liberation of free electrons.

At the same time, a serious difficulty was encountered, namely, how to explain the production of an atom, an electrically neutral body, from electrically negative particles, no electrically neutral or positively charged particle corresponding to the electron being known. Professor Sir J. J. Thomson assumed a sphere of positive electrification wherein the electrons are supposed to revolve. However, determinations made by him of the stoppage and scattering by various elementary and compound bodies of the electrons (B-rays) which are shot off when the radium atom decomposes, as well as other researches, seem to indicate that the number of electrons in any atom is of the same order as its atomic weight. Professor Rutherford has suggested, in consequence, that the atom may consist of a massive central nucleus (or ion = carrier of electricity), electrified positively, around which the electrically-negative electrons revolve, the atom thus being a sort of microcosmi solar system. The inertia or mass of the electron, as determined by Thomson and others, is about 1/7000 of that of the hydrogen atom. Moreover, everything indicates that this inertia or mass is entirely electrical in origin, the electron being, not strictly a particle charged with electricity, but simply an electrical charge—an indivisible unit or atom of negative electricity. Now, mass or inertia is the one characteristic property of what we call "matter," and it is because of this property that matter possesses weight; so that it would seem that the one essential character of matter can be explained electrically and that matter can be resolved into an electrical phenomenon.

The resolution of matter has, however, been carried a step further, and the view is everywhere gaining ground amongst men of science that the electron is nothing but a stress-center in the ether, and the atoms of matter etherial vortices. What then is the ether? The concept of the ether, like that of the atom, is exceedingly ancient and has undergone many vicissitudes. From the scientific point of view, the history of the theory of the ether may be dated from Huygens (17th century). It arose as the result of attempts to explain such phenomena as the diffraction and polarization of light, which the old theory, that light was propagated by means of small particles thrown out from the luminous body, was powerless to explain. According to Huygens undulatory theory, which was especially developed by Euler, Young and Fresnel, all space is tilled with a homogeneous, perfectly fluid medium, the ether. The luminosity of a body is due to an extremely rapid vibratory motion of its molecules, which, when communicated to the ether, is propagated in all directions. The vibrations of the ether take place transversely and not in the direction in which the wave is travelling.

Such a medium as the ether is, moreover, needed to fill the interspaces between the particles of matter, unless we are to essay the very difficult concept of action at a distance.

In the early days of the undulatory theory of light, and until quite recently, the ether was always thought of as a very tenuous and rarefied body, and attempts to calculate its density, yielding very small values indeed, based, as is now known, on erroneous hypotheses, were made. The researches of Sir Oliver Lodge have, however, entirely altered all this, and have given us an entirely different idea of the nature and properties of the ether—an idea which seems to take us back to certain esoteric and occult teaching. Lodge's researches prove, not merely that the ether is by no means a tenuous body, but that its density is enormously great compared with even the densest form of matter. Not only is the ether enormously dense, it also possesses tremendous energy. As Lodge himself puts it, "Every cubic millimeter of the universal ether of space must possess the equivalent of a thousand tons, and every part of it must be squirming internally with the velocity of light."

H. Stanley Redgrove

As Swedenborg so well divined, and modern research demonstrates, a fluid or normally non-rigid body, if moving with a sufficiently high velocity, becomes endowed with rigidity and the other characteristics of solidity; thus, as Lodge points out in the work to which I have referred, a disc of paper, if rotated sufficiently rapidly, will cut into steel, and a stream of water flowing at a high rate cannot be severed with a sword. So, by the rapid vibration of ethereal stress-centers may a solid atom be produced. Material bodies have such low densities compared with the ether, because, although made out of this very dense medium, they possess a grained structure, and the distances between the grains are so great. The density of the ether within any material body is as great as that of the ether without, but it is not this density we determine when we find, as we say, the density of a body, by means of weighing it and measuring its volume.

Matter in the light of this theory is seen to be something less than the ether—its properties faint shadows of those of its source. In itself ether is always ether, but to become manifested as matter, it must, if I may be allowed to personify it, humiliate itself and limit its splendor and powers. Rut if we may conceive the energy and mass of all material bodies to be that of the ether, limited in view of its manifestation, may we not carry the thought a step further and, with Swedenborg and many another bold adventurer into the unknown, regard the whole universe as continually created by the self-limitation of the infinite substance and power of God?

In connection with these recent conclusions of modern science, a work by Mrs. Besant and Mr. Leadbeater, which has just been re-issued in an enlarged form under the able editorship of Mr. A. P. Sinnett, is of peculiar interest. Clairvoyants claim to be able to see, through the veil of matter, the worlds that lie within and beyond. If this claim is a valid one, then the elements ought to be capable of analysis by means of clairvoyance. Now it is precisely this which Mrs. Besant and Mr. Leadbeater assert that they have accomplished, and the results of their investigation are given in the book in question with some considerable detail.

For full particulars of the investigation, I must refer my readers to the book itself, but it will be of interest here briefly to summarize the chief points. The researches, it is well to point out, were commenced in the year 1895, and the early results were published in *Lucifer* of that year.

According to Mrs. Besant and Mr. Leadbeater, all the chemical elements are built up of two sorts of constituents, the ultimate atoms of the physical plane. They may be roughly described as spiral whorls of force—which remind one of Swedenborg's views—and the two sorts differ from each other only in that in one ("positive" or "male") force pours into the physical realm from fourth-dimensional space, whereas in the other ("negative" or "female") the process is reversed. In other respects, they are identical. They are said to be very complex in structure, the spirals of which they are composed being in their turn made up of *spirillae*, and these again of *minuter spirillae*. The *minuter spirillae* themselves are made up of an immense number of the tiniest imaginable dots arranged like pearls threaded on an invisible string. It is estimated that there are about fourteen thousand millions of these dots in an ultimate physical atom. They are spherical and absolutely simple in construction, and consist of centers of vacuity in the all-pervading ether—or, as our authors term it, "koilon".

The ultimate physical atoms are built up, through three intermediate stages of increasing complexity, into the chemical atoms. The forms of these are more or less symmetrical, which show the appearance to clairvoyant sight of the atoms of sodium, gold, carbon and iron respectively. And it is thus possible to calculate the total number of ultimate physical atoms in any chemical atom, by counting the number in each of its distinct parts. Thus, in the sodium atom, the number of ultimate physical atoms in a funnel is found to be sixteen, the number in a central globe ten, and the number in the connecting rod fourteen. Since there are twenty-four funnels and two globes, this gives 418 as the total number. Now it was found that the hydrogen atom contains eighteen ultimate physical atoms, and 418 4-18 gives 23.22. This is a very close approximation to the atomic weight of sodium, which is 23.83, referred to hydrogen as unit. Similar results were in every case obtained, the number of ultimate physical atoms in a chemical atom when divided by eighteen giving a figure closely agreeing with the official atomic weight. It will hardly be suggested that Mrs. Besant and Mr. Leadbeater have deliberately concocted these results with a view to establishing credence for the clairvoyant powers they claim to possess. I merely mention this alternative in order to discard it. What explanation, then, is possible, of the striking agreement between their atomic weights, clairvoyantly determined, and those based on ordinary chemical methods? I can see only two possibilities. Either their sub consciousness has played a most elaborate trick on them—a very hazardous speculation, attributing to the sub-consciousness extraordinary powers in the way of mental arithmetic—or else what they claim to have seen does somehow correspond with reality.

I am by no means unaware of the difficulties involved in this latter view. Their ultimate physical atoms are far too large to be electrons—they are nearly a hundred times too large—whilst their centers of vacuity in koilon are far too small. Moreover, whilst, as a rule, they describe the atoms of elements which resemble one another chemically as having constitutions of the same type, the unlikeness of their sodium atom to those of sodium's chemical congeners (potassium especially) is rather marked; and we look at the diagram of radium in vain to see how helium could result therefrom, unless, indeed, the ultimate physical atoms sever themselves separately from the radium atom and recombine together as helium atoms.

The work of Mrs. Besant and Mr. Leadbeater presents a problem and a challenge. I certainly have no intention of proclaiming: Here is the mystery of the elements revealed; but also, I should be the last to tolerate ignoring the claims of clairvoyance. The mysteries of the world are manifold, and those who would see need every available source of light. He is a foolish man who scorns any means of approach—any hint that may lead to the solution of these mysteries. Research: that is what is called for—and it is only thereby that we may hope all finally to arrive at the same goal.

Before concluding this essay, there is one other curious matter to which reference must be made, a matter which raises questions no less difficult to answer than those created by Mrs.

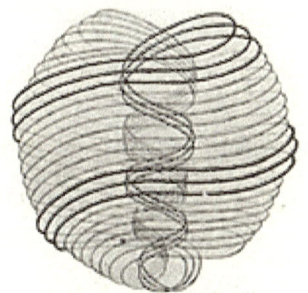

FIG. 1.—Positive (or male)

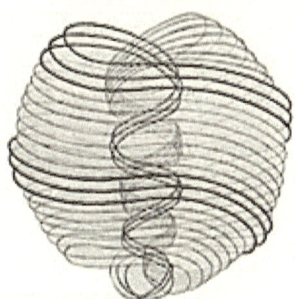

FIG. 2.—Negative (or female).
THE ULTIMATE PHYSICAL ATOMS.
(really observed, according to Mrs. Besant and Mr. Leadbeater.

Besant's and Mr. Leadbeater's work. The old-time occultists with one accord believed in a connection between the planets (including sun and moon) and the seven metals known to them—an idea in harmony with their belief in the symbolic, or to use Swedenborg's term, correspondential, relationship running throughout all planes of existence and binding them into a whole. There was also asserted by them to be a similar relationship between the planets and the days of the week, which belief is preserved in many cases in the names given to the latter. This is more particularly evident in the case of the French names, as may be seen from the Table herewith appended. And in the case of those English names which are derived from those of the gods of Scandinavian mythology, obvious connections can be traced between these gods and those of Greece and Rome, and a common astronomical origin for the gods of different mythologies is indicated. Thus, Tuesday is named after Tiw, a god of war, such as was Mars; Thursday, is named after Thor, a god of thunder, such as was Jove or Jupiter; and Friday is named after Frig, or Freya, a goddess, such as was Venus. It is not difficult also to connect Odin or Wotan, the god after whom Wednesday is named, with Mercury. Mercury, the fleet-footed, was the messenger of the gods, and Odin could send his thoughts afar. Both, it would seem, symbolize the mobility of thought.

Now the order in which I have enumerated the planets in the appended table—the Chaldean order—is the one invariably adopted by the ancients, and corresponds with the distances of the planets from the earth, and their periods of geocentric revolution. If, starting with the Sun, we select every third planet, and write in place of it the corresponding day of the week, we then have these days in their correct order. This fact, however, is less surprising than may appear at first sight, for the same result necessarily occurs if, instead of every third, we select every twenty-fourth planet, since twenty-four divided by seven (the number of the planets) leaves three as a remainder. According to the old-time belief, the planets, or the gods of whom they are the astral manifestations, rule each in order for a twelfth part of a day or a twelfth part of a night. And it seems probable that the days were named, each after that planet or god which ruled during its first twelfth part, and which in a special sense was the guardian of that day.

If, however, we start with Saturn, and select every fifth planet, a most surprising result is obtained, for if we then write for each planet its corresponding metal, we have the metals arranged in descending order of atomic weight. Fully to appreciate this extraordinary regularity we must bear in mind the unanimity that existed among the old-time occultists as to the allocation of the metals to the planets, and the fact that they could not possibly have been acquainted with the atomic weights of the metals (since the concept of "atomic weight" was unknown prior to Dalton) and, therefore, could not have deliberately allocated the metals to the planets in accordance with any rule based on their atomic weights. In fact, it seems fairly plain that the allocations were based upon certain obvious and seemingly rather superficial properties of the metals. Gold is yellow like the sun, silver white like the moon. Iron is reddish like the fiery planet Mars; it is also the metal chiefly used in making the instruments of warfare. Copper, on the other hand, was much employed for the making of mirrors, before the "silvering" of glass was discovered, and thus is connected with Venus, goddess of love. Mercury is the only metal fluid at normal temperatures, the mobile metal, assigned to the fleet-footed messenger of the gods and the rapidly moving planet of the same name; whilst dull and heavy lead is assigned to the slow-moving planet Saturn. And, finally, tin possesses the curious property of emitting a crackling noise when a sheet of it is bent—

H. Stanley Redgrove

thundering, so to speak, in miniature,—and is thus connected with Jove, lord of thunder.

I have to mention that the extraordinary regularity in question was first discovered and pointed out (to the best of my belief) by Mr. W. Gorn Old in his *A Manual of Occultism* (Rider, 1911), pp. 7 and 8, to whom full credit should be given. But the discovery passed almost without notice. This may have been due to the fact that Mr. Old in his book expressed the regularity in a rather obscure manner. Moreover, by a slip of the pen, I suppose, he wrote "specific gravity "instead of "atomic weight." As a matter of fact, the determination of the specific gravities of bodies, that is, of their densities compared with water as unity, was by no means beyond the experimental resources of the ancients; but as will be seen from the Table, no regularity of the sort indicated in the case of atomic weights can be traced in the case of the specific gravities of the metals concerned.

What is the explanation of the regularity? Is there, indeed, an occult connection between the seven metals and the seven planets known to the ancients? The discovery of numerous other metals, that of Uranus and Neptune, and the assignment of the sun and moon to categories other than those of planets, render this conclusion extremely hazardous.

TABLE OF OCCULT CORRESPONDENCES

Planet	Sign	Metal	Atomic Weight *	Specific Gravity	Day of the Week	
					English	French
Saturn	♄	Lead	207	11.4	Saturday	Samedi
Jupiter	♃	Tin	119	7.3	Thursday	Jeudi
Mars	♂	Iron	56	7.2 to 7.8	Tuesday	Mardi
Sun	☉	Gold	197	19.3	Sunday	Dimanche
Venus	♀	Copper	64	8.8	Friday	Vendredi
Mercury	☿	Mercury	200	13.4	Wednesday	Mercredi
Moon		Silver	108	10.5	Monday	Lundi

* These are here given to the nearest whole number only, expressed in terms of oxygen=16.

On the other hand, it can easily be calculated by means of the mathematical theory of probability that the odds against, not merely this regularity, but any such regularity, occurring by chance, are 119 to 1, so that the endeavor to explain the regularity away as a mere coincidence seems equally hazardous. I leave the problem for solution to a mind more capable than my own.

PHILOSOPHY AND TRUTH

IN a recent work, of no little importance in the world of thought. Professor Radharkrishnan, of the University of Mysore, has drawn up an indictment of modem philosophers and modem philosophy. "Skepticism," he very rightly urges, "is a better preparation for philosophy than dogmatism," for, whilst "criticism is the breath and being of philosophy, dogmatism is the enemy of truth and knowledge. Free thinking is the only guide to truth, but it is a risky game. It is far easier to defend popular beliefs and pet prejudices." And his charge is that philosophy is being prostituted to these base ends. No one acquainted with the philosophical literature produced during the years of the Great War, when "integrity of thought was lost and truth seeking had become the handmaid of state-policy," is likely to be so temerous as to combat the justice of this. But Professor Radharkrishnan's special charge is that of religious bias. "At the present day," he writes, "a system of philosophy is judged not by its truth and objective value, but by its conformity with the prevailing religious views." It must not be inferred, however, that he is in any way an opponent to religion *per se*. As a matter of fact, inasmuch as philosophy must take account of every form of experience, paying particular attention to the statements of the specialists in each department, he very rightly urges that the experiences of the mystics, those specialists in religion, must by no means be neglected. And in the constructive chapter of his work, he takes his stand on the reality of these experiences and the validity of the religious consciousness, utilizing in particular the results of this consciousness as revealed in the *Upanishads*.

Whether it be justified or not, Professor Radharkrishnan's indictment raises the interesting problem of the motive of philosophy, which may well occupy our attention for a few moments. *Why do men philosophize?* Man prides himself on his rationality, but, as Mr. W. Trotter, in his Instincts of the Herd in Peace and War, urges, he is fundamentally a creature of instinct. Rationality is something quite secondary. His most fondly cherished and firmly-held beliefs—those which he is incapable of doubting—are not rational, but instinctive and the product of herd-suggestion. Writes Mr. Trotter:

It is the belief, which is the primary thing, while the explanation, although masquerading as the cause on which the belief is founded, is entirely secondary, and but for the belief would never have been thought of. Such rationalizations are often, in the case of intelligent people, of extreme ingenuity, and may be very misleading unless the true instinctive basis of the given opinion or action is thoroughly understood.

If the truth of this be admitted, then the probability that every system of philosophy has at its very root and, if based upon non-rational belief—whether in the form of religious bias or otherwise—becomes very high.

But I think that an attempt to explain philosophy as simply and solely the outcome of man's efforts to rationalize his non rational and instinctive beliefs would by no means prove adequate to the task. Over and above this factor—potent though it be—something else remains to be posited. What it is in my opinion will, I hope, emerge in the course of these comments.

According to Professor Radharkrishnan, and the opinion is so commonly held that the expression of it sounds trite, the desire wherefrom philosophy—right philosophy—is born is the love of Truth for her own sake. But—what is truth? Wrote Francis Bacon, "What is truth? said jesting Pilate; and would not stay for an answer." Are philosophers—with few exceptions—any better? Do they stay for an answer? They write their great works to expound unto us the things which they envisage as true; but how seldom do they undertake to tell us what truth is. The absolutist worships logic; and yet, after all, what is logic? A machine, it may be replied, out of which you can get no more than you put in—indeed, very often you get less. A useful thing, no doubt; a true thing; but not truth.

I have referred to exceptions above, and there is, indeed, one school—that of the pragmatists—which has really tackled the question, What is truth? This may account for the fact that the pragmatists are so much disliked by other philosophic schools and so badly misunderstood by them. Pragmatism, we must observe, cuts the ground from under all other philosophic systems. The "other" perhaps should be deleted, for pragmatism is not strictly speaking itself a philosophic system, but a necessary introduction to all philosophy. Pragmatism tells us what truth is. To say, as is sometimes done, that pragmatism posits utility as a criterion of truth is an inadequate statement of its nature. Pragmatism does more than this: it identifies the utility of a statement with its truth. Utility is the meaning of truth, and a statement is true just in so far as—and no farther than—it is useful. According to pragmatism, writes Professor Radharkrishnan in the book to which I have already referred:

Truth is born into the world as any organic form, and perishes when it cannot stand the shock of new demands. The history of truth can be understood ... as the attempt of human intellect to meet the needs of life and action.

H. Stanley Redgrove

But we should misjudge pragmatism if we were to understand utility in the "bread and butter" sense only. There are needs of the soul as well as those of the body. The utility of art, for example, is above question; for its products are, for those who can appreciate them, immediately productive of pleasure by way of aesthetic satisfaction. Philosophy, it seems to me, is akin to art—is, in fact, the greatest of all arts. In man's soul, there is a yearning for an explanation of the seeming chaos of his experience—an explanation which can be realized in the sense that he can realize his own activity; a yearning which is unsatisfied by the thought-structures of science, for this aim not at explanation in this real and vital sense, but at correlation for the satisfaction of practical needs only. From this yearning is born philosophy, as from man's aspiration for the beautiful is born art; and the satisfaction it yields is, so it seems to me, a type of aesthetic satisfaction. Its capacity to yield this, and not its practical utility, is the meaning and measure of its truth.

If this view of philosophy as essentially an art leads to a profound skepticism, it nevertheless results in an attitude broadly tolerant and appreciative. I cannot say, categorically: This is beautiful, that is ugly. I can only say:

This is beautiful form, that is ugly for me. In a sense, it may rightly be said that everything is beautiful that has afforded man aesthetic satisfaction. So, too, must be our verdict concerning the truth and falsity of philosophic systems—the Monadism of Leibniz; the Spiritual Pluralism of James Ward; the Absolute Idealism of M. Bergson; the Radical Empiricism of Wm. James; the NeoIdealism of Rudolf Euken; the Neo-Realism of Bertrand Russell... all the systems which Professor Radharkrishnan criticized, and all the systems he passes by: have they not every one of them yielded satisfaction to innumerable minds? And shall we not say, therefore, that they are all true... and also all false? They are art-structures, each with a beauty and a value of its own, none being devoid of truth, and none attaining to perfection.

One further thought: Professor Radharkrishnan writes of the philosopher "as the spectator of all time and existence," aiming "at giving a unified account of the world as a whole." It is a magnificent ideal, but how many philosophers achieve it, or, indeed, approximate to its achievement? We are apt to criticize many of the old-time philosophers—Cornelius Agrippa, for example—for accepting without question, as the data on which to erect their systems, ideas current in their day, but now classed as superstition. But how many philosophers nowadays, accept modem scientific hypotheses with no better justification? The true philosopher must be at home in every department of human thought; must be capable of tracing to its roots every human belief. He can afford to neglect no source of knowledge, no avenue of inquiry; and it is one of the outstanding virtues of Professor Radharkrishnan's book, that he does not, like so many writers on philosophy, brush aside all those facts of experience which are comprised under the term "mystical." A philosophy which does do so is hardly worthy of attention. The facts brought to light by psychical research must also be taken into account, and the day is gone when treatises, dealing with the nature and destiny of the soul in which these facts are passed by, can be tolerated. Mr. Richardson's *Spiritual Pluralism and Recent Philosophy*, to which I have just referred, marks a great advance in this matter, and sets a good example for future philosophers to copy in the writing of those books which, for me at any rate, constitute the noblest works of art.

H. Stanley Redgrove

THE BOOK OF SECRETS

DURING Aristotle's own lifetime, the opinion was current that the peripatetic philosopher had two doctrines, an exoteric one given to the public generally, and an esoteric one reserved for his initiates. It is not surprising, therefore, that when in the Middle Ages a work in Arabic appeared, claiming to contain this secret doctrine, it was accepted at its own valuation. Concerning the authorship of the work in question, two different forms of which are known, nothing can be said with any degree of certitude, except that the author was not Aristotle. The claim made in the work itself that it was originally translated from Greek through Syriac may possibly be allowed, but no Greek or Syriac versions are extant. The origin of the work, perhaps, is of secondary importance; what is of primary importance is the tremendous influence it exerted on mediaeval thought. It is a veritable storehouse of occult learning, and, moreover, whilst we find in it much that in the light of modem knowledge is seen to be mere superstition, there remain certain principles and modes of thought to which modem Occultism, no less than that of the past, is pledged.

In the first half of the thirteenth century, this work—whose usual, though not invariable, title was *Secretum Secretorum*—was translated into Latin by one Philip, otherwise entirely unknown. Roger Bacon, some time prior to 1267, undertook a revision of this translation, making certain rearrangements of the text, and adding glosses, whilst later in his life he added an introductory treatise. The book had a very great influence on Bacon, and were it otherwise destitute of interest, it would be interesting for this alone. Bacon's edition of *the Secretum Secretorum* has now been published, forming phase V of the Opera *hactenus inedita Rogeri Baconi*, edited by Robert Steele and published by the Clarendon Press, Oxford. This valuable volume, for the publication of which all serious students of Occultism and of the history of the development of human thought must feel a deep sense of gratitude, contains, in addition to Bacon's edition of the *Secretum Secretorum* and his introductory treatise, a long introduction by the editor, an English translation of the Arabic version of the *Secretum Secretorum* an Anglo Norman version in verse, and a summary of Bacon's introductory treatise, as well as notes, bibliography, etc.

The form of the *Secretum Secretorum* is that of an address by Aristotle to Alexander for his guidance, not only in the government of the State, but also as to all matters relating to his private life. Concerning the former, there are a number of sage maxims which present-day rulers might very well put into practice; for instance: "It is necessary that he [a wise ruler] should lower all the taxes, especially in the case of those who come into his presence as merchants and traders." Again, Alexander is advised as follows: "Do not incline to that which does no good and is soon lost. But seek the wealth which is never exhausted, the life which never changes, the sovereignty which never ceases and permanency which never perishes, and a fair name, which is the greatest treasure." The following, too, may not be lacking in a certain truth and application nowadays: "A king or, for that matter, a minister of State, I presume, should spare loud words except in rare circumstances, lest he be heard too often, and the people, becoming familiar with his talk, despise his authority."

It is, however, more especially with the occult doctrines of the *Secretum Secretorum* that I propose here to deal; and, in the first place, we cannot but be struck by the insistence that is laid on the guidance to be derived from astrology. "Correctness of judgment," we are told, "depends upon nativity. Every one is born at a certain hour, and his subsequent proficiency in arts and his successes or failures in his undertakings depend upon the influence of the stars ruling over his nativity. Even if his parents try to turn him to engage in some other art or profession, he will turn to the one decreed to him by his stars"; and, in illustration of this, is told a story of the son of a weaver, in whose horoscope Virgo was rising, Mercury and Jupiter were in Gemini, and unfortunate aspects were absent, who became, in consequence, a minister of State. Alexander is thus advised: "Let all thy affairs, public or private, be guided by the approval of astrology." In accordance with this dictum, he is recommended neither to take medicine nor to open a vein, "except at the time chosen by astrology. For verily, the benefit of therapeutics is considerably augmented thereby." And, indeed, in one place. Pseud-Aristotle writes: "If it may be possible for thee do not rise nor sit nor eat nor drink nor do anything except at the time chosen by astrology, for thus you will prosper; because, verily, God has not created anything uselessly,"—advice, I am afraid, which the most fervent believer in the powers of the stars would find it irksome to put into operation. Bacon was a convinced believer in the truth of astrology; but he is very anxious to point out in his Introduction that the influence of the stars in no way negatives the free will of man.

Concerning medicinal magic, the author of the *Secretunt Secretorum* gives directions for the preparation of a medicine formed by the right combination of eight other medicines, which he describes as: "One of the greatest treasures of the world, and the most precious possessions of kings." In addition to curing every disease of the body, he says that: "One of its peculiar virtues is to create intelligence, that is the brain, to engender sagacity, to sharpen genius and improve the power of thought," and adds: "I do not know of any medicine prepared by philosophers excelling this one in preserving health and strength, and benefiting bodies and souls." This remedy, it is interesting to note, is, unlike so many early medicines, free from disgusting, materials, being prepared mainly from vegetable substances of medicinal value, with the addition of gold and precious stones. I am confident that it would prove as efficacious a cure-all as the majority of the nostrums which are greedily swallowed nowadays by a gullible public. It might prove more efficacious; it certainly would prove more expensive and difficult to manufacture.

Passing to a consideration of mental diseases, Pseud-Aristotle writes: "Know that mental diseases are also amenable to treatment. But their treatment is carried out by means of musical instruments which convey to the soul, through the sense of hearing, the harmonious sounds which are created by the motions and contacts of the heavenly spheres in their natural motion, which affect the right perceptions. And when those harmonies are interpreted in human language, they give rise to music which is pleasing to the human soul, because the harmony of the heavenly spheres is represented in man by the harmony of his own elements, which is the principle of life. Hence, when the harmony of earthly music is perfect or, in other words, approaches the nearest to the harmony of the spheres, the human soul is stirred up and becomes joyful and strong."

Concerning divination, the author of the *Secretum Secretorum* puts forward a theory which, in the main, is that held by most modem occultists, namely that a right forecast of the future is achieved, not by the mechanical reading of signs, but by means of a higher power of the soul making known its judgments to the-lower consciousness by the aid of such signs. "The soul," we read, "acquires the power of finding out inner truths, by external signs, when it happens to be free from lust and pain. This power is known by thought. And when the soul predominates, over the body and nothing intervenes between the spiritual substance which lies in the heart and the soul, and the animal part which lies in the brain, the intellect is freed from impurities and the object is reflected in it. Hence divination, which is mentioned in many books, and of the truth of which many wonderful instances are recorded." "But this," the author adds, remembering his faith in astrology, "also depends upon the conjunction of stars happening at the time of the creation of this power."

Not the least interesting fact concerning the *Secretum Secretorum* is that in it occurs the earliest known mention of the celebrated *Emerald Tablet of Hermes Trismegistus*, beloved of the alchemists. There are several different versions of this, and that appearing in the work of Pseud-Aristotle does not seem to state so explicitly the fundamental hypothesis of alchemy as do other versions which gained greater currency. "That which is below is like that which is above, that which is above is like that which below, to accomplish the miracles of The One Thing" here reads: "There is no doubt that the lower from the higher and the higher from the lower produces wonders from one single operation." But elsewhere in the *Secretum Secretorum* the principle of analogy between the material and the spiritual is expressed in no uncertain words. "Every physical body in the universe has its prototype in the spiritual world," we read, "the latter being the cause of the existence of the former, and ruler over it"—a statement of the Law of Correspondences almost as explicit as Swedenborg's. Who was it, one cannot help inquiring, who first formulated this idea?—an idea which has played so tremendous a part in the evolution of thought. In the *Secretum Secretorum* it is made the basis for a system of talismanic magic, and the student of Occultism will regret that, in the present edition of the work, the magical signs to be engraved on the talismans described are omitted; though I believe there is good reason for this in, the fact that the various Arabic MSS. differ from each other in this respect. However, not merely talismanic magic so-called, but the whole of magic—for in essence all magic is talismanic—is based upon the idea, more or less consciously held, of the correspondence between matter and spirit. This belief, indeed, must be held responsible for a tremendous mass of superstitious practices and beliefs, some of them of the grossest absurdity. And yet . . . and yet I think the modem occultist is justified in seeing in this doctrine of correspondences a great and permanent truth. Only by its aid can matter be reconciled to spirit; only in virtue of it can we grasp the Cosmos as a whole. Too easy has it been in the immediate past to discredit as mere superstition all that would not square with a truncated philosophy of the Universe. The present age is gaining wisdom. We are really beginning to prefer facts to theories, or, rather, to see that it is only through a synthesis of all available facts, none being discarded because of their awkwardness, that a theory of true worth is to be obtained. Not all the magic of the past was fictitious, nor magical theory fancy. Psychical research has disclosed, be it ever so slightly, a new world to our gaze; and it is in research that we pledge our faith. From this point of view, the speculations of the old occult writers assume a new value for us; and certainly this is true of the works of Roger Bacon and of the unknown man who wrote *Secretum Secretorum*.

ALCHEMY AND MODERN SCIENCE

THE science of radioactivity, by the remarkable nature of its achievements and the extraordinary advances it has already made during the few years of its existence, has perhaps more than any other caught the attention of the man in the street and fired his imagination. Its importance alike for philosophy and for its two sister-sciences, chemistry and physics, can hardly be overestimated; and to the serious student of Occultism it is of the greatest interest, not only because of its intrinsic philosophical significance, but also because it has provided something approximating to a complete vindication of the speculations of the old-time alchemists.

H. Stanley Redgrove

The science numbers amongst its workers many men of distinction. Not least amongst these is Frederick Soddy. Moreover, Professor Soddy possesses in a marked degree the happy power of putting scientific ideas into clear and simple language devoid of technicalities. His *The Interpretation of Radium* is essentially a work for the reader who desires a survey of the science of radioactivity at once scientific in its accuracy and popular in its mode of presentation. Professor Soddy has been so much impressed by the similarity between the fruits of modern science and those of ancient speculation, that he suggests that what we call the speculations of the alchemists may perchance be all that has remained of a body of knowledge, vaster far than is ours, which an ancient race of mankind, long since perished, had wrested from Nature. The hypothesis is frankly given as imaginative, but it will certainly be of interest to those who credit the existence of an Atlantean civilization in prehistoric times.

For my own part, I prefer to envisage the philosophical achievements of the alchemists as the result of highly intuitive minds pursuing the a priori method. Intuition is—so to speak—a shortcut to knowledge. It gives a splendid sweep, a magnificent survey. But it sacrifices detail to achieve this end. The inductive method of modern science proceeds far more slowly, but certainly more surely. Matters of detail are of the greatest importance when it comes to a question of making practical use of knowledge. A philosophy of the universe complete in broad outline is, no doubt, very satisfying to the mind. A philosophy less in its extent, but more precise in its details—a single mathematical formula summing up innumerable facts into one single generalization inductively achieved—is, perhaps, more useful.

The mistake is often made of supposing that the science of radioactivity has exploded Dalton's atomic theory. Nothing could be further from the truth. The most severe attack on Dalton's theory came from Professors Wald and Ostwald about twenty years ago: but their objections were not based

Forgotten Essays

on radioactive grounds. If radioactivity has considerably modified the atomic theory, it has at the same time greatly strengthened it, as Professor Soddy well shows, in as much as the at-first-sight inexplicable facts of radioactivity have received so complete and satisfying an explanation in terms of this theory. But no longer is the atom conceived to be the ultimate unit of matter—it is the unit for the purposes of chemistry only; and no longer can we regard the atoms of one and the same chemical element as necessarily identical in weight.

From its very inception, men of science resented the implication of the atomic theory that the physical universe was composed of some seventy-odd irresolvable elements. Their philosophical bias was towards monism. The hypothesis was put forward (by Prout in 1815) that all the varying elements are composed of hydrogen; but it failed then to be substantiated. We now know that Prout was fundamentally in the right. The alchemical hypothesis of the unity of all matter has triumphed.

Recent research has shown that an atom consists of essentially two parts, and resembles in a way a solar system. The sun of this system (the nucleus) is relatively massive. It is made up of hydrogen nuclei (i.e. hydrogen atoms each deprived of one electron or negative unit of electricity) and (or) helium nuclei or a-particles (i.e. helium atoms each deprived of two electrons) together with (in most cases at any rate) electrons or particles. The latter, however, are not sufficient to neutralize the positive charge of the former, so that the nucleus of every atom is positively charged. Around this nucleus, as planets around a sun, revolve particles or electrons, sufficient in number to neutralize its net charge.

The atomic weight of an element, and, in fact, all its mass properties, depend entirely upon the magnitude of the nucleus. Its chemical properties, on the other hand, depend solely upon the number of electrons (called "the atomic number") revolving about this. It is possible, therefore—and the fact necessitates a radical revision of ideas in chemistry—to have elements of different atomic weight (different size nucleus) with identical chemical properties (same "atomic number"), as well as those of identical atomic weight (same size nucleus) with different chemical properties (different "atomic number"). The former are called "isotopes," the latter "isobares." Many cases of each are now known. Isotopes cannot be separated by means of any chemical method, and the recent brilliant researches of Dr. F. W. Aston have demonstrated that many of the common chemical elements are mixtures of isotopes.

The radioactive elements are, as is now well known, spontaneously undergoing transmutation into other elements, as a result of the expulsion of either a- or β-particles from their nuclei. Their complicated but fascinating life-histories are well told by Mr. Soddy in the work already referred to. In every case, the final products appear to be the two elements: helium and lead (or rather isotopes of the latter). It is interesting to note that determinations of the atomic weight and density of lead from radioactive sources have shown slight divergences from those of ordinary lead, agreeing with those predicted by the theory of isotopy.

Not yet has science discovered how to modify these changes. Each radioactive element disintegrates in its own way and at its own speed, independently of whatever treatment is meted out to it. No doubt the non-radioactive elements are also undergoing similar changes, but at rates too slow to allow of this being perceived. The late Sir William Ramsay thought that by using the tremendous energy of radioactive changes, he might succeed in bringing about the transmutation of other elements, and claimed to have been successful in several cases. Repetition of certain of his experiments has, however, proved abortive; but the transmutation of minute quantities of nitrogen into hydrogen by bombarding it with a-particles does appear to have been achieved by Sir Ernest Rutherford.

Could the control of radioactive change be achieved, then the artificial production of gold—the *magnum opus* of alchemy—might be readily effected. Thus, the expulsion of two a-particles per atom from bismuth or one from thallium would yield the required result. Or lead could be converted into mercury by the expulsion of one a-particle and this into gold by the expulsion of an *a*- and a β-particle. In each case, it is interesting to note, in view of some of the remarks of the old-time alchemists concerning the qualities of philosophical gold, the gold made by such processes would have a slightly higher atomic weight than ordinary gold, and would, in all probability, be somewhat more dense.

It must be understood, however, that in radioactive changes the particles (whether *a* or β) are, as already mentioned, expelled from the nucleus. The outer ring of electrons seems to act as a barrier to the effecting of changes within, and the expulsion or addition of electrons to the outer rings of elements results, not in transmutation, but in ordinary chemical reactions.

But, as Professor Soddy has elsewhere remarked and again emphasizes in the present work: "if man ever achieves this further control over Nature, it is quite certain that the last thing he would want to do would be to turn lead or mercury into gold—*for the sake of gold*. The energy that would be liberated, if the control of these sub-atomic processes were as possible as is the control of ordinary chemical changes, such as combustion, would far exceed the gold in importance and value. Rather it would pay to transmute gold into silver or some base metal."

The recent lock-out in the coal-mining industry has brought vividly to our minds the value of energy and our absolute dependence on it. Energy is not only the Philosopher's Stone; it is also the *Elixir of Life*. In the course of the years, a new source of energy must be made available for man's use if he is to survive on this globe. That science will achieve this great end and discover the means by which interatomic energy may be utilized is, to my mind, certain. Not merely will transmutation then be achieved, but what is more important, the tremendous stores of energy then unlocked will make possible a life of ease and luxury—a paradise on earth—for all mankind. The old-time philosophers dreamt of such a world. It may be initiated in our own generation. Professor Soddy utters a wise word of warning: "Should that day ever arrive, let no one be blind to the magnitude of the issues at stake, or suppose that such an acquisition to the physical resources of humanity can safely be entrusted to those who in the past have converted the blessings already conferred by science into a curse. As suddenly and unexpectedly as the discovery of radioactivity itself, at any moment, some fortunate one among the little group of researchers engrossed in these inquiries might find the clue and follow it up. So would be diverted into the channels of human consciousness and purpose the full primary fountain of natural energy at its source, for use or misuse by men, according to whether the long and bitter lessons of the painful past and present have even yet been really learned."

Not idly did the old-time alchemists dream and not idly shall their dreams be fulfilled.

Forgotten Essays

A SUPERNORMAL ADVENTURE

THE following story of a curious and interesting psychical experience was related to me by a lady of my acquaintance, to whom I will refer as Mrs. Cedur. Mrs. Cedur's integrity is unquestionable, and I have no hesitation, therefore, in asserting that the account of her experience is true. By this term is implied the entire absence of any willful misrepresentation or distortion of facts by the narrator. I am, of course, well aware of the tricks that memory plays on us. I cannot, therefore, claim that the story possesses evidential value—psychic experiences to have this must be corroborated by contemporary documentary evidence. I am quite certain that those who wish to do so will be able satisfactorily to their own minds to explain away Mrs. Cedur's experience without resort to the supernatural, but I am by no means equally certain that such an explanation would be the true one; and for those who are prepared to believe in the possibility of the action of the thoughts of those we call dead, not only upon the minds of the living, but also upon material objects, the story will, perhaps, prove to be of some interest. Without more ado, therefore, I will proceed to relate it.

About twenty-two years ago, Mr. and Mrs. Cedur, with their infant son, took up their residence in a house in a small village in Berkshire. Previously to their arrival in the village, Mrs. Cedur had not seen the house, nor had she or her husband heard anything about it that would have caused them to believe it to be haunted. On the evening of their arrival, Mr. Cedur went into the village to secure some food, leaving Mrs. Cedur to move certain small articles of furniture into the house. It was twilight, but she could see distinctly, and entering the house by the back door was astonished to notice a woman standing in the kitchen. She naturally uttered an exclamation of surprise, and the figure gradually faded into nothingness. An examination of the various rooms of the

- 177 -

house, which she immediately undertook, showed that there was no person concealed in them. Mrs. Cedur had no feelings of fear, but the personal appearance and costume of the figure impressed her very vividly and became fixed in her memory. The figure was that of a tall woman, dressed entirely in brown. She had grey hair and a rather thin face, on which melancholy was expressed.

Some days after the Cedurs had been in their new residence, they discovered that it was rumored in the village that the house was haunted, one old villager assuring Mr. Cedur that he would not like to live there.

Some time later, Mrs. Cedur gained some very significant information regarding a married couple who had occupied the house previously to the tenants immediately preceding the Cedurs themselves. The wife had died in the house, and Mrs. Cedur's informant assured her that the woman had been exceedingly badly treated by her husband, who had even gone so far as to bring his mistress to the house while his wife was dying. Mrs. Cedur asked for a description of the dead woman: it tallied exactly, even to the details of the clothing, with the apparition which she had seen! The interesting point to notice, of course, is that when Mrs. Cedur saw the apparition, she knew nothing whatever concerning the woman in question, or of the rumor that the house was haunted.

Mrs. Cedur did not see the apparition again, although she continued to live in the place for many years; she asserts, however, that often, when she was alone in the house, she felt there was another presence with her. This feeling never gave rise to fear.

In the course of time, some building operations became necessary, which entailed the cutting off of the overhanging branch of an old elm tree in the garden of the house. One day Mrs. Cedur, who likes such exercise, decided to saw up this bough into convenient pieces for use as firewood. On sawing through the bough, she saw in the sap of the wood the figure in brown of the woman who had appeared to her. By cutting off further portions of the bough, she found that the impression continued for some considerable length of the wood, and then faded into indistinctness. It is no doubt very easy to say that she was misled by a merely fanciful likeness caused by some trivial and quite natural peculiarity in the growth of the tree; but Mr. Cedur, who strikes me as being a very hard-headed man, and who, unlike his wife, is not a believer in psychic phenomena, corroborates her statement as to the appearance of a woman in the sap of the tree.

Did the thoughts of the woman in brown continue, after her body was dead, to inhabit the spot where she had been so unhappy, impressing themselves, not merely upon the mind of Mrs. Cedur, but also upon the very material structure of the place? Or is the story to be discounted as just imagination? For myself, I do not know.

TALISMANIC MAGIC

IT is easy—and it may win a certain measure of applause—to dismiss the belief in amulets and talismans as a mere superstition, devoid of any serious interest. I do not think, however, that it is either profitable or wise. The belief in the power of the talisman or amulet is world-wide. It has won acceptance from generation after generation of men, and still persists, in one form or another, amongst many nations today. So ubiquitous and persistent a belief demands an explanation. Its very vitality indicates that, false and foolish as many of its forms undoubtedly are, there is at its root an element of truth. What this truth is has been well expressed by Mr. and Mrs. Pavitt, in their admirable work on the subject, of which a second edition has just been published. They write:

> The belief in [amulets and talismans] is by no means so universal as in olden times, and to the thoughtful person, many of the attributes claimed for them cannot be admitted; at the same time, with the growing knowledge of finer forces opening up new powers to mankind and with which we are slowly coming into touch, many people are prepared to admit that there may be some active power in a thought made concrete in the form of a talisman or amulet which may be made for some specific purpose, or for particular wear, becoming to the wearer a continual reminder of its purpose and undoubtedly strengthening him in his aims and desires.

Or, as I have myself ventured to express it: "The power of the talisman is the power of the mind (or imagination) brought into activity by means of a suitable symbol."

Superstitious folk nowadays who believe in the virtue of amulets, go to the nearest jeweler and purchase a lucky pig, or a black cat, or a bit of New Zealand green-stone. This is talismanic magic of the most foolish character. At its best, a talisman is something very different. According to the old occult writers, whether of Egypt, Greece or mediaeval Europe, the making of a talisman is no simple matter. For them, the talisman is the embodiment, in symbolic form, of an idea—nay, rather, at times, of a whole philosophy. It's making not only requires thought on the part of the operator, but usually more or less elaborate ceremonies are prescribed, well calculated to impress this idea upon his mind and to aid the concentration of his will upon the achievement of the desired purpose.

Strictly speaking, the terms "talisman" and "amulet" are not synonymous. Talismans proper are always astrological in their symbolism. The object of their use is to obtain the virtues of one or other of the heavenly bodies, which the ancients regarded as spiritual beings. But the term is seldom used with only this restricted meaning, and may, I think, be usefully extended to apply to any symbolic prayer or demand addressed to a spiritual being for aid in the achievement of man's purposes.

As so used, the term "talisman" will be found applicable to, if not all, certainly a large proportion of amulets. The peasant who nails up a horse-shoe on his cottage door, does so unthinkingly. The ancient Greek did much the same thing, but not unthinkingly: he was invoking the moon-goddess Isis.

In no other case, perhaps, is the connection between amulets and the gods so clear as in that of the amulets of the ancient Egyptians. These were not only carried by the living, but, owing to the great importance attached to the preservation of the bodies of the dead by the peculiar religious beliefs of the Egyptians, were lavished on their mummies. Mr. and Mrs. Pavitt devote many very interesting pages of their book to Egyptian amulets, and illustrate these by means of several plates, one of which is here reproduced.

Many Egyptian amulets, in addition to being symbolic in form, have words of power engraved upon them, by means of which they possess a double efficacy. Judging by the vast numbers that still exist, the scarab (Figs. 74 and 75) was the most popular of all the ancient Egyptian amulets. Our authors write:

The scarab was the symbol of Khepera, a form of the sun god who transforms inert matter into action, creates life, and typifies the glorified spiritual body that man shall possess at the resurrection.

H. Stanley Redgrove

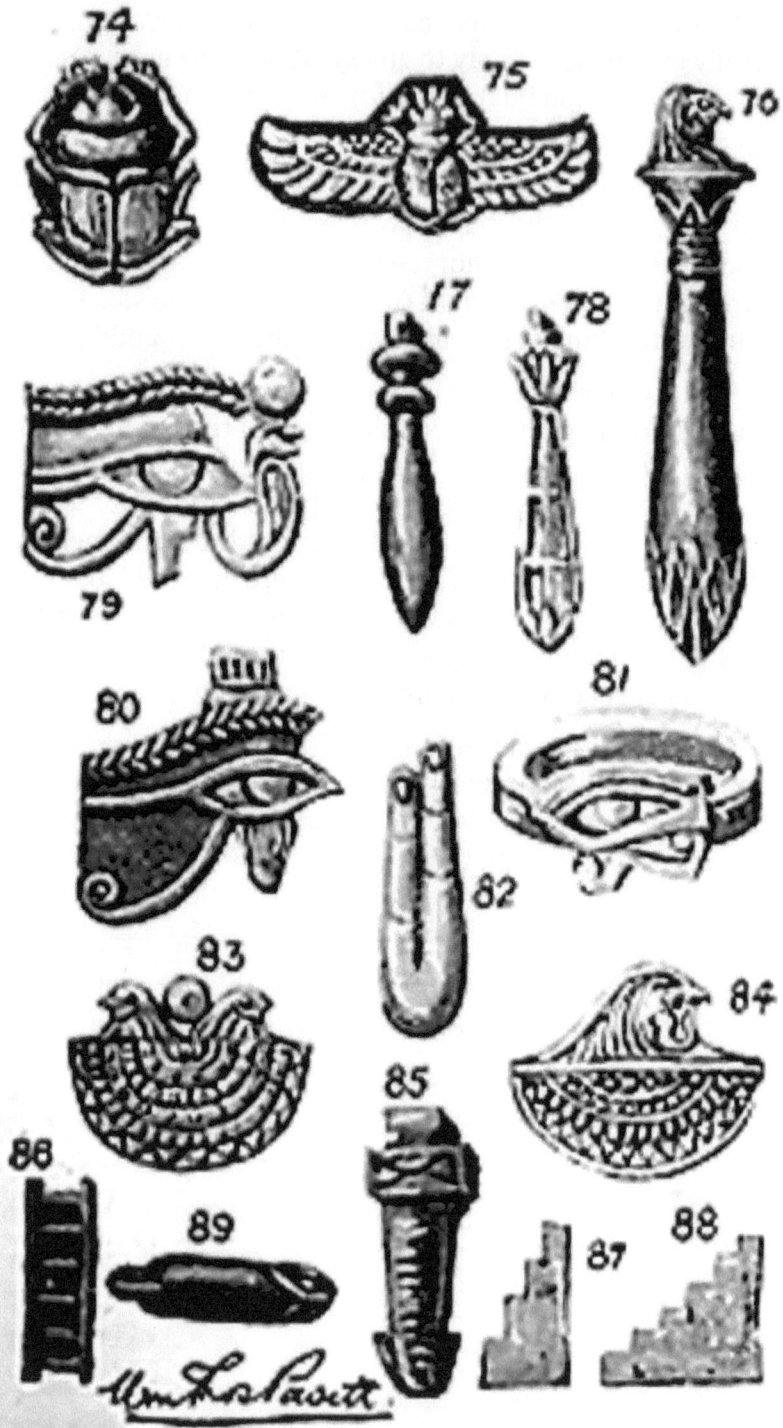

The scarab-beetle belongs to a family of beetles that feed on dung. It lays its eggs in a ball of this material, with the object of providing nourishment for its young, propels these balls by means of its hind legs, which are of peculiar structure adapted to this purpose, and deposits them in holes which it has prepared for their reception. The movement of these balls was likened by the Egyptians to that of the disc of the sun. Moreover, the beetles fly during that part of the day when the sun is at its hottest. These facts led to a magical identification of the scarab with the sun god. Furthermore, the Egyptians imagined that all these beetles were male, and that the young were produced in a special manner; concerning which idea Sir E. A. Wallis Budge writes:

The sun contained the germs of all life, and as the insect's ball contained the germs of the young scarabs, it was identified also with the sun as a creature which produced life in a special way.

Two other exceedingly important Egyptian amulets were the *heart* and the *ankh* or cross of life. The *heart* amulet was employed, not only to preserve the organ that it represented from the machinations of black magicians in this life, but also in the next. The heart was the seat of life, and at the judgment of the dead was weighed against a feather, symbolic of truth and right. Its possession was essential to the obtaining of the desired powers in the next world. It was customary to mummify the heart separately, and it was put under the special protection of the god Tuamutef.

The *ankh* cross was a symbol of life. According to Mr. and Mrs. Pavitt, the loop at the top represents a fish's mouth giving birth to water as the life of the country, bringing the inundations and renewal of the fruitfulness of the earth to those who depended upon its increase to maintain life.

They add that the symbol "was regarded as the key of the Nile which overflowed periodically and so fertilized the land."

The more usual theory regards the ankh as a phallic emblem symbolical of the dual generative forces of nature. Sir E. A. Wallis Budge says that its origin is unknown, and considers that "of all the suggestions which have been made concerning it none is more unlikely than that which would give it a phallic origin," though he gives no reason for this opinion. That other forms of crosses have evolved from the *ankh* is highly probable. Two other Egyptian amulets, the *menat* and the *sam* (Fig. 85) are also probably phallic in conception.

Figs. 79, 80 and 81 show examples of the *eye* amulet. This was the eye of Horus. It was a very common amulet, and was thought to bring the blessings of health and protection from evil influences.

Fig. 82 shows an example of the *two fingers* amulet. These were the fingers also of Horus, and symbolized those that he extended to assist his father, Osiris, to climb the ladder that led to heaven. It was used, of course, with the idea that similar assistance might be extended to the wearer.

The *collar* amulet, shown in Figs. 83 and 84, seems to have been less commonly employed. It was a symbol of Isis, and appears to have been a funeral amulet only, having for its object the giving of assistance to the deceased in freeing himself from his swathings.

The *ladder* (Fig. 86) is another amulet of Horus. It represented the ladder leading from this world to the next.

The *steps* amulet (Figs. 87 and 88) was dedicated to Osiris, and may be interpreted as having been a symbolic prayer to this god that he might assist the soul in its upward progress to the realms of heavenly bliss.

Fig. 89 shows an example of the amulet of the snake's head. This was a funeral amulet, used in order to protect the deceased against the attacks of the serpents of Set in the underworld. It was usually made of red stone, and as Sir E. A. Wallis Budge remarks:

As the goddess Isis is often typified by a serpent, and red is a color peculiar to her, it seems as if the idea underlying the use of this amulet was to vanquish the snakes in the tomb by means of the power of the great snake-goddess Isis.

Another amulet dedicated to Isis was the scepter, examples of which are illustrated in Figs. 76, 77 and 78. This was an amulet to preserve vigor and youth and to give assistance in agricultural pursuits, Isis having gained her scepter from her father, husband of Renenet, the beneficent donor of good harvests.

Such are a few of the amulets employed by the ancient Egyptians. Many others of equal interest might be mentioned, such as the *angle* and *plummet* amulets dedicated to Thoth, god of learning, which would endow the wearer with the high qualities of this god; the *tet*, a very important amulet dedicated to Osiris, which gave strength and stability and the power to reconstitute the body in the underworld; and the symbol of *Bes*, god of laughter and good luck, which Mr. and Mrs. Pavitt suggest may be the original of the modern Billiken. Not only the talismanic lore of ancient Egypt, however, but also that of China, Japan, Greece, Rome and Europe generally during the Middle Ages—and, indeed of other nations—is well worthy of exploration. If there is much folly here to be found, there is also something of wisdom. Mr. and Mrs. Pavitt's is not only a fascinating book, which will be read with interest by the general reader, but a guide which will be valued by the student in his researches in the mystic lore of bygone days.

H. Stanley Redgrove

A DEFENSE OF ALCHEMY

THE history of the science of chemistry, especially for the purpose of philosophical study, may conveniently be divided into four periods. The origins of the science go back far into the dim prehistoric past of mankind's history. When the historian first meets with man, he is already something of a chemist. The ancient Egyptians, for example, knew something about the smelting of metals, about the preparation of drugs, perfumes and poisons; they were expert in the art of embalming and had considerable skill in dyeing and the ceramic art. And much of this knowledge was certainly not of their own discovery, but was inherited by them from the past. We can, however, hardly dignify this primitive technical knowledge by the title of "science." It was not systematized: it lacked theoretic coherence, and consisted merely of a number of isolated formulae or rules-of-thumb known to artificers and mechanical workers, whose interest in the operations they carried out (sometimes with considerable skill) was limited to the practical needs of their particular craft.

Gradually, however, we find a body of theoretical doctrine arising; and we enter upon the second period in the history of chemistry, namely the alchemical period. Exactly what the theory of alchemy was and exactly how it arose are the questions with which we are immediately concerned; but, before entering upon a consideration of them, some few words seem necessary concerning the two subsequent stages in the history of chemistry. It was at one time customary to refer to the alchemist only in terms of scorn. His beliefs were mentioned only in order that they might be laughed at and to give the opportunity for the remark, "Behold how much wiser we are today!" This has always appeared to me to be a quite useless and profitless procedure. It seems to me far more interesting and useful to make the endeavor to understand why the alchemist held the particular beliefs that he did; and, in this connection, I would point out that, the more absurd the alchemical doctrines are supposed to be, the more urgent and the more difficult must this problem become. In any case, however, its adequate solution can hardly fail to be of great interest and value. If the alchemist committed intellectual follies, we may perhaps learn from his mistakes how not to commit similar follies ourselves. But recent advances in physical science have shown us that the alchemist was not quite such a fool as he has appeared in the immediate past. Somehow or other, he does seem at times to have hit upon certain fundamental truths concerning the nature of things. He may indeed have conceived them in so hazy a manner and with so many fictitious additions as to have rendered them useless for the purposes either of practical knowledge or of philosophical speculation; but, at any rate, we want to know how he managed to conceive them at all. His method may be capable of being improved, and adapted to the needs of the present day. In any case, and putting all other issues aside, the fact remains that the alchemical hypotheses gave a tremendous impetus to chemical research. A vast number of most useful and interesting discoveries were made, as a result of this impetus, which would never have been made had chemistry remained in its embryonic and merely technical stage. However, like most theories, those of alchemy, alter serving their purpose, had to be discarded by the growing science of chemistry; and we reach the third stage in the development of the science with the promulgation by Paracelsus, in the sixteenth century, of the doctrine that the prime aim of chemistry was the discovery of new and better medicines. This period is known as that of iatrochemistry. It must not, however, be supposed that alchemy was dead: practically all the iatrochemists were alchemists, in so far as they accepted the main alchemical doctrines and did not question the validity of the alchemical quest. The difference between the iatrochemist and the alchemist pure and simple resided in the fact that the former had a new and additional impetus to experiment and investigation and one which tended enormously to the enlargement and enrichment of chemical science.

But chemistry was not always to remain a handmaid to the healing art. The fourth and final stage in the history of chemistry is that of chemistry itself as a pure science devoted only to the discovery of a certain aspect of the truth of things. We may date its origin from the time of Robert Boyle, who, in the seventeenth century, first laid down the definition of a chemical element as this term is understood by modem science. By Boyle's day, we should note, alchemy was seemingly dead. It had failed to fulfil its promises: its quest had been abandoned by natural philosophers and was used only as a cloak for fraud by such dishonest men as could find foolish people to believe in them. At the same time, hypotheses having some resemblance to those of alchemy still continued to be formulated until Dalton put forward his momentous atomic theory in the opening years of the nineteenth century. This theory constitutes a landmark of essential importance in the history of chemistry; and, for those who are interested in the philosophy of the subject, it is convenient to subdivide the last stage in the history of chemistry into three subsidiary stages: the first being the period prior to Dalton; the second, the period dominated by the Daltonian theory; and the third, that which we have only just reached, being characterized by the discovery of the complexity of the chemical elements.

I should be sorry, however, if, by speaking about a post Daltonian stage in the history of chemistry, I should seem to give support to the idea that recent advances in chemical and physical science have rendered Dalton's atomic theory obsolete. This idea has, it is true, somehow got abroad, but it is altogether erroneous. As Mr. Soddy has well pointed out in his Interpretation of Radium, these very researches which are supposed to have shaken the truth of Dalton's atomic theory to its foundations have done more than any other researches to substantiate it. On the other hand, however, they have necessitated certain modifications in the theory of very great importance philosophically. The inductive method of modern science rarely, if ever, leads to a cul-de-sac, and it would be difficult to find an instance of a scientific theory which has had, in the light of more recent knowledge, to be abandoned as altogether worthless. On the other hand, scientific investigators do often (from an excess of enthusiasm, shall we say?) imagine that the end of a journey has been reached when, in fact, only the first stage has been achieved. Scientific theories supposed to be absolute are continually being discovered to be only approximate. As experimental knowledge grows, so do theories grow, becoming more comprehensive and complex, which is precisely the case in regard to the atomic theory. The alchemists had one maxim which certainly seems altogether erroneous. It was that Nature is simple. Modern investigation seems to indicate, on the other hand, that she is almost infinitely complex.

As I have hinted above, it is as regards the ultimate nature of the chemical element that the philosophy of modern chemistry differs from that of the Daltonian theory; and, perhaps, one cannot so well exhibit the difference between alchemy and chemistry as by asking each of them the question, "What is an element? "The Greek philosophers, and following them the mediaeval alchemists, regarded earth, air, fire and water as the four elements from which the whole material universe was made. But we shall miss the whole point of their philosophy if we misconstrue the nature of this" making, "A house is made of bricks, we say, and a plum-pudding of suet, flour, dried fruits, spices, and I know not how many other ingredients. But not in such manner was the universe made from its elements for those for whom these elements were earth, air, fire and water. For Dalton, it is true, the atoms of the elements were the bricks wherewith the edifice of the universe was constructed, or, alternatively, the ingredients of this strange plum-pudding of a world. The alchemical notion was entirely different, and I cannot perhaps better illustrate it than by referring to a passage in the writings of a seventeenth-century iatrochemist and alchemist, to wit, Jan Baptista van Helmont.

Van Helmont was an original thinker. He did not accept the current doctrine of the four elements, but his very criticism of it was the logical outcome of a conviction of the validity of the alchemical notion of what the nature of an element was. Van Helmont thought that he had discovered the element earth in the substance we now call "silica," one of the forms of which is sand. Van Helmont called it "quellem," and he carried out a very important series of experiments with this substance. Now glass is made from sand and clay: van Helmont discovered that, by appropriate chemical means, from a given quantity of glass, the same weight of silica or quellem could be obtained as was used in making it. The method is to fuse the glass with an alkali, extract with water, and add a suitable quantity of acid. This was a discovery of lasting importance, and must be described as a brilliant piece of work, especially if we take into consideration the comparatively slight importance that was attached in van Helmont's time to the use of the balance. It is not, however, this aspect of the matter upon which I wish to dwell, but upon the conclusion that van Helmont drew from his discovery. He did not break with tradition so far as to deny the elementary nature of earth, but he deprived earth of all potency and power in the production of other bodies. "The sand, or the element of *earth*," he writes, "doth never concur to natural and seminal generations." He sought to explain chemical processes by likening them to physiological and psychical ones. Life, for him, explained matter, not matter life; and the origin of minerals (like that of plants and animals) was to be sought in a seminal principle, wherefrom they had been developed by a process analogous to that of growth in the organic world. Elementary earth played no part in this because it did not undergo development—it could, as we have seen, be obtained unchanged from its products.

Let us now turn to the view of another natural philosopher, a man I have already mentioned, namely Robert Boyle. When van Helmont died Boyle was nearly of age, so that the two men are almost contemporaries; but their views concerning the nature of the elements and the formation of other material bodies from them are as poles asunder. Boyle's definition of an element, which, slightly modified, is still accepted today, is that it is a substance which cannot be decomposed, but which can enter into combination with other elements producing more complex forms of matter, capable of decomposition into these original elements. It will be seen that the very reason that almost caused van Helmont to deny that earth is an element, and which, at any rate, did cause him to assign to it a very subsidiary and unimportant position in his chemical philosophy, is just the reason, according to Boyle's definition, that would make us suspect it to be an element. As a matter of fact, silica was for some time so regarded, until early in the nineteenth century it was proved that, by submitting this substance to highly drastic chemical treatment, it could be decomposed into two separate bodies, namely, oxygen and a hitherto unknown element which was christened "silicon."

To the alchemist, the elements developed: more complex bodies were produced from them by a process analogous to the growth of a living organism. To the Daltonian chemist, elements combined: more complex forms of matter were produced from them, as I have already indicated, in a manner somewhat resembling the way in which a house is produced from bricks and mortar. The modern chemist, however—whilst accepting Dalton's theory in the main—realizes that chemical combination is something more than the merely mechanical addition of one element to another. He finds it necessary to explain why the properties of compound bodies are usually entirely different from those of their constituent elements: water, for example, is a compound of the two gaseous elements, hydrogen and oxygen, which are unlike it in every way; whilst common salt is a compound of a metallic element called sodium, which has the remarkable property of reacting violently with water, producing a very caustic solution and liberating hydrogen-gas (which may catch fire), and chlorine, a greenish-yellow gaseous element, which possesses an unbearable odor and is poisonous. It must have been noticed in the very earliest days of chemical experimentation that chemical changes always took place either with the absorption or the emission of heat; but in spite of a certain amount of experimentation, the real significance of the fact escaped attention until well into the nineteenth century, when, with the formulation of the concept of "energy," it began to be recognized that an energy-change is an essential part of every chemical reaction. Water, for instance, is not merely hydrogen plus oxygen: it is hydrogen plus oxygen minus so much energy; similarly common salt is sodium plus chlorine minus so much energy. Thermochemistry, as the department of study dealing with this aspect of chemical change is called, is now an important branch of the science of chemistry. Many other lines of research have converged to demonstrate the importance of the idea of energy: so much so that the concept of energy can now rightly be said to play a far more important role in modern scientific theory than the concept of matter. The hard mechanical atoms of Dalton have gone: modern research has penetrated within the atom, and the atoms are now regarded as elaborate structures containing, locked within them, almost incredible stores of energy. Since the atoms are complex, the chemical elements can no longer be regarded as being truly elementary; but the term "element" is still retained for what is, strictly speaking, the class of compounds impervious to purely chemical action. The modern view of matter, therefore, is not without kinship to the alchemical; for the alchemical view, as I have indicated, was essentially vitalistic, and to endow the atom with energy is not so very different from endowing it with life. Thus, by its profound modification of the philosophical basis of Dalton's theory, modem science has rendered possible a more sympathetic attitude towards the speculations of the alchemists than would have seemed legitimate to scientific thinkers during the century that has just passed. The late Dr. James Campbell Brown well remarked, concerning these theories:

I have just said that the alchemical view of the elements was vitalistic: if we bear this fact in mind, we shall find that it sheds considerable light, even in the darkest places of alchemical speculation. A plant is first a seed; then it puts forth roots; stem and leaves appear; it blossoms; its blossoms fade and die: yet we say it is one and the same plant throughout all these changes. John Smith may change in his appearance or his character; he grows from boyhood to the full estate of man; yet we call him "John Smith" all the time. So too, thought the alchemists, might metals and minerals undergo similar mutations of form. To the Daltonian chemist, to say that lead and gold (for example) are elements is to deny the possibility of transmuting one into the other. The alchemists did not regard the metals as elements, but, had they done so, it would have been no obstacle to their crediting the possibility of transmuting them. The art of dyeing, as I have pointed out, was one of man's earliest achievements, and it no doubt played an important part in the genesis of alchemical theory. The color of a fabric could be altered by dyeing it, why should not something similar be possible in regard to its other properties? As concerns the metals, a process somewhat analogous to dyeing was also known in the pre-alchemical days. By alloying suitable metals together, imitations of the precious metals, silver and gold, could be obtained: that is to say, commoner metals could be tinged, so as to resemble them in the one property of color at least. It seems hardly possible that the early workers in metals, having proceeded so far as this in their experiments, should not have speculated as to the possibility of altering the other properties of metals, such as their ductility, density, etc., so as to obtain from common metals bodies resembling silver and gold in all their properties and not merely in the property of color alone. A papyrus is known—the Leyden papyrus—of undoubted authenticity, dating from about the third century a.d., which contains a number of recipes for what we should now call the falsification of metals. It was almost certainly the notebook of an artisan. Great importance has been attached to this papyrus by M. Berthelot, whose view of the origin of alchemy would seem to be that a belief in the possibility of transmutation arose as the result of a misunderstanding of such practical recipes of Egyptian workers in metals as are contained in it by Greek speculators who confused the falsification of metals with their transmutation. To my mind, the theory is hardly adequate. If the Greeks misunderstood the practical recipes of the Egyptian workmen it was because of certain notions they already entertained concerning the nature of things, and to understand the origin of alchemy we shall have to inquire as to what these notions were. It must be noted, moreover, that the alchemical texts, which according to M. Berthelot are derived from the Leyden papyrus, are, on his own showing, of an entirely different character therefrom; and these texts commonly distinguish between the achievement of the magnum opus, that is, the transmutation of base metal into silver and gold, and the making of mere spurious imitations of these metals. I think, therefore, that whilst, in an endeavor to unveil the origin of alchemy, due importance must be attached to notions derived from the practical work of dyeing textiles and alloying metals, other and more important factors have to be taken into account. Why, for instance, were the alchemists so exclusively concerned with the problem of transmuting base metals into silver and gold, when so many other chemical problems presented themselves for solution? The natural cupidity of human beings is not adequate to account for this, for it is quite evident, from both their lives and their writings, that many of the alchemists were animated, not by avarice, but by the love of knowledge. Why was the solution of this problem regarded as so intimately bound up with that second great object of the alchemical quest, the discovery of the Elixir of Life? Indeed, for the later alchemists at any rate, the two problems became one, to be achieved by a single agent, possessed of magical and almost incredible powers, the marvelous Philosopher's Stone. In this connection it is significant that the doctrine of the Philosopher's Stone does not figure in the writings of the Greek alchemists. It is essentially a product of Christian thought, which fact alone should make us suspect that alchemical theory owes a debt to theological doctrine.

The alchemical theories, let me repeat, were vitalistic: the alchemist, imbued with the philosophical notion of the unity of all things, that "what is below is like that which is above; what is above is like that which is below," and, using analogy as his guiding principle, likened the metals to man. There is nothing, to my mind, surprising in this. Indeed, I would even go so far as to say that it was inevitable. The mind must proceed from the known to the unknown: the early philosophers knew, or thought they knew, something about the origin of living things. It could not have been otherwise than that they should have attempted to explain the origin of inorganic substances by the aid of concepts derived from the world of life. Moreover, in addition to their theories and actual knowledge concerning man as an inhabitant of this world, there was, in Christian days at any rate, a vast body of doctrine concerning man as a spiritual being, which was regarded as the most indubitable truth. The likening of metals to man, therefore, made possible two means whereby chemical phenomena might be explained: they might be likened to the processes of animal life, or to those of the life of the soul. Both were adopted, the result being an extraordinary fabric of speculation, made up of analogies drawn (a) between chemical phenomena and physiological processes, and (b) between these same phenomena and the life of the soul. These two factors in the genesis of alchemical theory I have called the "phallic" and the "mystical" respectively—although I am aware that neither term is altogether unobjectionable—and, in my Alchemy: Ancient and Modern (Rider, second edition, 1922) and the two chapters devoted to alchemy in my Bygone Beliefs (Rider, 1920), I have dealt with them in some detail, tracing to their roots in physiology and theology the outstanding doctrines of alchemical philosophy. In the main, then, we may say that alchemical philosophy was an a priori structure having its foundations in the crude physiology of bygone ages and the doctrines of Christian theology, to which must be added certain mystical notions derived from Neoplatonism and other sources.

The central doctrine of alchemy was that of development. Here, at any rate, the principle of analogy did not mislead the alchemists. Modern scientific research has demonstrated what the Daltonian theory denied, that the metals and other chemical elements are being produced by an evolutionary process. The alchemists grasped this general principle, even if they erred in all its details. Nature, they thought, or rather the vital spirit which animated her, produced the metals by a gradual process, which might be likened, on the one hand, to the growth of living things; on the other, to the development of the soul in man. Nothing to them was purely material: "Copper," declares an early work, *The Book of Crates*, "like man, has a spirit, soul and body." But not all the metals were equally mature and perfect—various impurities impeded Nature's processes. These processes they sought to understand and to control, so that what Nature slowly affected, they might accomplish in a moment. The aim of religion is the spiritual perfection of man, which, according to Christian doctrine, is to be achieved by the spirit of Christ. In accordance with this principle, the alchemists sought to perfect the metals, that is to say, to transmute the base and common ones into silver and gold, by means of the extraordinary agent they called the Philosopher's Stone. And just as in Christian theology, Christ is conceived to be, not only the means, but also the type of man's perfection, so, writes one of the alchemists concerning the Philosopher's Stone, "in species it is gold, more pure than the purest." It was the quintessence of Nature's powers, and, therefore, not only the medicine of the metals, but the Elixir of Life, the medicine that would restore man to the flower of youth.

About the time of the Reformation, when the trichotomy of personality became popular, the idea—probably first put forward by Isaac of Holland during the latter part of the fifteenth century, and vigorously championed by Paracelsus—that the metals, and, in fact, all bodies, are produced by the interaction of three principles, became an essential element in alchemical philosophy. These three principles were called "salt," "Sulphur" and "mercury," and were the metallic analogues to the body, soul and spirit in man. We must not confuse these principles with the common substances so called. Just as to the modem chemist the term "salt" is a general one, being applied not only to common table-salt (sodium chloride), but to all compounds formed by the interaction of an acid and an alkali, so too were "salt" and "Sulphur" generic terms for the alchemists, though their application of them was by no means consistent. I am not quite sure whether the same can be asserted of "mercury"; the mercury principle, however, was certainly not ordinary quicksilver, but rather a hypothetical substance that might, in the opinion of some of the alchemists at any rate, be obtained from ordinary quicksilver by purificatory processes. In fact, all three principles were hypothetical rather than actual substances, though no doubt many alchemists thought they had obtained one or other of them in the course of their experiments. It is this fact that leads to so much confusion in the interpretation of the writings of the alchemists, since what one alchemist, for instance, called "philosophical Sulphur" or "philosophical mercury" might by no means be the same substance as that to which another alchemist gave the same name. The properties of these three principles were generally considered to be as follows: Salt conferred fixity and resistance to the power of fire. Sulphur endowed a body with color and made it combustible. Mercury was the essentially metallic principle: it endowed metals with luster and the property of fusibility.

For many of the alchemists, philosophical mercury was the first principle of all things, and by the action of pure philosophical sulphur on pure philosophical mercury was the Philosopher's Stone to be obtained. This hypothetical reaction was often likened to the conjunction of the sexes in marriage, and much curious speculation was engaged in as a consequence. The earlier alchemists do not appear to have recognized the existence of the principle "salt"; and, failing any certain knowledge as to who first definitely formulated the idea of metals being generated by the action of philosophical sulphur on philosophical mercury alone, it is not possible to say whether the analogy which guided him was a sexual one or was one based upon a mystical dichotomy of the spiritual side of man into an active element and a passive one: ideas derived from both these analogies are common in alchemical writings. Certainly, the sexual theory of the origin of the metals, though very crude, is not without interest, especially in view of the findings of modern science that the atoms of the chemical elements are dual in their constitution, being products of the balanced interaction of particles of negative and positive electricity.

In order to achieve the transmutation of the metals, it was usually regarded as essential to strip them of their outer properties, so as to make it possible to get at and manipulate their hidden essence or spirit. This was the first matter or, alternatively, philosophical mercury, in their search for which the alchemists were unwearying. Many descriptions of the first matter are to be found in the writings of the alchemists: some of which, as I have already intimated, refer no doubt to actual chemical substances; others are descriptions of hypothetical bodies and are the result of philosophizing by the a priori method. Certain of these latter descriptions are of considerable interest, and show an approximation in general outline to the modem concept of the ether of space, though devoid of the element of mathematical exactitude, which, of course, is the chief merit of the modern theory. Thus, in *The Book of the Revelation of Hermes*, interpreted by Theophrastus Paracelsus, concerning the *Supreme Secret of the World*, we read that the alchemistic essence of all things "is of a mysterious nature, wondrous strength, boundless power," that "it exists in everything in every place, and at all times," that "it has the powers of all creatures; its action is found in all elements, and the qualities of all things are therein, even in the highest perfection." And in the "Smaragdine Table" attributed to Hermes Trismegistos, the mythical father of alchemy, we read of "One Thing" from which "all things were produced by adaptation," which is "the cause of all perfection throughout the world," which is "the fortitude of all fortitude, because it overcomes all subtle things and penetrates all solid things," and by means of which "all things were created."

The writings of the alchemists, as is obvious to all who essay to read them, are excessively obscure. This obscurity is partly only seeming, being the result of the fact that our present mode of thought is so different from that of the days in which the alchemists lived. Partly it was involuntary; the alchemists' views were on the whole obscure, and naturally the expression of them was obscure also. The use of the a priori method, even when, as in the case of alchemy, it was fortified by experiment, inevitably leads to obscurity. We may ultimately discover that the Universe is, indeed, a unity, and that the principles that hold on one plane of being are true also of all others; but even so, it still remains true that the use of analogy is attended with many dangers. The alchemists, I think, too frequently allowed analogy to run away with them, with the result that often it seems practically impossible to capture the meaning of what they wrote, even when we assiduously endeavor to follow the advice of one of them who says that "we must . . . consider the several analogies and similitudes of things, or we shall never be able to understand the philosophers." Partly also their obscurity was voluntary, and was the result of a not altogether unreasonable desire for secrecy. Alchemy in the Middle Ages was, it is true, not looked upon with such hostility as was magic, but it was nevertheless suspect. It was not wise in those days to know too much concerning Nature, or to reveal too explicitly her mysteries. Moreover, the language of alchemy provided a means whereby heterodox theological doctrines might be expressed. There is nothing fantastic in the suggestion that some alchemical books may have had nothing whatever to do with chemical processes whatever, their authors having used alchemical terms in which to expound mystical doctrine not in agreement with that of the Church, or to describe mystical experiences or investigations in the domain of what we now call psychical research. One alchemical book of a purely mystical nature is certainly known, namely *The Aurora* by Jacob Boehme, and in Boehme's other mystical treatises, considerable use is made of alchemical terms. There is, indeed, a school of thought, represented by two well-known works, namely Mrs. Atwood's *A Suggestive Enquiry into the Hermetic Mystery* and Hitchcock's *Remarks on Alchemy and the Alchemists*, which takes the view that alchemy was a purely mystical study, concerned only with spiritual processes relating to man and having nothing to do with metals or ordinary chemical processes at all. This view is an exaggerated one, since, apart from all other evidence, we know, as I have already stated, that the alchemists enriched chemical science by many valuable discoveries of a purely chemical nature. At the same time, we must bear in mind that the sharp distinction now drawn between matter and spirit did not exist for such men as could write about the soul of metals. We find, as a matter of fact, that many of the alchemists thought that they were dealing with spiritual beings, when, in modem terminology, we should say that they were merely handling gases and vapor. But if they sometimes imagined that they were discovering things concerning the mysteries of the spiritual realm when in fact they were carrying out purely chemical manipulations, it is equally possible that from chemical investigations certain of them may have been led into the domains of psychical research. A recent writer in the Occult Review, Mr. S. Foster Damon, has, for example, made out a very good prima facie case for believing that Thomas Vaughan—who wrote under the name of "Eugenius Philalethes," and is usually regarded as a mystical, rather than a physical, alchemist—discovered in the course of his experiments that amazing substance which is known to modem psychical research as "ectoplasm," in whose existence we are only just beginning to believe, of whose extraordinary properties we know but little, but that little enough to astound us, and of whose nature—whether, indeed, it should be regarded as physical or super-physical—we know nothing. Henry Khunrath is another alchemist whose concern appeared to have been with spirit rather than with matter; and the possibility remains that these and other alchemists may, in the course of their investigations, have encountered phenomena not known to modern science. There are, moreover, strange stories of the actual transmutation of base metal into gold, given on the authority of men like van Helmont and Helvetius, which seemingly are not to be explained away as mere tricks of mal-observation or as the result of the malpractices of fraudulent alchemists whose powers of legerdemain were in excess of their honesty; but which also cannot be accounted for by any theory of transmutation based on the modem doctrine of the mutability of the chemical elements. It is related of Alexander the Great that he sorrowed for the fact that no more worlds remained for him to conquer. Something of the same emotion, in its unwisdom, was experienced by nineteenth-century science. We are now wiser. We are now beginning to realize something of the majestic mystery of the Universe. We are awed, but we are not dismayed. Man, by patient investigation, by the utilization of the whole of his powers and energy, may succeed in the final and complete conquest of Nature. But no possible means of advance must be neglected, and for that reason, if for no other, I would commend the study of the writings of the ancient alchemists, those old-time thinkers who, with all their faults and follies and far-fetched allegories, were in many cases men, not only of unwearied patience in research, but possessed, it would seem, of extraordinary intuitive powers.

THE SOUL OF THE BEAST

THE soul of the beast, writes Swedenborg, "considered in itself is spiritual. It must, however, be observed, that the souls of beasts are not spiritual in the degree in which the souls of men are, but they are spiritual in a lower degree; for there are degrees of spiritual things." This view marks a great advance on the old-time orthodox teaching that man alone possessed a soul. Man alone was supposed to be a spiritual being, he alone could think and reason, he alone possessed the gift of immortality: the animal was a mere automaton moved by blind instincts. Such teaching as this, of course, is rendered quite untenable by the theory of evolution. Whether we accept Darwinism or one of its modern modifications, we are compelled to recognize man's animal ancestry: his body is related to that of the beasts, and, if this is true of his body, it can hardly be otherwise than that there is some relation between his mind and the mentality of the lower animals. Yet, on the other hand, there are obvious differences, which become glaringly so if we compare extremes at either end of the scale, as, for example, the mind of Newton and that of a shrimp. In my *Matter, Spirit and the*

Cosmos (popular edition, Rider, 1916), and Purpose and Transcendentalism (Kegan Paul, 1920), I have attempted to formulate a theory along the lines of that of Swedenborg's, indeed, it can be called a modern exposition of Swedenborg's own theory, to reconcile the view that, whereas man's physical part is derived from that of the lower forms of life, his soul or mind is essentially, or to use Swedenborg's term, discreetly, different from theirs, the difference being equivalent to that between "consciousness" and "self-consciousness." At the same time, in putting forward this theory, I have always contemplated (at the back of my mind, at any rate) the possibility of certain animals, under exceptional conditions perhaps, attaining to some degree of self-consciousness, and of some human beings falling short thereof.

To leave philosophic speculations aside for a moment, however, and to concern ourselves with facts: some very interesting experiments have been carried out in recent years dealing with the intelligence of animals, which may ultimately cause many of us to revise our views considerably on the subject. In the early part of the present century, the world of psychological investigation was startled by the extraordinary claims made for the thinking horses of Elberfeld. The performance was hardly less extraordinary than the claim, and the cry of fraud which was first raised was shown to be quite unfounded. It is perhaps remarkable that the controversy concerning the intelligence of animals has been carried on with as much acrimony as that concerning the nature of spiritualistic phenomena, and the coincidence, as we shall see later, may be more than a chance one.

Following the work on the horses of Elberfeld came a number of remarkable experiments with various dogs, which have culminated in those of Fraulein Henny Kindermann with her Airedale terrier-bitch, Lola. These experiments were carried out mainly during the stress and deprivation of the war period. Their results are of the most astounding nature, and although we have to rely on Fraulein Kindermann's word for most of them, I do not think there is the least reason to doubt her *bona fides*.

The dog was first taught to count by means of tapping with its paws, and various arithmetical exercises were then attempted and achieved with the greatest ease. Lola then learnt to associate numbers with sounds and the shapes of letters, and thus to spell and express its thoughts in words, which were tapped out on its mistress's hand. It is impossible in the course of a short article such as the present to recount one iota of the interesting experiments that were done, and of the remarkable results that were obtained. The reader must consult the book for himself. The following, however, are amongst some of the most extraordinary results. Lola was taught to tell the time from a clock, but so accurate ex *hypothesi* was her sense of time that she was able to tell her mistress the time without consulting this instrument on which we human beings have to rely. She not only recognized persons by their smell, as we know dogs are capable of doing, but could also accurately record their psychic states by this means. Thus, on one occasion, after some pressing, she described her mistress as smelling of lying, after the latter had promised to take her to Munich, but at the time was thinking of doing otherwise. Her abilities at arithmetical problems I do not stress, since in this respect she does not seem to have excelled the Elberfeld horses, whose powers of mentally extracting roots seem to have been more highly developed than those of human beings, but her capability for correctly forecasting the weather must not be passed over without mention. It should be noticed, however, that all these and similar remarkable feats were, according to Fraulein Kindermann, only achieved by the dog when they were novel: as the novelty wore off, so Lola's powers appeared to decrease also. Some of the recorded conversations between the dog and her mistress are most extraordinary. On one occasion, Fraulein Kindermann asked Lola why dogs preferred being with human beings rather than with other dogs. Lola replied: "Because of their eyes and their sorrows without ceasing." Fraulein Kindermann even attempted such philosophical questions as "Why are you living?" to which Lola replied, "*Egal ich lebe gern!*" (It's all the same to me, I like living!).

What is the explanation? If we are to accept these experiments as evidence of the dog's intelligence, it would almost appear that the intelligence of animals is superior to that of human beings. Their meaning, however, is not quite upon the surface. In a paper by Dr. F. C. S. Schiller, "On the So-called Thinking Animals," which appeared in the Journal of the *Society for Psychical Research* for June, 1914 (vol. 16, pp. 244 et seq.), he urges that the real test of knowledge must be the pragmatic one. Such tests of this type as have been attempted on Lola appear signally to have failed. Fraulein Kindermann writes: "The dog's thinking seems to be at variance with her acts: thought can therefore have little influence on a dog's behavior, for—as has been the case with dogs of every kind, from time immemorial—its actions are due to the excitement of the outer senses, such as scent, taste, and hearing, and any emotions observable are but the direct and inward continuation of those external sensations, and, as such, last but for a given time. What we may term the 'thought form' that is bound to any given *word*, representing objective thought in its simplest form, rotates within a very limited circle, and is powerless over the animal's feelings. . . . An animal can be got to understand and carry out certain injunctions such as, 'Sit up and beg,' 'Lift up your paw,' 'Go to your bed,' 'Go out of the door,' and much more of the same description, while after instruction it will understand 'Behind the stove lies a biscuit,' yet action seldom results from such knowledge. The dog's eyes will brighten, and it is evident that it has perfectly well comprehended the meaning of the words—indeed, this much can be easily ascertained by questioning it—but the dog will seem incapable of translating what it has comprehended into action."

Fraulein Kindermann here unconsciously begs the question of what constitutes a valid test of knowledge. One might say that it appears as though there were two minds at work in the dog: one the mind that produces the dog's normal actions, the other the mind that produces its replies by means of tapping. We are once again reminded of the phenomena of spiritualism, and it is along these lines that Dr. Mackenzie explains the whole of the phenomena with the exception of the arithmetical feats. In the arithmetical phenomena, Dr. Mackenzie finds nothing remarkable. I cannot quite follow his reasoning, but it would appear to be that since animals involve mathematical principles in their constitution, there is nothing impossible in their achieving such feats of mathematics as have been related of Lola and other so-called thinking animals. The idea would seem to be that if you could only endow an atom with a modicum of consciousness, it might accomplish all sorts of mathematical marvels because of its mathematical constitution. Certainly, it must be admitted that ability at mathematics is no proof of general intelligence, but I must confess I find Dr. Mackenzie's explanation of the mathematical feats of "thinking animals" far-fetched. But his correlation of the other phenomena with those of mediumism is in my opinion very striking. Certainly, there seems to be needed some rapport between the human being and the animal before such results as those recorded of Lola can be obtained, and in very many ways the phenomena recall those of mediumism and indicate the possibility that the intelligence operating through the animal is the subconsciousness of the human being who is experimenting with it. But the present moment is not the time to dogmatize. What is needed is more research, and an end of acrimonious argument engendered by theological prejudices. Whatever explanation of the phenomena may finally come to be accepted, the thanks of all students of psychology are due to

Fraulein Kindermann for her painstaking work, and her book will be found not only of great interest to students, but no less fascinating to the general reader.

A MASTER OF MAGIC: ALPHONSE LOUIS CONSTANT

THE history of Occultism might not inaptly be described as a series of biographies of extraordinary personages. Not least extraordinary amongst these stands Alphonse Louis Constant, better known under his literary pseudonym of Eliphas Levi. Knowledge of the man and his works is one of the many debts English students of Occultism owe to the indefatigable labors of Mr. Arthur Edward Waite. In 1886, Mr. Waite gave us, under the title of The Mysteries of Magic, a digest of Eliphas Levi's occult writings, of which a second and revised edition appeared in 1897. The previous year Mr. Waite published a complete translation of Eliphas Levi's *Dogme de la Haute Magie and Rituel de la Haute Magie*, and in 1913 a translation of his *Histoire de la Magie*. The *Dogme* and *Rituel* form together possibly the most brilliant work on Occultism that has ever been written, a work justly prized by students representative of all schools of occult thought, and, in fact, regarded by the majority of them as an indispensable guide. Very welcome, therefore, is the new and sumptuous edition of Mr. Waite's translation which has just been published by Messrs. William Rider & Son, Ltd. Like the first, it contains all the original engravings, a portrait of the author and an important Biographical Preface by the translator and editor, and in addition there are now added a large number of very useful annotations containing many references to Eliphas Levi's other works. The translation, moreover, has been fully revised.

H. Stanley Redgrove

The year 1810 was that approximately in which Alphonse Louis Constant was born. He was the child of humble parents, his father being a shoemaker, but a kindly disposed parish priest, who noticed signs of unusual intelligence in the boy, secured for him the position of scholar at the school of St. Sulpice, where he was educated with a view to the priesthood. Apparently, these early signs did not belie the boy's intellectual ability; but his was not the mind to be fettered by the bonds of orthodoxy, and some time after his appointment as professor at the *Petit Seminaire de Paris* (he had previously taken minor orders, and become a deacon), he was expelled for teaching heterodox doctrines. Alternatively, according to another account, he voluntarily relinquished his post. Exactly how he proceeded to make his living in a somewhat hostile world is, like many other details in his life, obscure, but he was soon destined to come into conflict again with orthodoxy—this time political, not religious—being imprisoned for six months for writing a book on the Gospel of Liberty which contained socialistic ideas. Some time after his imprisonment, he contracted a runaway marriage with Mile. Noemie Cadiot, a beautiful girl of sixteen, who bore him two children and afterwards deserted him and succeeded in getting the marriage annulled on the grounds that it was contracted without her parents' consent while she was still a minor. It appears that it was after this event that Constant's attention became directed to the study of Occultism, and the year 1855 saw the publication of his first work on the subject, namely the *Dogme de la Haute Magie*. This was rapidly followed by other works of an occult character, namely the Rituel de la Haute Magie, in 1856; Histoire de la Magie, 1860; La Clef des Grands Mysteres, 1861; a second edition of the *Dogme et Rituel*, 1861; Fables et Symboles, 1862; *Le Sorcier de Meudon*; and *La Science des Esprits*, 1865. The year previous to the publication of the Dogme, Eliphas Levi was in London, where he carried out his celebrated ceremonial evocation of Apollonius of Tyana, a full account of which will be found in chapter thirteen of this book. In this connection his insistence on the facts as he experienced them, and his characteristically skeptical attitude as to their meaning and significance, are both worthy of note. Whilst in this country, it is almost certain that he came in contact with Lord Lytton, and the point is of interest because of the strong similarity between the mysterious *vril* of Lytton's *The Coming Race* and Eliphas Levi's central hypothesis of the Astral Light.

During his lifetime, Eliphas Levi's works do not appear to have achieved any extraordinary degree of popularity, but they attracted a circle of disciples, and many inquirers came to him for advice on occult matters. We are told that when at home he invariably wore a long red robe, such as that in which we see him garbed in his portrait. Mme. Gebhard, as quoted by Mr. Waite in his "Biographical and Critical Essay," prefaced to The Mysteries of Magic, writes of him as follows: "He was a short and corpulent figure; his face was kind and benevolent, beaming with good nature, and he wore a long grey beard which covered nearly the whole of his breast. His apartment resembled a *bric-a-brac* shop, with specimens of the most beautiful and rare old china, tapestry and valuable paintings. . . . He lived a quiet and retired life, having few friends. . . . His habits . . . were simple, but he was no vegetarian. . . . He had a wonderful memory, and a marvelous flow of language, his expressions and illustrations being of the choicest and rarest character. . . . Never did I leave his presence," she adds, "without feeling that my own nature had been uplifted to nobler and better things, and I look upon Eliphas Levi as one of the truest friends I ever had, for he taught me the highest truth which it is in the power of man or woman to grasp."

Eliphas Levi died in 1875. The closing years of his life were unmarked by any literary activities. He never openly left the Church of Rome, and it has been asserted that in his later years, he renounced the errors of his heterodox magical doctrines. Certainly, his later works show some attempt at approximating the teachings of the *Dogme* and *Rituel* to a more orthodox standpoint; but if Eliphas Levi clung to the Church and died as one of her sons, we may be certain that it was because he was capable of interpreting her teachings for himself in a manner which would certainly not have appealed to her orthodox adherents.

I have characterized the *Dogme* and *Rituel* as forming together possibly the most brilliant work on Occultism that has ever been written; but that is not to say that it is beyond criticism. Mr. Waite has briefly summed up those characteristics that are most estimable in the work of Eliphas Levi and those which most detract from its value. He writes concerning him: "Intensely suggestive on the mere surface, he is at the same time without evidence of depth; splendid in ready generalization, he is without accuracy in detail, and it would be difficult to cite a worse-guide over mere matters of fact." Yet in spite of his defects, it is emphatically true, as Mr. Waite remarks, that "no modern expositor of occult claims can bear any comparison with Eliphas Levi, and among ancient expositors, though many stand higher in authority and are assuredly more sincere, all yield to him in living interest, for he is actually the spirit of modern thought forcing an answer for the times from the old oracles. Hence, there are greater names, but there has been no influence so great during the last two centuries: no fascination in occult literature exceeds that of the French Magus."

Mr. Waite charges Eliphas Levi with insincerity, and, in the "Biographical and Critical Essay" prefacing The Mysteries of Magic, he has exhibited a number of contradictory statements drawn from the different works of this Master of Magic. I should prefer myself to say that, like most people, Eliphas Levi sometimes found occasion to change his views, but he had an unfortunate literary knack of always writing authoritatively, as a high hierophant in possession of absolute truth, so that he gave expression to theories which were really only tentative as though they were (as perhaps at the moment he believed them to be) the last word on the subject. Whether his first thoughts or his last were always the best is, of course, another question.

The doctrine of the *Dogme* and *Rituel* is a doctrine of power—the invulnerable power of will. Underlying all religious dogmas, teaches Eliphas Levi, is one absolute truth. This truth is magic, and the dogmas of theology are, as it were, faint reflections of it, fables adapted to the intelligence of children. As concerns his hypothesis of the Astral Light, the quasi-material agency of all magical phenomena, the universal force that is governed by the will, I am inclined to think that it is at once too indefinite and too wide in its applications. It seems, moreover, to have been based, in its inventor's mind, on scientific concepts which are now tending to become obsolete. But that the words "will" and "imagination" connotes very real and potent powers and that in terms of these powers is to be found, a rational explanation of many seemingly inexplicable phenomena is, to my mind, almost beyond doubt.

I must not conclude this brief notice of Eliphas Levi and his work without quoting some of his brilliant utterances—so apposite, in their wording, and rich in their suggestiveness—on the subject of the will and its magical powers. Symbols and ceremonies, according to him, have but one function, namely, to educate the will, and are of value only in so far as they are, so to speak, the crystallized form of magical doctrine. "Ceremonies, vestments, perfumes, characters and figures, being . . . necessary," he writes, "to apply the imagination to the education of the will, the success of magical works depends upon the faithful observation of all the Rites, which are in no sense fantastic or arbitrary. They have been transmitted to us by antiquity and obtain permanently by the essential laws of analogical realization and of the correspondence which interbinds ideas and forms." "The sign," he tells us, "is nothing by itself, and has no force apart from the doctrine of which it is the summary and the logos"; whilst in a chapter of his work devoted to the subject of Talismans, he defines a pentacle "as a synthetic character resuming the entire magical doctrine in one of its special conceptions," adding, "it is therefore the full expression of a completed thought and will: it is the signature of a spirit."

There is nothing superstitious in the use of ceremonial as advocated by Eliphas Levi. Ceremonial only becomes superstitious—as it invariably tends to do—when its true meaning is lost sight of "Superstition," he writes, "is derived from a Latin word which signifies survival. It is the sign surviving the thought; it is the dead body of a Religious Rite." But even a superstitious and insensate practice may possess efficacy, he points out, in so far as it is the realization of the will. "A prayer is more powerful," he writes, "if we visit a church to say it than when it is recited at home, and it will work miracles if we fare to a famous sanctuary for the purpose—in other words, to one which is magnetized strongly by the great number of its frequenters—traversing two or three hundred leagues with bare feet and asking alms by the way." Again, he writes, "If a peasant rose up every morning at two or three o'clock and went a long distance from home to gather a sprig of the same herb before the rising of the sun, he would be able to perform a great number of prodigies by merely carrying this herb upon his person, for it would be the sign of his will, and in virtue thereof would be all that he required it to become in the interest of his desires." Even the bizarre stories of witchcraft, according to Eliphas Levi, are not devoid of a certain element of truth, nor are the practices of Black Magic without a certain horrible efficacy. "Witchcraft, properly so called," he writes, "that is, ceremonial operation with intent to bewitch, acts only on the operator, and serves to fix and confirm his will, by formulating it with persistence and travail, the two conditions which make volition efficacious;" for the will may be educated and strengthened in evil as well as in good, and it is indeed true that "he who affirms the devil creates or makes the devil." Is it objected that Eliphas Levi claims too much for the will when he asserts it to be capable of effecting miracles? "The supernatural," he replies, "is only the natural in an extraordinary grade, or it is the exalted natural. . . Miracles are effects which surprise those who are ignorant of their causes, or assign them causes which are not in proportion to effects."

The king is he who can control the multitude. This would appear to be the last word in Eliphas Levi's doctrine of power. "The Great Work in Practical Magic," he writes, "after the education of the will and the personal creation of the Magus, is the formation of the magnetic chain, and this secret is truly that of priesthood and of royalty. To form the magnetic chain is to originate a current of ideas which produces faith and draws a large number of wills in a given circle of active manifestation." This may, indeed, be a dangerous doctrine, but that it is true can hardly be doubted, and it is as well that we should be acquainted with it. He who would be himself must learn to rise superior to the emotions that sweep over crowds, emotions which those who understand crowd-psychology so often utilize for their own personal ends to the detriment of their servitors. The Absolute Key to the Occult Sciences! Perhaps—though it may seem unlike what we expected—Eliphas Levi has, in a sense, really given it to us. At any rate, his writings—in spite of their defects—have a high excellence and value that is characteristically their own, and the thanks of all English students are due to Mr. Waite for the work he has done towards making them available in English.

H. Stanley Redgrove

HERB-MAGIC

SOME one, I believe, has remarked of the English that they are characterized by their especial love of flowers. I do not know how true this is; but certainly, if it is true, the affection is one of which we have no need to be ashamed. To the vegetable kingdom man, in common with other animals, owes the greatest of all debts, namely, that of his continued existence. The chlorophyll of plants is the agency adopted by Nature for maintaining the oxygen of the atmosphere which is essential to the life of man and all creatures that breathe, and to the plant-world man is entirely indebted, either directly or indirectly, for his supply of food-stuffs, for it is only plants that have the power of converting mineral substances into forms that can be assimilated by the digestive organs of man and other animals. Moreover, the beauty of flowers, the charm of their varied forms and colors and the deliciousness of the odors that many of them exhale, cannot be denied. Finally, it is from the world of plants that man obtains many of the most potent drugs (e.g. quinine) with which to combat the various diseases that afflict him. The medicinal value of plants is the characteristic that appears most to have excited the interest of the ancients. Convinced that everything in Nature existed for the service of man, they were eager to find some medicinal property, some magical virtue, in every plant, even the seemingly most unlikely. No wonder, therefore, that there came into existence a vast body of folklore associated with plants, folklore that has died hard, and of which very many traces indeed may still be found lingering in the country today.

The study of the old herbals embodying the ancient knowledge and beliefs concerning plants, a curious medley of fact and fiction, has a charm which is all its own. It has not, perhaps, been explored as widely as it deserves to be, for there are few books which reveal to us as intimately as do the old herbals the thought and beliefs—the mental atmosphere—of days that are gone. We ought, therefore, to be especially grateful to Miss E. S. Rohde for her beautiful book on the old English herbals which has recently been published by Messrs. Longmans, Green & Co. It is one of those discursive books which the reader feels must have given great enjoyment to the author to write, and which it gives him equal pleasure to read. It is essentially a popular book, in the best sense of that rather misused term; and if it is not free from certain inaccuracies, we can readily forgive Miss Rohde for these because she has succeeded in conveying to us the spirit of the old herbals, and that is what is of primary importance.

So fascinating are the old herbals, so alluring are the many quaint beliefs of Herb-Magic, that it is difficult to select for treatment one book, or one belief, rather than another. But something of that sort has to be done in a brief article such as the present. Personally, I find Gerard quite irresistible. His Herbal, which is one of the best known, was published in 1597. The manner of its production, it is true, does Gerard little credit. A considerable portion of the material for it he obtained, and used without acknowledgment, from an unpublished translation of a work by Dodoens; but the man, in spite of the fact that he could descend to this literary theft, was by no means devoid of genius, and he transfused this genius into the work, transmuting the somewhat dry bones of Dodoens into one of the world's most fascinating books. Some parts of it, indeed, are his own work. Very interesting is it to read his accounts of the plants that grew about London in his day, and to picture the charm of the place as it then was. And no less interesting is it to know, as an illustration of the tenacity of plant-life, that some of them are still to be found by those who have eyes to see. Whortleberries and the Small Earth-nut are still to be found at Hampstead, and, although I have not seen the Hemlock Dropwort at Battersea, it may very well be there, for I observed it in a seemingly equally unlikely place—near the canal bridge at Stratford—but a few years ago.

Writing of the beauty of plants, Gerard says in "*The Epistle Dedicatorie*" to his work: "What greater delight is there than to behold the earth appareled with plants, as with a robe of imbroidered worke set with orient pearles, and garnished with great diversitie of rare and costly jewels?" "But," he continues in that spirit of nature-mysticism which we are perhaps unfortunately beginning to lose, "these delights are in the outward senses: the principal! delight is in the minde, singularly enriched with the knowledge of these visible things, setting foorth to us the invisible wisdome and admirable workmanship of almightie God." Of the medicinal or magical (one can hardly distinguish between medicine and magic in these days) virtues of plants, Gerard has naturally much to say. There were for him plants not only to cure physical ills, but also those to cure ills of the mind and heart. The odor of Basil, he tells us, removes melancholy and makes a man glad. Much the same was also said to be true of Balm; and it is pleasing to think that, in the days when so much use was made of medicinal preparations of the most disgusting and nauseating character, the herbalists stoutly maintained the medicinal efficacy of sweet-smelling herbs and plants. The virtues of Rosemary were, of course, much extolled by Gerard. "The flowers made up into plates with sugar after the manner of Sugar Poset and eaten," he writes, "it comforteth the heart, and maketh it merie, quickeneth the spirits, and maketh them more lively." The belief in the sovereign virtues of Rosemary is a very old one, and Rosemary was one of the ingredients in Roger Bacon's celebrated recipe for the cure of old age and the preservation of youth.

No account of Herb-Magic would be complete without some reference to the Doctrine of Signatures, to the idea, that is, that the hidden virtues of plants were indicated by some external sign. The notion is a very ancient one. Roger Bacon gives expression to it as follows: "Wheresoever God hath placed such an unspeakable Virtue, he hath added a certain Similitude, that every Man, who is of a clear and vivacious Wit and Understanding, may conceive its Operation." The doctrine became very generally accepted during the seventeenth century, no doubt owing partly to the vigorous championship of it by the great Paracelsus. William Coles, a late seventeenth-century herbalist, writes concerning the doctrine as follows: "Though Sin and Sathan have plunged man kinde into an Ocean of Infirmities (for before the Fall, Man was not subject to Diseases) yet the mercy of God which is over all his Workes, maketh Grasse to grow upon the Mountaines, and Herbs for the use of Men, and hath not onely stamped upon them (as upon every Man) a distinct forme, but also given them particular Signatures, whereby a Man may read, even in legible Characters, the use of them...........*Heart Trefoyle* is so called, not onely because the Leafe is Triangular like the Heart of a Man, but also because each Leafe contains the perfect Icon of an Heart, and that in its proper color, viz. a flesh color. *Hounds tongue* hath a form not much different from its name, which will tye the Tongues of Hounds, so that they shall not bark at you: if it be laid under the bottomes of ones feet.......... Wallnuts bear the whole Signature of the Head, the outwardmost green barke answerable to the thick skin wherewith the head is covered, and a Salt made of it, is singularly good for wounds in that part, as the kemell is good for the braines which it resembles being environed with a Shell which imitates the Scull, and then it is wrapped up againe in a silken covering somewhat representing the *Pia Mater.*"

With the Renaissance and the revival of ancient astrological doctrines going back to the days of the Babylonians, the belief became current that the virtues of plants were derived from the planets. Every plant was in correspondence with one of the heavenly bodies, many of them bore the impress or seal of the planet wherefrom it derived its virtue, and hence it was necessary for the

H. Stanley Redgrove

herbalist to be acquainted with the virtues of the planets and to read their signs aright. Astrology, it must be remembered, for these old-time thinkers, was more than a mere method of foretelling the future; it was, rather, a philosophy of the universe. Cornelius Agrippa, in his Three Books of Occult Philosophy, that heroic attempt to work out all the correspondences of the universe, tells us the means whereby we may assign not only plants, but, it would seem, almost all other terrestrial objects to their appropriate planets. Thus, the Marigold—a very sun-like flower in appearance—we learn, is solary. So also are those plants which fold their leaves when the sun is near upon setting, but unfold them little by little when it rises. Solary also are plants which never fear the extremities of winter; as well as many others, such as Mint, Saffron, Balsam, Calamus or Sweet Flag, Sweet Marjoram, etc., for less obvious reasons. Amongst the names of seventeenth-century British herbals in which astrological doctrines predominate, that of Culpeper's is perhaps pre-eminent. Miss Rohde regards Culpeper as a charlatan. Perhaps, to some extent, he was. Yet in spite of all its fantasticality, my own feeling is that he believed in much of what he wrote; and he certainly achieved—however many its absurdities—the most popular herbal, judged by the enormous number of times it has been reprinted in one form or another, that has ever been produced.

Forgotten Essays

BLAKE AND SWEDENBORG:

A STUDY IN COMPARATIVE MYSTICISM

THE question of the relation between Swedenborg and Blake is an exceedingly difficult and involved one. It will not, of course, be possible, within the confines of a brief study such as the present, to present anything approaching a complete answer to this question; but, at least, I shall attempt to throw some light on an obscure problem, and to point out certain facts connected therewith which seem to me to be of importance.

In dealing with Swedenborg's and Blake's works, we are not confronted with two independently constructed systems of thought. Blake's father is said to have been "a dissenter," and it is possible that he was amongst the early converts to Swedenborg's doctrines; at any rate, Blake began to be acquainted with these at an early age. This fact, one might think, ought to simplify the question with which we are concerned: in truth, however, it complicates it. For to Blake's early acquaintance with the doctrines of the Swedish philosopher-seer were, no doubt, largely due (i) his very thorough assimilation of certain of Swedenborg's teachings and modes of thought, and (ii) his capacity for so very thoroughly disliking Swedenborg on occasion. It is this fact, namely, that Blake is at once so Swedenborgian and so anti Swedenborgian, coupled with the inherent difficulty of interpreting Blake's frequently obscure language, that renders the question with which I am concerned one of the hardest in a region of hard and obscure problems. Moreover, it must be remembered that Blake was subjected to other potent influences, particularly that of Boehme, the inspired shoemaker of Goerlitz; and although Boehme's and Swedenborg's teachings have much in common—especially do they agree in regarding Christianity as primarily a matter

- 219 -

of life—Boehme and Swedenborg seem to have pulled against one another in Blake's mind.

Swedenborg was essentially a man of science, and when he gave up his scientific calling to enter upon another sphere of labor, he did not leave his scientific attitude of mind behind. Blake, on the other hand, was essentially an artist, who distrusted science, as tending, he thought, to bind down imagination. In one poem, for example, he writes:

> You don't believe—I won't attempt to make ye:
> You are asleep—I won't attempt to wake ye.
> Sleep on! sleep on! while in your pleasant dreams
> Of Reason you may drink of Life's clear streams.
> Reason and Newton, they are quite two things;
> For so the swallow and the sparrow sings.
> Reason says "Miracle": Newton says "Doubt."
> Aye I that's the way to make all Nature out.
> "Doubt, doubt, and don't believe without experiment":
> That is the very thing that Jesus meant,
> When he said "Only believe! believe and try I
> Try, try, and never mind the reason why!

whilst in his picture entitled "Newton" (1795), Newton, as a symbol of Science, is represented by a naked, youthful figure, intent upon a geometrical figure upon the ground, the dark sky in the picture corresponding to Blake's concept of the mind of empirical science.

Swedenborg, though he claims to have passed through assuredly the most extraordinary and exciting experiences, never exhibits excitement. He is always cool, level-headed, analytical. Blake, on the other hand, is always in a state of intellectual excitement: he is bubbling over with exuberance, or exploding with honest indignation. Swedenborg saw that no detached statement could be altogether true: he is, therefore, always qualifying, supplementing, defining, with an eye to scientific precision; and he is always alive to that element of truth present in the current opinion of his day. But if Swedenborg would convince by accuracy and precision, Blake would convince by violence and paradox. Swedenborg could denounce when conciliation was impossible, Blake always denounces—his opponents in art or philosophy are invariably "murderers," "liars," or "slobbering fools." Blake never expresses a great truth unless he does so in an exuberant and excessive—perhaps some will say, exaggerated—form. In a word, Swedenborg was a Swede, whilst Blake, if the tradition that he was an Irishman is not true, let me say, ought to have been one.

There are some persons who react as intended to Blake's fiery words, to whom Swedenborg's more precise style proves boring or (as to Blake himself) irritating. There are others who find intellectual satisfaction in Swedenborg's works, but are repelled by Blake's paradoxes. And there are some more fortunate minds, and I count myself amongst their number, who can admire both these great geniuses and appreciate their several different qualities. To such, any attempt to value one at the expense of the other would appear invidious and repellent. In her Mysticism in English Literature, an excellent work on a subject concerning which sane books are rare, Dr. C. F. E. Spurgeon says:

Blake knew some, at least of Swedenborg's books well; two of his friends, C. A. Tulk and Flaxman, were devoted Swedenborgians, and he told Tulk that he had two different states, one in which he liked Swedenborg's writings, and one in which he disliked them. Unquestionably, they sometimes irritated him, and then he abused them, but it is only necessary to read his annotations of his copy of Swedenborg's Wisdom of the Angels (now in the British Museum) to realize in the first place that he sometimes misunderstood Swedenborg's position, and secondly, that when he did understand it, he was thoroughly in agreement with it, and that he and the Swedish seer had much in common.

H. Stanley Redgrove

It was assuredly in that state in which he disliked Swedenborg's writings that Blake wrote, probably in 1790, The Marriage of Heaven and Hell, in many ways the greatest and most forceful of his works. There Blake wrote as follows:

I have always found that Angels have the vanity to speak of themselves as the Only Wise. This they do with a confident insolence sprouting from systematic reasoning. Thus, Swedenborg boasts that what he writes is new; tho' it is only the Contents or Index of already published books... he shows the folly of churches, and exposes hypocrites, till he imagines that all are religious, and himself the single one on earth that ever broke a net. Now hear a plain fact: Swedenborg has not written one new truth. Now hear another: he has written all the old falsehoods. And now hear the reason. He conversed with Angels who are all religious, and conversed not with Devils who all hate religion, for he was incapable thro' his conceited notions. Thus, Swedenborg's writings are a recapitulation of all superficial opinions, and an analysis of the more sublime—but no further. Have now another plain fact. Any man of mechanical talents may, from the writings of Paracelsus or Jacob Behmen, produce ten thousand volumes of equal value with Swedenborg's, and from those of Dante or Shakespear an infinite number...

Of the items of this violent criticism, it will not be necessary for those who know Swedenborg, to point out that not one is justifiable. The highest of Swedenborg's angels never reason, because they have divine truth inscribed on their hearts, and perceive as true that which is true. Swedenborg's "Memorable Relations," contained in his works, relate conversations and other experiences with evil spirits as well as good, and it is surely inconsistent to deny the validity of the former whilst admitting that of the latter. And I know of no philosopher more free from conceit, and of a more humble temper of mind. Nor was it Blake's constant or final attitude towards Sweden's great philosopher-seer. The year previously, at any rate, Blake appears to have been a whole-hearted disciple of Swedenborg. In that year, the first General Conference of the New Jerusalem Church—a religious organization based upon Swedenborg's theological doctrines—met in Great East Cheap, and according to the Minute Book, the signatures "W. Blake" and "C. Blake" are, together with those of other persons who attended, attached to the following declaration of faith:

We whose Names are hereunto subscribed, do each of us approve of the theological Writings of Emanuel Swedenborg, believing that the Doctrines contained therein are genuine Truths, revealed from Heaven, and that the New Jerusalem Church ought to be established, distinct and separate from the Old Church.

These signatures are almost certainly those of William Blake and his wife Catherine—unfortunately the original Minute Book is lost, so that a slight doubt as to their identity must remain. A large number of resolutions of this conference, asserting belief in the various distinctive doctrines of Swedenborg's theological and philosophical writings, are reported as having been passed unanimously, so that presumably they had Blake's assent. It seems probable, also, that for a time at any rate, Blake was an attendant at the New Jerusalem Church opened in Cross Street, Hatton Garden, in 1797, though later in his life he ceased from attending public worship. There are, moreover, some explicit references to Swedenborg in Blake's later works, written in a different spirit from that in which the Swedish mystic is referred to in *The Marriage of Heaven and Hell*, in Milton (1804), Swedenborg is entitled—rather ambiguously, it is true—"strongest of men, the Sampson shorn by the Churches," whilst in the *Descriptive Catalogue* (1809) he is a "visionary" whose works "are well worthy the attention of Painters and Poets; they are foundations for grand things," and he is referred to as agreeing with Blake in his denunciation of learning without imagination. Further, in

H. Stanley Redgrove

1825, towards the close of his life, Blake spoke of Swedenborg to Crabb Robinson—according to the latter's Diary—as "a Divine teacher," who "has done much good, and will do much," adding, however, that Swedenborg "was wrong in endeavoring to explain to the rational faculty what the reason cannot understand."

Blake's criticism of Swedenborg in *The Marriage of Heaven and Hell*, it is important to note, is not at all an orthodox criticism. It is not the criticism of a materialist, but of one spiritualist or idealist (there is no univocal term) directed against another. The genuineness of Swedenborg's spiritual experiences, that he was vouchsafed a revelation and conversed with the inhabitants of the other world, Blake never questions (at least, so far as these conversations are with angels), but takes, as it were, for granted and beyond dispute—though it is just this claim which to the ordinary mind must seem so extraordinary and difficult to credit. The reality of vision and the substantiality of spirit were facts of prime importance with both Swedenborg and Blake. Swedenborg never tires of reiterating that the spirit is the real man, perfectly organized and possessing senses and functions corresponding to every one which is associated with the body; and he invariably contrasts the natural and the spiritual realms on the ground that, whereas the things of the latter are substantial, those of the former are merely material. In *Heaven and its Wonders and Hell*, for example, he writes:

From all my experience, which has now extended over many years, I can declare and solemnly affirm that angels as to their form are in every respect men; that they have a face, eyes, ears, a body, arms, hands and feet; that they see, hear and converse with one another, and, in a word, that they are deficient in nothing that belongs to a man except that they are not clothed with a material body. I have seen them in their own light, which exceeds by many degrees the noonday light of the world; and in that light, all their features could be seen more distinctly and clearly than the faces of men on earth.

Now hear Blake:—

The Prophets describe what they saw in Vision as real and existing men whom they saw with their imaginative and immortal organs; the Apostles the same; the clearer the organ, the more distinct the object. A Spirit and a Vision are not, as the modem philosophy supposes, a cloudy vapor or a nothing: they are organized and minutely articulated beyond all that the mortal and perishing nature can produce. He who does not imagine in stronger and better lineaments, and in stronger and better light, than his perishing mortal eye can see, does not imagine at all. The painter of this work asserts that all his imaginations appear to him infinitely more perfect and more minutely organized than anything seen by his mortal eye. Spirits are organized men.

Swedenborg's concept of spirit as essentially substantial and organized is logically connected with his teaching that "God is Very Man." "It is because God is a Man," he says, "that all angels and spirits are men in perfect form." Again, he writes:

Everyone who believes that God is a Man can confirm in himself the truth that there are infinite things in Him. For since he is a Man, He has a body and everything belonging thereto; thus, He has a face, breast, abdomen, loins and feet; for without these, He would not be a Man. And having these, He has also eyes, ears, nostrils, mouth and tongue; and further the internal organs, as the heart and the lungs, and the parts connected with these; all of which, taken together, are what constitute a man. In created man, these things are numerous, and in their structural details innumerable; but in God-Man they are infinite and complete, and therefore to Him belongs infinite perfection. A comparison is made between uncreate Man, who is God, and created man, because God is a Man, and it is said by Him that the man of this world was created after His image and in his likeness (Gen. i. 26, 27).

This doctrine of Swedenborg's has been criticized as excessively anthropomorphic. But the Swedish philosopher realized that only a God who is Very Man can satisfy the heart's desire and call forth adoration and worship. It is in the Glorified Savior that he saw the perfect manifestation of God, and that manifestation is as perfect man. Moreover, it may be urged that only a God who is Very Man can satisfy the reason in its demand for a final explanation of the phenomenal world, for the only true cause known to reason is the human will, and it is the will (or love) which, so teaches Swedenborg, essentially constitutes the man. The organs of the material body are only the symbols of states of will and intelligence. The true organs it may be said, therefore, are spiritual—what we observe are merely their material shadows,—and it is in this sense that the passage I have already quoted from Swedenborg is intended to be understood. Blake annotated II (quoted above) of his copy of Swedenborg's *Divine Love and Wisdom* as follows:

Man can have no idea of anything greater than Man, as a cup cannot contain more than its capaciousness. But God is a man, not because he is so perceived by man, but because he is the creator of man. Think of a white cloud as being holy, you cannot love it; but think of a holy man within the cloud, love springs up in your thought. For to think of holiness distinct from man is impossible to the affections. Thought alone can make monsters, but the affections cannot.

He had thoroughly assimilated Swedenborg's views concerning the nature of God. In his "Auguries of Innocence" we read that:

> God appears, and God is Light,
> To those poor souls who dwell in Night;
> But does a Human Form Display

To those who dwell in realms of Day.

The meaning is evidently that, whilst the perception of God as a pantheistic light-giving principle enlightens those who sit in darkness, clearer vision perceives him, not as a Principle, but as a Personality. One has only to turn to the illustrations of Job, to that wonderful picture in which the Ancient of Days measures out infinite space by the span of his hand (1794), or to that grand invention "Elohim creating Adam" (1795), to see how deeply imbued Blake's mind was with the concept of the Humanity of God. As Mr. Chesterton remarks:

God was to him [Blake] the magnificent old man depicted in his dark and extraordinary illustrations of Job, the old man with the monstrous muscles, the mild stem eyebrows, the long smooth silver hair and beard. In the dialogues between Jehovah and Job, there is little difference between the two ponderous and palpable old men, except that the vision of Deity is a little more solid than the human being. But then Blake held that Deity is more solid than humanity. He held that what we call the ideal is not only more beautiful but more actual than the real. The ordinary educated modern person staring at these Job designs can only say that God is a mere elderly twin brother of Job. Blake would have at once retorted that Job was an image of God.

Solidity and strength are essential elements in Blake's concept of Deity: God, to him, is the Superman. He thus repeats Swedenborg to the letter; and if anyone thinks that Blake was wrong in this, let him attempt a picture that will better convey the concepts of omnipotence and omnipresence than the wonderful creations of Blake's I have already mentioned, without employing the human (i.e. the truly divine) form.

H. Stanley Redgrove

Blake was a fervent Christian, with an ardent faith in and love for his Savior. In this he resembles Swedenborg, and, as I have already indicated, his early initiation into Christianity was most probably into Christianity as Swedenborg conceived it. In a lecture I delivered to the Blake Society on August 12, 1914, it was pointed out, I believe for the first time, that in "The Lamb" Blake clearly identifies the Savior with the Creator. "The Lamb"—an exquisite, child-like poem—is as follows:

> Little Lamb, who made thee?
> Dost thou know who made thee?
> Gave thee life, and bid thee feed,
> By the stream, and o'er the mead;
> Gave thee clothing of delight,
> Softest clothing, woolly, bright;
> Gave thee such a tender voice,
> Making all the vales rejoice?
> Little Lamb, who made thee?
> Dost thou know who made thee?
> Little Lamb, I'll tell thee,
> Little Lamb, I'll tell thee,
> He is called by thy name,
> For He calls Himself a Lamb,
> He is meek, and He is mild;

He who made the Lamb is he who, becoming a child, is called by the lamb's name. Such words could not be uttered by one who accepted the orthodox Trinitarian doctrine of Three Persons in the Godhead, and clearly reflects Swedenborgian teaching. The astute Swedish theologian denied the ordinary Trinitarian doctrine on the grounds that it involves a contradiction in terms, and throws men's minds into intellectual confusion and darkness. He teaches that Father, Son and Holy Spirit are three aspects or functions of one Divine Person—who is revealed to us in the Glorified Savior—corresponding to the will, understanding and consequent action in finite man.

In his later works, however, Blake seems to separate Jesus, the forgiving Savior, and Jehovah, the supposedly-revengeful Law-giver, and to set these two in opposition to one another. This view of Blake's is associated with an antinomian doctrine of forgiveness to which at times he seems strongly to incline. But Swedenborg asserted that this was not the true sense, and sought a deeper mystical import.

Many other points of contact between the thought of Blake and that of Swedenborg, no less important than those I have already indicated, might be dealt with did space allow. Possibly I may have something more to say on this subject on another occasion. But in closing the present contribution to the subject, I wish to add one word lest the significance of "influence" should be misunderstood. Blake, as we have seen, was certainly influenced by Swedenborg; in all probability he had assimilated from the works of the Swedish seer more than he was himself aware. But he was the very antithesis of a slavish disciple. Sometimes he misunderstood Swedenborg; but at others, he reinterpreted him. What he accepted from Swedenborg, he accepted because it was in agreement with his own genius and squared with his own experiences; and when the two men spoke with one voice, they spoke thus because the realm of spiritual truth presented itself similarly to both of them.

H. Stanley Redgrove

THE SCIENCE OF SMELLS

THEY haven't got no noses, They haven't got no noses, And goodness only knowses, The noselessness of man. Perhaps things are not quite so bad as Mr. Chesterton suggests, in an endeavor to portray the thoughts of that celebrated dog, Mr. Quoodle, on the subject, but certainly for animals in whom the olfactory is the most highly developed sense, as for example, dogs, and especially such insects as ants, the world must be a vastly different affair from what it is for us. To such creatures' odor is, in all probability, a sense of forms, such as sight, is for normal human beings. I owe the suggestion to Dr. Dan McKenzie, who brings out the point very effectively in a most interesting and original work that has just been written entitled *Aromatics and the Soul*. The idea, I believe, is due originally to Forel, and Dr. McKenzie explicates it as follows:

When an ant sets out from her nest, she distinguishes the various odors and varying strengths of odors she comes upon, noting and memorizing them as in two main fields, one on her left side, the other on her right. In order to find her way back again, all she has to do is to unwind, so to speak, the roll in her memory, transposing right and left, and this successfully accomplished will bring her back to the point she started from. If we ourselves were endowed with such a perfect olfactory mechanism situated in long, flexible whip-lashes, which we could move and tap with each step, the world for us would be transformed. Odor would become a sense of forms. Thus, the orientation of ants can be explained without assuming the existence of an unknown sense.

This is by no means the only thought of interest on the subject of olfaction that Dr. McKenzie's book contains: indeed, the volume is packed with suggestions for further thought and study, some of which should make a special appeal to the serious student of Occultism. "Olfaction is," as Dr. McKenzie says, "generally felt to be the lowest, the most animal, of the senses." Yet, nevertheless, it is in many ways the most mysterious of them all. It is true, of course, that the transmutation of stimulus into sensation is, as concerns any of the senses, an absolutely unsolved mystery; but in the case of the sense of smell, the mechanism is especially mysterious just because it is seemingly so simple. Scientists are not yet even agreed as to the exact nature of the olfactory stimulus. Is it purely a matter of chemical reaction? Or, alternatively, is the process in any way analogous to that whereby color is perceived? The latter view is that held by Heyninx; and Dr. McKenzie gives an adequate account of it, together with a useful summary of the arguments for and against. Now it has been shown that the vapor of odorous bodies absorb certain ultra-violet rays whose periods of vibration have been determined. Heyninx argues that the vapor are composed of molecules vibrating with a period equal to that of the light rays they absorb and, further, that it is to these vibrations that their odorous qualities are due, differences in odor being the result of differences in the rate of vibration: It is a fascinating theory, and, although several objections to it have been advanced, it is just possible that the theory may ultimately surmount them. One curious phenomenon that Dr. McKenzie omits to mention, and which might be urged in support of Heyninx's theory, since it seems analogous to color-blindness, is partial anosmia, or the inability to smell certain odors. I believe, for example, that many persons are anosmia **(a loss of smell)** to prussic acid. At any rate, I have personally come across more than one such case; and the instance, I think, is particularly interesting because the absorption bands of prussic acid and steam are practically identical, and therefore, on Heyninx's theory, these two substances should have practically identical odors, that is to say, prussic acid should be odorless.

H. Stanley Redgrove

Any theory of olfaction, to be satisfactory, has got to explain the fact that, in the case of certain substances, the most ultramicroscopic particles can be detected by the olfactory sense. Indeed, Fabre's experiments, seem to indicate in the case of certain insects a degree of delicacy of olfaction which is well-nigh incredible. I quote the following abridged account from Dr. McKenzie's book:

Having by chance a living female Great Peacock moth captive in his house; Fabre was surprised one night by the advent of some forty others of the same species-males in search of a mate. At once, the question arose in his mind: How was it that they were attracted? Sight could not have guided them, because, apart from the comparative rarity of this moth in that particular district, the night of their arrival was dark and stormy, his house was screened by trees and shrubs, and the female ensconced under a gauze cover. He observed, besides, that the males did not make straight for their objective, as is characteristic of movement when directed by sight. They blundered and went astray, some of them wandering into rooms other than that in which the female was lying. They behaved, that is to say, as we ourselves do when we are trying to locate the source of a sound or a smell. But sound was ruled out by the fact that they must have been summoned from distances of a mile or a mile and a half. Olfaction remains, and with this in his mind, Fabre undertook several experiments. . . When the female was sequestered under the gauze cover, and in drawers or in boxes with loosely-fitting lids, the males always succeeded in discovering her. But when she was placed under a glass cover, or in a sealed receptacle, no male at all appeared. Further, Fabre found that cotton-wool stuffed into the opening and cracks of her receptacle was also sufficient to prevent the summons reaching the males. . . In watching the behavior of the third moth on his list, the Banded Monk . . . Fabre discerned a circumstance very strongly suggestive of the operation of an odorous lure. He found that, if the female was left for a time in contact with some absorbent material and was afterwards shifted, the males were attracted, not to her new situation, but to the place where she had originally been lying. Subsequent experiment showed that a period of about half an hour was necessary to lead to the impregnation of the neighborhood with the effluvium she elaborated.

Most of us, perhaps, can give instances from our own experience in which an odor has produced an action on our part a moment or two before it has attained to conscious perception, and Dr. McKenzie throws out the interesting suggestion that possibly man's olfactory sense is finer than he is aware, certain faint odors invariably escaping consciousness but being subconsciously perceived and thereby affecting his conduct. Cases of antipathy and sympathy between strangers might thereby be explained, and even perhaps some instances of supposed telepathy. It may seem ridiculous at first sight to say that one person can convey his thoughts to another by an odor unconsciously produced on the one hand, and unconsciously perceived on the other. Yet certainly something of this sort does seem to take place in the case of certain of the lower animals; and although mankind has ceased to rely, except to a very inconsiderable extent, on the sense of olfaction for guidance in the affairs of life, it is possible that his subconscious mind still possesses something of the powers that belonged to his ancestors. At any rate, the suggestion is a very interesting one, and should be borne in mind by psychical researchers.

The psychology of olfaction is, in any case, no less mysterious than its physiology. No satisfactory reason, for example, has yet been given for the astonishing power odors have of recalling memories. Nearly everyone, I think, can testify to these powers from his own experience. They constitute, perhaps, a heritage from the past, and provide some indication of what this now despised sense signified in days when mankind was yet young.

To the chemist, smells have an intellectual value, an informing quality, which for most other folk is non-existent. To the man in the street smells are just classified as pleasant and unpleasant, and as we know, very few folk can make a good show at the game, frequently played at bazaars and the like, of identifying a score or so of common substances by their odors alone. Indeed, as Dr. McKenzie points out, "Our native language does not possess a terminology descriptive of smells. We never name an odor, we only say it is a 'smell like' something or another." The same is true, I believe, of the French language, and the fact may be taken as indicative of our general state of ignorance concerning olfaction and of the neglect of its cultivation by mankind.

It might be maintained, however, that the old-time occultists did recognize the importance of odors from the point of view of their psychological effects. The weird and wonderful recipes for aromatic ointments, suffumigation's and the like which are to be found in the books of magic are evidence of this. Not the least interesting chapter of Dr. McKenzie's admirable book is that on "Smell in Folklore, Religion, and History." Many of the old-time medical practices that he details seem very absurd in our modern eyes; yet, as he indicates, "out of these most absurd and to us meaningless methods of treatment modern medicine has here and there selected recipes which experiment and experience have proved to be of value." Valerian and *asafetida* may have been originally prescribed because it was thought that their vile odors would drive away evil spirits: they have truly remedial virtues nevertheless, and one wonders sometimes whether the old occultists were always such fools as it is nowadays customary to portray them.

Dr. McKenzie is a man of science, the fact is evident from his work, apart from the "M.D." on the title page-yet he is keenly aware how dull a scientific book can be made, and, skillfully avoiding all the pitfalls, has produced a volume which the general reader, not less than the student of philosophy, will read from cover to cover with the keenest pleasure.

EYELESS SIGHT

THE fact appears to be fairly well established that many somnambulists are able to guide themselves with remarkable ease during their nocturnal wanderings with their eyes closed or even bandaged, and the idea has been expressed, and has to some extent passed into popular belief, that this guidance is effected by means of the fingertips to which, in some way or the other, the sense of sight is transferred. Allied to this phenomenon are many well-established instances, in the case of hypnotized subjects, of the apparent transference of the seat of sensibility, as concerns vision, to the knee, stomach or other part of the body. Exactly how such transference is possible, however, remains obscure, and, as an explanation of the phenomena in question, the theory of transference can hardly be regarded as satisfactory. "The common theory," wrote F. W. H. Myers in his Human Personality, and the remark is still true today" would be that these [phenomena] are merely cases of erroneous self-suggestion; that the subject really sees with the eye, but thinks that he sees with the knee, or the stomach, or the finger-tips." Myers own suggestion is that, although in some cases this theory is the true one, in others there is actual telaesthesia, a perception by the spirit in wholly supernormal fashion, represented as visual, but in an incoherent manner, and thus referred to some part of the body other than the retina.

H. Stanley Redgrove

It must be confessed, however, that none of these theories, nor that which assumes hyperesthesia of the sense of touch sufficient to acquaint the percipient with properties of an object placed in contact with his skin usually regarded as only perceivable through the sense of sight (e.g., the color and form of words written on a sheet of paper) can be regarded as wholly satisfactory; and, indeed, in view of the remarkable character of the phenomena in question, the amount of attention bestowed on them, apart from the extraordinary researches of M. Jules Romains with which I shall deal in a moment, seems remarkably meagre. For if the phenomena in question are genuine, which certainly appears to be the case-their observation constitutes a discovery in the realm of psychology analogous-shall I say?—to the discovery of a new element in chemistry or a new star in astronomy.

Previous to the period of Psychical Research, the science of Psychology was singularly lacking in such discoveries. It was concerned, almost entirely at any rate, with phenomena which were in no sense new. Certainly, I would not imply that this work of accurately observing such phenomena and, as far as possible, correlating them was in any sense lacking in value, seeing that it constituted the essential groundwork without which further progress in psychological research would have been impossible. One at least of the generalizations it reached—namely the *Weber-Fechner Law*—has that quality of quantitativeness typical of the laws of nature formulated by physical science. But whereas in the domain of the physical sciences the tendency is towards the generalization of new phenomena, the correlation of that which is newly discovered with that which was hitherto known—in experimental psychology this seems hitherto to have been the case only to a very limited extent. For example, no sooner was the first radio-active element discovered, and its radio-active properties seem to be due to the disintegration of its atoms, than chemists and physicists began to feel that other radio-active elements must exist, and indeed that possibly all elements were radio-active to a lesser or greater degree. This attitude of mind on their part has led to all the many important discoveries in the domain of radioactivity which the last few years have witnessed. On the other hand, as concerns psychology, the tendency has been to treat new phenomena as abnormal and to regard subjects exhibiting them as being in a pathological condition. This may be due, perhaps, to the fact that the observation and study of these phenomena have been so largely carried on by medical men. The attitude of mind which thus expresses itself is, however, wholly unscientific and the consequent treatment of psychical phenomena is detrimental to research. To label a phenomenon "abnormal" or "pathological" explains nothing. Indeed, the very word "hypnotism," and all terms derived from it, are somewhat tainted, owing to the fact that hypnosis has come to be regarded as essentially an abnormal state. It would perhaps be better to substitute for it the alternative expression "regime of consciousness" and to recognize the fact that more than one regime of consciousness is possible, such regimes having certain elements in common, but others peculiar to each.

I am indebted for this suggestion and indeed to a large extent for the, whole of the above line of argument, to the brilliantly-written chapter, entitled "From Histological Physiology to Experimental Psycho-Physiology," of M. Jules Romains recently-published work *Eyeless Sight*. It is, so to speak, his *apologia* for the belief that if the "transference of vision" or "paroptic vision," to use a preferable term which implies no hypothesis as to the nature of the phenomenon, is possible in the case of certain subjects, then it should be possible, to some extent at any rate, to all persons. This is the author's justification for undertaking an investigation the results of which are published in the present work. Judging from these results, the investigation has been a brilliantly successful one, and, unless we are to regard the investigator as a deliberate impostor or one subject to an extraordinarily complicated delusion, he must be credited with having made one of the most remarkable psychological discoveries of the century, and a discovery moreover capable of valuable practical applications. That the cry of "charlatan" was raised when M. Romains first announced his discovery in France, I gather to have been the case; but since that time various test-sittings have been held, which have satisfied some of the leading savants in France, including M. Anatole France, of the genuineness of the phenomena, and it is to be hoped that other scientific men will repeat and extend the experiments and observations of M. Romains so that this may be confirmed if possible. The point is made that, although we are here concerned with phenomena that certainly come within the purview of the student of Occultism, they are of a perfectly general nature, and the experiments can be completed by any scientific man with the necessary leisure.

To put the matter in few words, M. Romains claims to have discovered that it is possible to see, not only by means of the eyes, but also by means of any not too small area of the skin, especially in the vicinity of the face, chest or hands. The sense, he argues, resides in certain microscopic organs (the menisci of Ranvier) situated in the epidermis, whose existence is already known to histologists, but whose functions, in common with those of many other microscopic organs which are to be found in the skin, are obscure, though assumed by Ranvier to be those of the tactile sense. In brief, it may be stated, according to M. Romains, that our skin is one mass of eyes: a heritage from long-distant ancestors belonging to some simple class of creature devoid of differentiated sense-structures. We have, however, forgotten how to use these eyes; but the power is there, and may be regained, either by a mutation of the regime of consciousness or, less effectively and easily, by conscious effort, achieved after much practice, entailing the most rigid attention. No doubt such a claim as this is of the most extraordinary character, and the most convincing experimental proofs should be insisted upon before it is accepted. For an account of these experiments, the book itself must be consulted. The general procedure, however, may be indicated as follows: The subjects were chosen at haphazard from those willing to submit to the experiments. The subject to be experimented upon was put into a certain regime of consciousness, i.e., he was hypnotized, to use a term to which M. Romains objects. He was then kept in this regime, his eyes were effectively bandaged, and he was assured that he would be able to see without the use of them. He was asked to make the necessary effort to do this, and, it is claimed, was successful in this effort, giving correct descriptions of various objects, including the reading of a newspaper, the deciphering of numbered cards, and the distinguishing of colors. It is stated that necessary precautions were taken, at any rate in preliminary experiments, to obviate; the possibility of telepathy, though my own feeling is that fuller details as to these precautions are desirable, because the elimination of telepathy is as difficult as it is important for the establishment of the author's thesis. Experiments carried out in the dark were unsuccessful, and it is stated that it was necessary for success that a ray of light should pass from the object to be seen to a not too small area of the skin of the subject's body. Experiments were also devised to show that the information concerning the objects described was not derived from the sense of touch in the ordinary meaning of the term, though as a matter of fact many of the results obtained are inexplicable even supposing direct contact between the subject and the object, unless we are to assume hyperesthesia to an incredible degree.

The series of experiments in which the powers of paroptic vision were made possible in subjects by means of mutation of consciousness were followed by a series of subjective experiments, in which M. Romains attempted to acquire the paroptic sense for himself, without mutation of consciousness, but by mental effort and the training of attention. The account of this series of experiments is not less interesting and important than the preceding. M. Romains claims that it was successful, although the task was by no means easy and the degree of paroptic sensibility attained appears to have been much less than in the case of subjects undergoing mutation of consciousness.

Finally, M. Romains started experimentation on the blind. A special technique has been developed for use in the case of such persons, the details of which the author prefers not to reveal, not involving mutation of consciousness. "By means of this technique the first manifestation of the paroptic function," to quote M. Romains, "appeared after the fourth or fifth sitting, in a blind person taken absolutely at random, and completely lacking all retinal sensibility." Apparently, the experiments on blind persons have suffered some opposition and interruption; it is to be hoped, however, that they will be continued, as their importance can hardly be over-estimated if all that M. Romains claims for his discovery is true.

Naturally, the question of a paroptic sense raise some metaphysical questions concerning the nature of space. Paroptic space apparently resembles ordinary visual space, except that its field seems to be circular, or, rather, spherical, as distinguished from the flat space of ordinary sight. M. Romains appears to think that his experiments go to confirm the metaphysical theory of the objective reality of space. But the conclusion seems hardly warranted in view of the fact that all the persons experimented upon were acquainted with ordinary visual and tactile space, and would naturally tend to interpret any new sensations in terms of those with which they were already acquainted. Experiments on persons born blind might be more instructive on the side of metaphysics of space. It is not, however, in its metaphysical implications that the phenomena of the paroptic vision appear to be important, but in their practical applications, especially as concerns the blind, and in their significance for psychology (and not less for the serious study of Occultism) as explanatory of many hitherto obscure phenomena. M. Romains claims cannot be ignored. If they are just—and this alone further independent research can demonstrate-then he has made a discovery of the first magnitude. It is hoped that no time will be lost in determining this momentous question.

THE ROSICRUCIAN'S

CONCERNING the Rosicrucians, there is a considerable body of literature. I cannot claim to be acquainted with it in its entirety, but what I have sampled of it I believe to be typical; and the literature impresses me as being singularly uninformed and uncritical. The word "Rosicrucian," in fact, has, in the mouths of some, come to be merely a vague expression covering such implications as are more precisely indicated by the terms alchemist, kabbalist, occultist and the like; and this common misuse of the word appears to offer the only excuse possible for the existence of some of the books purporting to deal with the Rosicrucians. Indeed, until the publication of the work which is the occasion of these remarks, there was, I venture to state, so far as books in the English language are concerned, only one dealing with Rosicrucianism which really gave reliable Information on the subject and displayed that element of criticism which is so essential. This book was Mr. Arthur Edward Waite's *The Real History of the Rosicrucians*. It was published by Mr. George Redway in 1887, has been out of print for many years, and is much sought after by students. In preference to preparing a second edition of it, Mr. Waite has written an entirely new work on the subject, of a far more bulky character than its predecessor and containing the results of long-continued research into the knotty problems involved. How great an amount of labor there has been necessitated by the Compilation of this work, only one who has endeavored to unravel problems connected with the origin of occult theories and institutions can judge. It is a work of vast erudition, and can be characterized aptly only by the description "monumental." The main conclusions of *The Real History* remain; they are fortified by further evidence; and much more is now made plain concerning modern developments of Rosicrucianism. The central problem of the Rosicrucians is a peculiar one.

At the present moment, more than one Organization exists embodying the term "Rosicrucian" in its title; but there is little or no evidence for regarding this name as being other than borrowed—indeed all the evidence points to such borrowing—and so far as the lesser claim is concerned that these organizations are founded in the likeness of the original Rosicrucian Fraternity, the question with which we are confronted is, Did this Fraternity ever exist in fact, and not merely in the imagination of the author of certain anonymous tracts (to be specified in a moment) published in Germany early in the seventeenth Century? Uncritical authors have envisaged the Rosicrucian Fraternity as being of immemorial antiquity; others, not less uncritical, have, in their turn, postulated as its originator Raymond Lully, Paracelsus, Cornelius Agrippa, Dr. John Dee, and, naturally, seeing that he was (in their dreams) the author of all the works of Shakespeare and nearly every other work of genius that was written during his life and after, Francis Bacon. The fact is, however, that the term "Rosicrucian" is first to be found in a pamphlet that was published in Germany and probably at Cassel, round about 1614. It appears to have been circulating in MS. for a few years previously, but the claim to antiquity can be pushed no farther. This pamphlet, *Fama Fraternitatis* or, "a Discovery of the Fraternity of the most *Laudable Order of the Rosy Cross*," to adopt the title given it by an English translator, addresses itself to "the learned in general, and the

Governors of Europe" whom it informs of the existence of a secret association founded over one hundred years ago by the famous C.R.C., grand initiate in the mysteries of Alchemy, whose history (which is clearly of a fabulous or symbolic nature) is given. According to its own Claims, the Fraternity was versed in the Higher Magic, the mysteries of Kabbalism, and the secrets of Alchemy, both as concerns the art of healing and the transmutation of metals. In regard to this last, however, it is declared that true philosophers esteem the art but little, for their concern is not with gold, but with a spiritual quest having, it would seem, as its end the general reformation of the world. Finally, the pamphlet concludes by inviting the wise men of the time to join the Fraternity, directing those who wished to do so to indicate their desire by the publication of printed letters or pamphlets which would not fail to come into the hands of the Brotherhood. This *pronunciamiento* was closely followed by a second pamphlet—presumably from the same pen—being, to anglicize its title, *The Confession of the Rosicrucian Fraternity*, again "addressed to the learned of Europe," which appears to have been written originally in Latin but first published in a German translation. It contained further information concerning the Brotherhood as promised in the *Fama Fraternitatis*, though still leaving many things obscure. Certain facts do, however, stand out prominently. One is the intense Protestantism of the author or authors of the pamphlets. The other is the implied recognition of a spiritual side to Alchemy. A third pamphlet, written in German, *The Chemical Nuptials of Christian Rosencreutz* appeared at Strasbourg in 1616. This work is very different in style from the two preceding; it shows considerable literary ability, and is a remarkable allegorical romance, describing how an old man, a life-long Student of Alchemy, was present at the accomplishment of the *Magnum Opus* in the year 1459. There appears to be little doubt that this last pamphlet was the work of one Valentine Andreä, a young Lutheran divine, who had a passion for Protestantism and for the general reformation of mankind; and a commonly accepted theory on the part of those who are not prepared to accept such wild fantasies for its origin as I have already mentioned is to regard the Fraternity of the Rosy Cross as being nothing more than a sort of hoax perpetrated by this ingenious gentleman—not, I should say, just a hoax merely, but one with a serious purpose. As the late Mr. R. A. Vaughan wrote in his well-known Hours with the Mystics:

... this Andreä writes the *Discovery of the Rosicrucian Brotherhood*, a *jeu-d'esprit* with a serious purpose, just as an experiment to see whether something cannot be done by combined effort to remedy the defect and abuses—social, educational, and religious, so lamented by all good men. He thought there were many Andreäs scattered throughout Europe—how powerful would be their united systematic action! ... He hoped that the few nobler minds whom he desired to organize would see through the veil of fiction in which he had invested his proposal; that he might communicate personally with some such, if they should appear; or that his book might lead them to form among themselves a practical Philanthropy confederacy, answering to the serious purpose he had embodied in his fiction.

The publication of the pamphlets, it need hardly be said, caused an immense amount of excitement. In the early days of the seventeenth Century, Alchemy was a subject of outstanding interest; and in the philosophy of Occultism, it was hoped, would be found the Solutions to the many problems that confronted mankind. As Mr. Waite remarks: "Whatever our opinions concerning the occult Sciences, whether we regard them as connoting a body of secret knowledge or as fantastic and illusory arts, there is no question that at the beginning of the seventeenth Century they were pursued with the uttermost zeal by untold numbers who were in search of light and certitude on the mysterious relations between God, man and the universe." The time was certainly ripe for the formation of such an association as was portrayed in the pamphlets. There is no evidence, however, that of the many who applied by way of the written word to be initiated into the ranks of the Rosicrucian's a single one had his request granted. A hot controversy raged for four or five years, some maintaining that the Society had deluded them, whilst others—they being, however, so far as the evidence allows one to say, still outside its ranks—as keenly maintained its integrity. That Valentine Andreä was numbered amongst the Fraternity's keenest critics is accounted for, by those who hold him to have been responsible for the *Fama* and *Confessio* as well as the *Chemical Nuptials*, on the ground that he realized his scheme to have been a failure, no one having seen through the veil in which he had clothed his ideas.

The fact that the pamphlets were not merely successful from the bookseller's point of view, but were—in view of the mental atmosphere of the times in which they appeared—so well calculated to be successful in this sense, suggests the possibility that they may have been written by some person unknown, with no more serious intention on his part than to be the author of the "best sellers" of his day. I am not quite sure that the possibility of this being the true explanation of the mystery has been negatived; but certainly Mr. Waite has marshalled many interesting facts in support of his alternative thesis that the Rosicrucian Fraternity was real in fact and that its origin is to be found in the *Militia Crucifera Evangelica*, a secret society, whose nature is indicated by its title, founded by Simon Studion in Germany at the end of the sixteenth Century. Studion was even more militantly Protestant than Andreä, and it is important to note that in Martin Luther's seal, the Rose and the Cross are to be found in combination. Moreover, this unusual combination is also to be found in Studion's unpublished MS., *Naometria*, preserved at Stuttgart, which, owing to the kindness of the librarian, Mr. Waite has been able to examine, and of which he gives most important details in the Appendix to his book. The only point militating against Mr. Waite's conclusion is the fact that *Naometria* is devoid of those alchemical and occult elements so prominent in the *Fama* and *Confessio*.

Whether there was a real society behind the *Fama* and *Confessio* or not, and whatever, if there were such an Organization, its true character was—and it is unlikely after the herculean labors of Mr. Waite that further research is likely to unearth any facts of importance—it seems certain that sooner or later secret societies did begin to be formed along the lines laid down in the pamphlets in question, societies concerned with occult research and especially with Alchemy. And certainly, if the voices of Robert Fludd and Michael Maier, which were raised in defense of Rosicrucianism in England and Germany respectively, counted for anything, the fact that Alchemy connoted a spiritual quest as well as a physiological and metallic one was not forgotten. In 1710 we hear in Germany of an Organization calling itself "*The Brotherhood of the Rosy and Golden Cross*," which may have been the descendant of the original Rosicrucian Fraternity (assuming there to have been one) or which, alternatively, may have been founded in its likeness. According to its Claims, this Organization would appear to have been in possession of the arch-secrets of Alchemy. But there is nothing to substantiate these Claims, and the probability is that it was an association of seekers in the alchemical quest who hoped that by a certain pooling of knowledge the attainment of their object might be achieved. By 1777, a remarkable change appears to have taken place in this Organization. It had developed ceremonial forms, and admitted only to membership those who had attained the degree of Master Mason. This grafting of Rosicrucianism on to Masonry is so curious that one is tempted to question whether the Organization of 1777 was the same Organization as that of 1710. It seems more feasible to suppose that the first Organization, having become defunct, was revived in a modified form by those whose chief concern was Masonry, rather than to suppose that all the surviving members of the first Organization had not only become Master Masons but were so convinced of the value and importance of Masonry, that they decided that the qualification in question was necessary to cooperation within their ranks in the work of Alchemy.

With the later history of Rosicrucianism and its Connection with Masonry, I do not propose to deal. Those who are interested can read the story at large in Mr. Waite's book. There have been and there are many Rosicrucian associations which have made use of the name by way of popularizing their occult investigations. Yet, after all has been said in criticism, the fact remains that there is a heart of truth in Rosicrucianism—that it shadows forth, even if the shadows ofttimes distort, secrets which are not revealed in the works of materialist philosophers. It is now thirteen years since I first took upon myself the task of defending the alchemists from that hasty criticism, rooted in mental inertia, which declared their works to be meaningless and their philosophy to be nonsense. That they erred in many things hardly needs to be said. In the light of that knowledge gained by the experimental investigation of Nature, which we call "Science," much that they believed and taught must be rejected. Certain generalizations, however, which they appear to have gained by intuition, remain; and in view of this fact it seems worthwhile not to reject out of hand because they carry us beyond what is in the region of demonstrated knowledge, but rather to treat as working hypotheses certain other generalizations of seemingly like origin. There is a spiritual as well as a physical side to Alchemy, and it is this which I have in mind. It connects with Kabbalism and with Occult Doctrines generally, and it would appear to have been this aspect of Alchemy with which Rosicrucianism at its best was concerned. For this, Mr. Waite is a good guide. Not once,

H. Stanley Redgrove

but often, has he earned the gratitude of students, but never more than by the Compilation of The Brotherhood of the Rosy Cross.

ARABIAN ALCHEMY

THE debt that learning owes to Islam, frequently forgotten, is a considerable one. During those centuries of Christendom, which are well called the Dark Ages, it seemed as though all the culture of Greece and the wisdom of past ages were to be lost to Europe. But they were preserved in Arabia; to be rediscovered by European thought in due course, when a new light had burst upon it and a new impetus to knowledge had made itself felt. The wisdom of the Greeks was not, however, merely preserved by Islam, but something thereto was added, the gift of the genius of Arabian thought. Especially is this true of Alchemy: it is generally admitted that the Science—if Science it should be called—made wonderful strides during its sojourn in Arabia, and yet it is nevertheless true that very little detailed knowledge is available concerning the history of Alchemy during this time, say between a.d. 600 & a.d. 1000, and very little has been done to make available to students the numerous alchemical texts of the period. I suppose few names in the history of Alchemy are as celebrated as that of Jäbir ibn Hayyän, better known in its Latin form of Geber, and the fact may perhaps be quoted as testimony to the importance of the Arabian period in the history of Alchemy. Few alchemical works can be compared in point of lucidity and the practical knowledge of Chemical operations displayed with Summa *Perfectionis Mettalorum, De Investigatione Perfectionis Mettalorum, De Inventione Veritatis* and *De Fornacibus Construendis* attributed to this great master, and moreover in these works is to be found for the first time (assuming their authenticity) the remarkable sulphur-mercury theory of the metals: a theory which, however false we may see it to be in the light of modern Chemical knowledge, had the two essential characteristics of a genuine scientific hypothesis, i.e., it gave an intelligible explanation of the known facts and provided an impetus to further investigation. The Sulphur mercury theory, moreover, I might add in parenthesis, is one of especial interest to the serious Student of Occultism, inasmuch as it lends itself to a mystical Interpretation and in all probability had a mystical origin, being based upon an intuitively perceived analogy between the metals and man. It is true that the luster of Geber's name has been considerably dimmed by the researches of the late M. Berthelot. Not only was M. Berthelot unable to discover the original Arabic MSS of the works quoted above, but undoubtedly genuine works of Geber which he was enabled to unearth were of a purely mystical character and provided no warrant for regarding their author as either (a) an expert chemist, or (b) the originator of the sulphur-mercury theory, and the conclusion which he drew, and which in the light of the facts then available I was also compelled to adopt in Alchemy: Ancient and Modern, was that the Latin works attributed to Geber were forgeries.

The possibility now emerges, however, that M. Berthelot was mistaken. The crucial proof of this, namely the discovery of the missing Arabic Originals of the Latin works in question, has, it is true, not yet been achieved, but Mr. Edward J. Holmyard, who has the advantage of being both a chemist and an Arabic scholar, has discovered other Arabic MSS. undoubtedly by Geber—in particular one entitled *The Book of Properties*, which is preserved in the British Museum— which in the two chief essentials closely resemble the Latin works under discussion, that is to say the sulphur-mercury theory of the metals is clearly stated, and many practical recipes for the preparation of various Chemical substances are contained in them. As concerns the works of Geber which

H. Stanley Redgrove

misled Berthelot, Mr. Holmyard suggests that these are, strictly speaking, not Chemical works, but mystical writings in which Geber—as a chemist—employed Chemical symbolism to express his religious ideas. As I have already stated, and the above few remarks concerning Geber well illustrate the point, we really know very little about Arabian Alchemy. Mr. Holmyard has taken upon himself the task of enlightening us. It is his intention to publish the more important original texts, together with adequate translations and introductions. Personally, I await with very considerable interest the publication of Geber's The Book of Properties. But meantime I give a very hearty welcome to the first of the projected texts and translations, namely the Book of Knowledge acquired concerning the Cultivation of Gold, by Abu'l-Qāsim Muhammad ibn Ahmad al-Träqi.

Concerning the author, practically nothing is known. Mr. Holmyard chose the work for publication out of a host of other available texts for three good reasons, (1) the book is comparatively short, (2) it was held in high esteem by the Arabian alchemists themselves, and (3) "it gives us a very clear account of the Arabic Chemical theory of transmutation written by a man who realized the importance of experimental work."

The possibility of transmuting the metals was not universally credited by the Arabian alchemists. The influence of Aristotle was strong (it is very marked in several places in the Muktasab) and the question presented itself in this form: Are the metals different species or only one? Abu'l-Qāsim al-Träqi was a transmutationist and brings forward both practical and theoretical arguments in favor of the view that the metals are "of one species essentially." "Each of them" [namely gold, silver, copper, iron, lead and tin], he writes: is marked off from the others by accidental distinguishing properties, and it should be possible to effect the necessary removal of these properties, the specific nature remaining constant. Of the practical arguments in favor of this view that he puts forward, one of the most interesting is that based on the fact that in the cupellation of lead, a small residue of silver not infrequently remains behind. As Mr. Holmyard remarks, the interpretation of this fact as being due to a partial transmutation of lead was "a very natural mistake." He adds:

This is not the place to undertake an estimate of the value of the theory of transmutation, but it must be admitted that it served very well to explain many facts (and was therefore scientifically "true" at the time) and to stimulate research.

Abu'l-Qāsim al-'Irāqi's theoretical arguments in favor of transmutation are not less interesting, and serve to show how dominant in his mind was the idea of development as applicable to the metals. "To the alchemist," as I have remarked elsewhere, "the elements developed: more complex bodies were produced from them by a process analogous to the growth of a living organism." The idea is well conveyed by the very title of the book "The Cultivation of Gold"—gold was to be cultivated—to be caused to grow and to increase—as barley or rye was cultivated. Gold, to our author, was the pure metallic species: the other metals were not gold because of some accidental impurity or imperfection—thus, "the imperfection of silver is due to the excess of coldness" whilst "it was, indeed, known that the two coppers are held back from the state of being gold only by their excessive hotness." How were these imperfections to be removed? How was gold to be cultivated? The process, it is explained, must be a gradual one:

Natural things do not reach their limit of perfection except by natural degrees. A cotton-seed, for example, cannot immediately become a garment. Its seed-form must first pass away, then it clothes itself in the form of a plant, and, after decay and change, takes many forms. Then it casts off the form of a plant and takes the form of a thread; then it casts off the form of a thread and takes the form of a piece of cloth;

then it casts off the form of a piece of cloth and becomes a garment.

Plants and animals need appropriate food and he who wishes to cultivate plants or to breed stock must pay attention thereto. More especially, must the alchemist study what is the appropriate food of the metals; for these, according to our author,

Have these three powers, namely, feeding, growth, and reproduction, and reproduction is served by feeding and growth, and growth is served by feeding. But here, feeding is served by a single power, namely, digestion, for the food is mixed in the metal without attraction on its part, and digested without retention. Hence, this power does not raise the food to its highest point, since retention is necessary in Order to render the digestion able to do this. Moreover, the metal does not possess the power of rejection, by which it can reject what is not appropriate for it. For the power of rejection, rejects only that which resembles the chyme of the Constitution. So that since the metal does not possess the power of rejection, when food is administered to it, it assimilates both the suitable and unsuitable and that which is born from it is not of the same species. Now since the metal is such that it does not possess the power of rejection philosophers found it necessary to prepare the foodstuff in such a way that there was removed from it what was not suitable for the substance fed, for fear lest they should introduce it into the (metallic) species, which has no power of rejection, and that thus there would be mixed with the material appropriate for the Constitution that which was not appropriate, in which case the species on reproduction would be confused and no advantage would be derived."

Again:

The remedy which is administered to the man who is lacking in health is like the Elixir which is administered to this metallic species.

So far, the theory of the Arabian alchemist—the ideas at the back of his mind, the analogies which guided (or misguided) him—is perfectly easy to follow and is as logical as a proposition in Euclid's Elements. It is when we come to the part of his work dealing with the practical method of transmutation that, in the words of Mr. Holmyard, "we begin to feel at sea."

The vexed question as to the intellectual honesty of alchemy [writes the latter], at once arises, and upon this subject every one is entitled to his own opinion. Charlatans there must have been, but personally I find it difficult to believe that men of the caliber of Jäbir ibn Hayyän, Abu'l-Qasim al-'Iräqi, Lully and van Helmont were all willfully dishonest. Inspired by a wonderful theory, which, in a way undreamt of, is at last coming back into its own, they performed stupendous amounts of Chemical research and must time after time have encountered facts which appeared to them to prove the theory beyond reasonable doubt. The crucial test of their allegorical writings is, surely, whether modern chemists can interpret any of them and find, not indeed a recipe for gold making, but a description of a reaction which might easily have misled a mediaeval scientist. In point of fact, many of the allegories of the alchemists can easily be interpreted in this way.

There is one further consideration I feel ought to be emphasized. There is a seemingly inherent tendency in the human mind to carry every analogy to its (frequently bitter) end. Metals resembled living things and these latter could be cultivated, improved, perfected by such-and-such means: especially—to pass from biological to mystical analogies—could man be perfected spiritually. Therefore, such-and-such means would suffice for the transmutation of the metals, and such-and-such signs would be observable at each stage of the experiment. Undoubtedly in their writings on transmutation, the alchemists frequently described in veiled terms actual Chemical experiments; but not infrequently. I think they also described what their theories led them firmly to believe ought to be the results if the experiments in question were rightly carried out. Descriptions of imaginary experiments are certainly alien to the Spirit of chemistry; but the alchemists were not only chemists: they were also philosophers. Perhaps their philosophy was childish and fantastic; yet the very fact that in their wild philosophic dreams, they seem at times intuitively to have grasped great truths should make us hesitate before passing upon them any sweepingly destructive criticism.

THE LIMITATIONS OF THE LAWS OF NATURE

IN spite of all that Education has done for mankind, it is still very common to find the Laws of Nature referred to as though these laws were similar to the statutes devised by man for the purposes of government. How often, for example, are we told, in connection with matters of health, morals, etc., that it is unwise for man to act contrary to the Laws of Nature, as though these laws were enactments, statutes which ought to be obeyed, which it is advisable to obey, but which—if one is prepared to pay the price—can be broken.

On the other hand, those who steer clear of the rocks of Scylla not infrequently fall into the whirlpool of Charybdis, and the error of regarding the Laws of Nature as principles inherent in the Universe, and as having the character of an inflexible necessity, is as serious an error—perhaps one more serious—than that of supposing them to be enactments.

It cannot be too often or too emphatically pointed out that the Laws of Nature are neither enactments nor principles, but organons of thought, that is to say, mental tools devised by man's thought to enable it to deal with experience—to reduce the chaos of experience to something approximating to order.

There is a popular story to the effect that Sir Isaac Newton discovered the Law of Gravitation by observing the falling to the ground of an apple from a tree. The story, like most of its sort, is untrue. But there appears to be just an element of truth in it, namely that it was this particular phenomenon that first drew Newton's attention to the problem of falling bodies for ages mankind had observed things fall, and a great deal of information had been collected about how things fall. Galileo, for example, had discovered—that is, had first observed—the startling fact that different objects dropped on to the earth from the same point fell to ground in the same time. And in particular, much information had been gleaned about the falling of those bodies we call the planets, which are continually falling round and round the Sun.

Kepler had investigated the motions of the planets and had formulated certain laws concerning them. These were as follows: (1) The planet describes an ellipse, the sun being in one focus. (2) The straight line joining the planet to the sun sweeps out equal areas in equal times. (3) The squares of the times of revolution of any two planets about the sun are proportional to the cubes of their mean distances from the sun.

The movement of the planets as presented to experience are chaotic: each traces out a complicated curve in space with respect to the earth, each moves at a rate different from that of the others, and the rate of each itself undergoes a most complicated series of changes. The mind of Kepler brings a measure of order into this chaos. His laws render easy of calculation the motion of any planet, and enable us to predict with a very fair measure of accuracy the position of any one planet with respect to any other at any point in time. It is to the genius of Newton that we owe the further generalization, which shows the motion of the planets to be a sort of falling; or, rather, which correlates the motions of the heavenly bodies with that of bodies falling on the earth. Every particle of matter in the Universe, according to Newton, attracts and is attracted by every other particle with a force directly proportional to the product of the masses of the two particles and inversely proportional to the square of the distance between them.

In effect, the three Laws of Kepler are replaced by the one Law of Newton—one tool is devised which will do the work of three. More: Newton's Law of Gravitation enables us to make predictions, not only about the motion of the planets, but about all other falling bodies as well.

Such a wide generalization as Newton's Law of Gravitation has been, is, and will remain a mental tool of immense service to mankind. But—this being recognized—let us look a little at some of its limitations. In the first place, let us avoid the common error of saying that Newton discovered the law which bears his name. He did not. He invented it. He did not dig the law out of Nature, as though it were a hitherto existent but unknown thing. His mind put it there. And what is true of this great Law of Nature is true of all others. The Laws of Nature are emphatically human inventions.

Let us, also, cease to say that one particle of matter attracts another. Whether it does or not, we simply don't know. Let us rather say that bodies move as though particles of matter attracted each other in the way Newton's Law states. Further, let us not delude ourselves into the belief that Newton's Law explains anything. It is only explanatory in the sense that it brings an immense number of seemingly diverse problems:

Why does the moon move in this manner, and Jupiter in that? Why does the apple fall from the tree in such a manner and at such a rate? What is the cause of the tides? etc., etc.—under one head. But in so far as it does this, it raises a multitude of new problems. What is matter? What is mass? What is attraction? What is force? How does one particle attract another, and why does it attract it with one force rather than another? Or if bodies don't really attract each other, why do they move as though they did?

One could go on piling up question after question. But the plain fact is that it is not the function of Newton's Law to explain: its function is to enable us to predict. And what is true of this Law in this respect is true of all others. They are humanly-devised tools of scientific prediction.

Finally, let us not make the error of supposing Newton's Law to be absolutely accurate. All Laws of Nature are based on observation, and all observation is liable to error. We can claim, therefore, for no Law of Nature anything greater than a high degree of accuracy, dependent upon the accuracy of the observations of which it is the generalization.

I have chosen Newton's Law of Gravitation as an example, because this Law is so wide in its application, so simple in its form, so precise in its accuracy, and has stood the passage of time and the constant growth of human knowledge so well that it had become to be almost universally regarded as a fundamental principle of Nature, and as one giving warranty to the idea of the old time alchemists—an idea which was the one serious blunder in their philosophy—that Nature, at heart, is very simple.

Alas for the materialists, for those whose philosophy demands principles inherent in Nature, and who pin their faith in matter and force as fundamental realities. Einstein has demonstrated that Newton's Law is after all, only an approximation—an approximation of exceptional accuracy and therefore a mental tool of great utility. Matter and force themselves are seen to be no more than creations of mind, and a new Law of Gravitation, far more complex than Newton's, is formulated to meet the needs of man's growing experience.

The history of every science tells the same story. Simple Laws suffice when knowledge is in its infancy. As knowledge grows, as experience widens and deepens, Nature (which is simply a word denoting the totality of sensuous experience) becomes increasingly complex. Finer tools are needed and the human mind formulates more precise Laws.

Nothing could be simpler, for example, than the law concerning the behavior of gaseous substances under changes of temperature and pressure, formulated partly by Boyle and partly by Gay-Lussac over a century ago. "The volume of a gas is directly proportional to its absolute temperature and inversely proportional to its pressure." But no gas actually obeys it. The Law is a first approximation only, but none the less a very useful mental tool. Comes Van der Waal with a more complicated formula. Yes, this is better: it is more accurate. But still it falls short of absolute accuracy.

Thus, as I have intimated, knowledge grows and the scientific mind improves its tools, formulating Laws of increasing complexity to meet the needs of growing experience, of observation becoming ever more precise. Has knowledge any bounds? I think not. The field is infinite, and, if this be true, no Law of Nature can achieve absolute accuracy unless it be infinitely complex. Such a Law would be useless, because impossible of application. It would involve the whole of human experience.

This fact, apart from the essential character of a Law of Nature as a human invention, sufficiently indicates that the Laws of Nature are contingent. It deprives Natural Law of that quality of necessity so much admired by materialist philosophers. How dull would be the world if their

Forgotten Essays

philosophy were really true—how exciting the world is, in fact.

There are those, however, who would carry the principle of iron necessity into the domain of Mind itself. More deadly in its stultifying effects than ordinary Materialism is that philosophy which would evolve the universe out of what it pleases to call the Laws of Thought.

I suppose all my readers, at some time or another, have read Euclid's Elements of Geometry, or at any rate a modernized edition of the work of the great Greek geometrician. How wonderful is the way in which, seemingly out of nothing but the mere necessity of logical thought, he evolves space and its manifold possibilities of forms—lines, curves, angles, surfaces, and solids of varying types—demonstrating to us, seemingly beyond question and in harmony with experience, their many properties.

But I think Euclid himself realized better than some of his more modern expositors the limitations of his work. For it was amongst his postulates—or things which he asked might be granted—that he placed what has sometimes been wrongly entitled the "parallel-axiom." "If a straight line meets two other straight lines so as to make the two interior angles on one side of it together less than two right angles, these straight lines will meet if continually produced on this side."

Yes—if! In this very assertion, Euclid defines a sort of space, and his "Elements" are a description of this space. It is a space invented by the human mind, and, as the human mind has evolved and the knowledge of mathematics increased, it has invented other sorts of space, types of space in which lines do not behave in the way postulated by Euclid and in which, for example, the three angles of a triangle do not together make exactly two right angles, but either more or less than this.

Are any of these spaces identical with actual space, that is the space of experience? Euclid's space fits ordinary experience very well. But like Newton's Law of Gravitation and the Boyle Gay-Lussac Law of Gases, may not Euclid's Geometry be but a first approximation? Einstein has answered Yes, and has shown us how extraordinarily complex actual space is. Its complexity is the very complexity of human experience itself. But even Euclid's general axioms—which are the Laws of Thought (or their first derivations) by means of which a certain school of philosophers would evolve Experience out of Logic— are not devoid of limitations. Is it invariably and of necessity true, for example, that the whole is greater than the part? "The two infinite series

$$1, 2, 3, 4, 5, 6, etc.$$
$$2, 4, 6, 8, 10, 12, etc.$$

obviously contain the same number of terms, since there is a one-to-one correspondence between them. Yet it is equally obvious that the second series is a part of the first, and contains only half its number of terms. This is no mere mathematical quibble, but a demonstration that the laws of finite quantity do not apply to infinitude. The law that the whole is greater than its part is not universally valid." It is therefore neither axiomatic, necessary nor inherent in thought or nature; but, like all other laws, it is a mental tool. It is a human invention, whereby all quantities may be divided into two categories: (i) the finite, to which the Law applies, and (ii) the infinite, to which it does not.

Take for consideration another so-called axiom: "Things which are equal to the same thing are equal to one another." Yes, this might be absolutely true of things, if things-in themselves existed—a proposition incapable of proof. But it is not true—not absolutely, but only approximately, true—of sensations; that is, of things as they exist in experience.

According to the Weber-Fechner Law of Perception, "equal difference between sensations means proportional difference between stimuli." This means, for example, that if a person could just barely perceive, by weighing in his hand, a difference of one ounce added to twenty ounces, two ounces would be the smallest difference he could detect when added to forty ounces, four ounces when added to eighty ounces, and so on. The Law was first formulated as a result of numerous experiments on the perception of weight, but has been demonstrated for other forms of perception as well. It is, of course, only a first approximation: but, even so, it is in conflict with the axiom in question. Indeed, this axiom is contradicted by the very fact that there is a least perceptible difference in experience, the existence of which is undeniable. For, to keep to the illustration already given: If a person to whom one ounce in twenty is the least perceptible difference compares the following weights: (a) 20 oz., (b) 20.5 oz., (c) 21 oz: the perception of weight he gets from a is the same as that he gets from b, and the perception of weight he gets from b is the same as that he gets from c, but the perception of weight he gets from a is not the same as that he gets from c. In other words, if A, B, and C represent the three percepts derived respectively from the three stimuli a, b, and c, then whilst $A = B$ and $C—B$, A does not $= C$.

Let us admit that the equality axiom is true of stimuli. It is certainly not true of percepts, and this indubitable fact deprives it of absolute validity.

When once the true character of the Laws of Nature is clearly understood, life and experience present a new and exciting aspect. The theories of those who stand against Materialism are certainly not to be accepted blindly and in an uncritical spirit. But these dreamers are those who adventure in the realm of Mind. And it is only in the spirit of adventure that the unknown is to be won.

H. Stanley Redgrove

THE QUEST FOR TRUTH IN ALCHEMY

IN 1921, I conceived the idea of founding a Society for the study of the writings of the alchemists. Trained as a chemist and interested in the theories of the occultists and the strange workings of the human mind, it was perhaps inevitable that my attention should be directed to the study of these old-time thinkers and experimentalists, their fantastic writings, their very real achievements and their ultimate failure.

I was shocked to observe how these men were treated in the majority of the books dealing with the history of chemistry and of science in general. They were cursorily dismissed as a set of charlatans and fools.

Yet the facts remained that they had performed a most useful function in the evolution of chemistry. Their actual discoveries and inventions were considerable, and, if they had not exactly lain the foundations of chemical science, they had, at any rate, performed an essential part in preparing the ground.

The works of alchemists were, I felt convinced, worthy of scientific study. But there was a further incentive. At the close of the nineteenth century, discoveries were made which shook the prevalent scientific philosophy to its very foundations, and a new philosophy—a new view of the nature of things—began to be formulated. In several respects, this philosophy exhibited striking points of agreement with the views of the old-time alchemists.

Let it be admitted that the new philosophy was the product of an entirely different method; let it be admitted that the a *priori* method of the alchemists—their reliance on strange analogies between metals and the soul of man, and, indeed, between matter and spirit in all their myriad manifestations—is quite unreliable. Even so, it cannot be urged that this method which, in spite of all its aberrations, sometimes yielded the gold of truth, is so contemptible as to be totally devoid of interest.

Moreover, it seemed, and still seems, possible to me that the alchemical writings may contain *some* facts discovered—if I may so phrase it—before their time. It is, I think, possible that, in the general replacement of the Hermetic philosophy by Scientific Materialism, some genuine facts were discarded along with a great deal of theoretical rubbish. Scientific Materialism now reposes in the world's dustbin. It might be as well, in the light of the New Philosophy, to rummage over what we previously discarded.

In December 1910, Messrs. William Rider and Son had published, under the title of *Alchemy: Ancient and Modern*, a preliminary study of the subject which I had undertaken. The book enjoyed a most remarkably favorable reception by the Press and an American edition was called for.

However, the task of investigating all the problems which the alchemists and their works presented was not a problem to be successfully essayed by one mind. I felt there was a need for a united effort on the part of those who were attracted to this study. I made it my business, therefore, to discover people sufficiently interested in the matter to form a Society, and the Alchemical Society was founded in November, 1912.

One of the first persons—I think the very first—that I approached was the late Madame Isabelle de Steiger. I am reminded of this fact by the publication by Messrs. Rider and Co. of her *Memorabilia*, in which there are several kindly references to the Alchemical Society and myself. Mme. de Steiger had then already published her book, On a Gold Basis, and, it was announced, was undertaking the republication of the late Mary Anne Atwood's remarkable work on the alchemists, A Suggestive Enquiry into the Hermetic Mystery—a project not realized until 1918. I wrote to her with reference to this project, which greatly interested me, and had the pleasure of meeting her shortly afterwards. She received my plan of forming an Alchemical Society very sympathetically.

I was particularly glad to have Mme. de Steiger's support because, as a disciple of Mrs. Atwood, her views concerning the real nature of alchemy differed widely from my own. I was most anxious that the Society should not become a cult, but that all earnest students of the subject—and there was none more earnest than she—should, whatever their opinions, feel at home in it.

The objects of the Society were set out, in the broadest terms, as follows: "The study of the works and theories of the alchemists in all their aspects, philosophical, historical and scientific, and of all matters relating thereto."

The late Professor John Ferguson, M.A., LL.D., F.I.C., F.C.S., of Glasgow University, an eminent authority on the early history of chemistry and a man of wide knowledge and sympathies and possessed of a charming personality, accepted the Honorary Presidency of the Society, and took a great interest in its proceedings. I was elected Acting President. Mr. Arthur Edward Waite, Mme. de Steiger, and Mr. W. Gorn Old, were the Society's first three Vice-Presidents.

The Society held regular monthly meetings, except in the summer, to which visitors were invited. Each meeting was usually devoted to the reading of a paper and a discussion thereon.

Reports of the meetings, including the full text of papers read thereat, were printed in the Society's journal, which was edited by myself and published by the firm of H. K. Lewis, of 136, Gower Street, W.C. In addition, the journal contained reviews of all books bearing in any way on the subject of alchemy, and, occasionally, other contributions bearing on the Society's work. The journal was supplied to all members free of charge, a few additional copies being printed for sale;

and, owing to its relatively small circulation, it has now become exceedingly rare. Altogether, the Society held twenty-two general meetings.

According to the Suggestive Enquiry, alchemy was a spiritual science, its great experiment being concerned with the union of the soul with God, and having nothing to do with mundane matters. As Mr. Waite remarks in his Preface to Memorabilia, "Mme. de Steiger's paper on 'The Hermetic Mystery' . . . is to be understood as a defense of these views and their summary presentation from her own standpoint, as one who had studied and corresponded with Mrs. Atwood during a long period of years". It was, Mme. de Steiger remarks in her book, extremely well received, though, I should add, interest did not necessarily mean agreement with views so hard to reconcile with the known facts concerning the lives of the alchemists and the part they played in laying the foundations of chemical knowledge.

In the early part of 1914, an *entente cordiale* was established between the Society and *La Societe Alchemiquede France*. Professor Ferguson and myself were created *Membres d'Honneur* of the French Society, others members of the Council, including Mme. de Steiger, being created *Membres Titulaires*. M. Jollivet Castelot, the President of the French Society, was elected an honorary member of the Alchemical Society, and an interchange of journals between the two societies was set up.

During 1915, the Society's work was carried on under considerable and increasing difficulty owing to the continuance of the European War. At the Third Annual Meeting steps were taken to increase the Society's revenue in order that the journal might continue to be published, but, in spite of all efforts, it had to cease publication with Parts 20 and 21.

Looking back now on the work of the Society, I cannot express entire satisfaction with its work. Some of the papers it published were contributions of outstanding value to the scientific study of the problems of alchemy; all were of interest. But, in too many, the tendency to speculate upon insufficient material rather than to collect the essential data for a real understanding of the subject is perhaps too much in evidence.

Nevertheless, I am confident that the Society did good and useful work in helping to stimulate interest in a highly obscure subject, and that most emphatically, therefore its labors were not in vain.

Writing in her eighty-eighth year (she died on January 1st, 1927, in her ninety-first year), Mme. de Steiger says of the purpose of her existence, "Put briefly, I think I had one dominant idea, the quest of what I feel Solomon sought all his life, i.e., Understanding." There could be no better quest. It was this quest which united in the Alchemical Society men and women holding the most diverse views. I am glad to think that, in spite of the differences between us in our philosophical outlook and our estimation of the significance of alchemy, I retained Mme. de Steiger's friendship—testified to by a stack of interesting letters on alchemy and cognate subjects—to the day of her death. And I prize, because of the donor and the motive of the gift, a little eighteenth-century volume of mystical philosophy she gave me shortly before her life reached its term.

Forgotten Essays

THE SENSE OF CERTITUDE: SOME NOTES ON INTUITION AND REASON

THE other day I had to meet, in a public spot, a friend whom I had not seen for a considerable time. I arrived at the meeting place somewhat early for the appointment. My mind was rather ill at ease; I was a little disturbed by the thought that I should not recognize my friend. I endeavored to picture him in my mind; but I am a bad visualizer. I remembered certain characteristics, which stood out boldly in my mental image. The rest was vague, so that what I had before me was a caricature rather than a picture of the man.

A man approached. Was he my friend? I reasoned rapidly. Yes! he was the right height, his carriage was that of my friend and he wore clothes similar to those in which I had been accustomed to see him. Certainly, this was the right man. But when he got nearer, and I saw his face clearly, I realized that I had made a mistake.

I caught sight of a face in the crowd. By Jove! I said to myself, this must be the man. I remember that he had a nose of just this peculiar shape and a rather small mouth without a moustache. But another look at him convinced me that I had again made an error. This man was not my old friend, after all.

I became more perturbed than ever. I had, I thought, certainly not remembered his appearance accurately or I should not have made these two mistakes. I should certainly not recognize him at all; and, no doubt, he would similarly fail to recognize me. Was this the man, or this, or this?

And then a man appeared, and at once I knew that he was my old friend. I knew beyond question or doubt. How I knew was another matter. Certainly, I was not conscious of having arrived at the result by any process of reasoning from this peculiarity in the appearance of the man or that. I just knew he was the right man. I could have confirmed this knowledge in a multitude of ways. But this was unnecessary. I greeted him and plunged at once into the business that was the occasion of the meeting.

In the sense of being unique or merely unusual, there was nothing remarkable to me in this occurrence. I have had similar experiences before, and I imagine that many of my readers have experienced much the same sort of thing. The remarkable character of the experience only appears on reflection and resides in the overwhelming sense of certitude which seems spontaneously to arise from nowhere and without the aid of reason.

I can see analogies to this sense in other forms of experience. There will be those of a romantic turn of mind who will say that it is not unlike the certitude of love. The young man may be attracted by this girl and that, and may ask himself: Do I love her—or her? And then his true mistress comes into his life, and he asks no more. It is certainly analogous to the intuition of which the mystics speak. Perhaps an analysis of the sense of certitude in connection with a simple mundane experience such as the one I have related of myself may assist us in arriving at a better understanding of the mystery of intuition.

Undoubtedly, the mind is larger than our consciousness of it. The term "subconsciousness" has been introduced to connote the sum of those of its activities, of which we are not aware. Seeing the remarkable character of these activities, the term "super-consciousness" might be better; but quarrelling with terms is an unprofitable business, and I will use the generally accepted word. It seems to me certain that, in any act of observation, a great deal is lost to the conscious mind, which is stored in the subconscious, and equally certain that the subconscious mind is able to form judgments based upon the material which is presented to it. These judgments may or may not be conveyed from the subconscious to the conscious mind; but, if they are they seem to arise from nowhere, and they possess a force and power peculiarly their own. They carry with them *the sense of certitude*.

Intuition, therefore, can be regarded as the form in which a subconscious judgment is conveyed to the conscious mind. Such a judgment is, of course, not infallible, and intuition is seen to be a sort of reasoning, superior, however, to ordinary reasoning because based upon far wider observation.

In the case under consideration, for example, I must have observed a multitude of little peculiarities characteristic of my friend, which I had forgotten. The memory of these, however, persisted in my subconscious mind, where there was a perfect picture of the man, unlike the caricature, which was the best image my conscious mind could produce. The first glance at my friend when he actually appeared was all my subconscious mind, armed with these memories, needed to establish his identity, and the judgment of this identity surged into consciousness as an intuition, a conviction seemingly coming from nowhere and carrying with it the sense of certitude.

In claiming for intuition, however, that its sense of certitude is one on which we can rely, the fact has to be noted that conviction and truth are not necessarily identical. Men have clung and still cling with the utmost tenacity to ideas of a highly preposterous character; and, if such a one challenges me on the score of the quality of his ideas, I can meet him by acquiescing in his particular set of delusions and pointing to the other fellow who holds a contradictory set. The question arises: How is intuition to be distinguished from that which resembles it but is of an unreliable character?

Modern theosophical writers draw a useful distinction between impulse and intuition. These, in theosophic terminology, are, the first a surging of the astral body (desire), the second an item of knowledge coming from the higher mental plane. They seem at first to be alike. Calm consideration and delay, according to Dr. Besant, causes the first to die away, the second to increase in strength.

I would add, moreover, that it seems typical of intuition that the sense of certitude accompanying it leaves no room for doubt, not even that subconscious doubt that causes the mind to seek for reasons to bolster up its most cherished beliefs.

However, I question, in the light of the history of man's thought and its strange aberrations, whether either of these two peculiarities provide an infallible criterion for distinguishing between intuition and the conviction, which is borne of desire, though as guides both are certainly useful.

I have a profound faith in and a considerable distrust of that wonderful faculty of the mind we call Reason—a confession of faith of, seemingly, so contradictory a character that some explanation is necessary.

Let me say, then, that if we give up reason, we are not merely like mariners adrift in a rudderless ship, we are in the sea without a ship at all. But just as a ship is a machine, so must we remember is reason a machine. A ship will carry us in this direction or that according to our desires, and it is desire that uses reason to achieve its ends.

As Mr. W. Trotter points out in his *Instincts of the Herd in Peace and War*, many of our reasons are mere afterthoughts. We do this, we believe that, because we desire so to do. Afterwards, we invent reasons to justify our actions and to validate our beliefs, the process being largely a subconscious one which deludes us into thinking that we really acted as we did and really hold the beliefs that we do because of these reasons. As the old adage has it, "the wish is father to the thought."

Listen to almost any argument: how great a display of reason is there here—and what an unprofitable business it is.

Each disputant wishes to prove the other wrong (and probably does to his own satisfaction). Neither really desires to attain to the truth about the matter under discussion, though possibly both delude themselves into believing this to be their aim.

I am convinced that the Quest for Truth is a much more difficult task than appears at first sight. In the domain of the physical sciences much has been achieved, though even here petty personal strife and men with pet theories are not quite unknown. But outside, in the domains of Religion and Philosophy, and of all those things which affect man most intimately and at first hand, the Quest is hardly yet begun. We have not yet learnt to follow the advice of good old Locke, who admonishes us that "we should keep a perfect indifferency for all opinions, not wish any of them true, or try to make them appear so; but, being indifferent, receive and embrace them according as evidence, and that alone, gives the attestation of truth."

Perhaps it is difficult for us to do this until we know more concerning our own minds, and have learnt to control our desires and thoughts. Here are problems with which the occultist is particularly concerned. They are problems of the highest moment.

H. Stanley Redgrove

THE STAR OF PERFECTION

MAN is almost entirely dependent upon symbols for making his desires known to his fellows, for communicating to them his ideas and sharing with them his experiences. Language has become, in a manner, so much second nature to us that we conduct a great deal of our thinking by means of it, and are thus apt to forget its symbolic character. Yet the fact remains that the written word "hunger," for example, the spoken word "hunger" and hunger itself are three totally distinct things The written word is no more than a symbol of the spoken word which itself is no more than a symbol of the reality. Indeed, language, whether spoken or written, would appear to consist mainly of symbols of a very arbitrary character. The study of the derivation of words and the evolution of language tends to remove—to some extent at any rate—this impression of arbitrariness. Some spoken words are clearly onomatopoeic, and the hieroglyphics of the Egyptians were definitely pictorial. Perhaps all spoken words are derived from onomatopoeic roots, and all alphabets are pictorial in origin. Language might, if these suppositions could be demonstrated, be shown to be free from arbitrariness: its symbolic character would remain.

Words, however, are by no means the only symbols mankind finds it necessary or convenient to employ. Mathematics is essentially a system of symbology—it is symbolic logic—and its symbols have many advantages, in regard to both precision of meaning and convenience of use, over words. Indeed, most of the modern advances in the physical sciences would have been impossible without the aid of mathematics; and, as I have endeavored to show elsewhere, mathematics provides us with symbols applicable to the realm of the psychical as well as those adapted to the needs of the physical sciences.

He would be a curious mathematician, however, who, because of the superiority of the symbols of mathematics, despised the use of words, and endeavored to carry on the ordinary affairs of daily life by means exclusively of mathematical formula. Our mildest criticism would be that he was unwise.

Is it not unwise of us if we despise the symbols of the ancients? Embodied within them is the wisdom of the past. Is it not worthwhile to endeavor to unravel something of their meaning?

Of these symbols, undoubtedly the most important is the pentagram—the Star of Perfection. This figure is most conveniently drawn by producing the sides of a regular pentagon—an equilateral and equiangular plane figure having five sides—so that they meet together in pairs.

Now, whilst it is a very simple matter to construct equilateral and equiangular plane figures possessing three, four, or even six, sides, the construction of a regular pentagon involves considerably more mathematical skill and knowledge.

It was the mind of Pythagoras who first rendered the accurate solution of this problem possible. Contemplating the curious fact known to the Egyptians that a triangle having sides 3, 4 and 5 units in length respectively possessed a right angle opposite its longest side, Pythagoras sought to understand the reason of this fact and to generalize it so as to apply to other right-angled triangles. He was thus led to discover the theorem in geometry, which to this day bears his name, a theorem necessary for the correct construction of the regular pentagon.

In his investigation of the properties of solid figures, Pythagoras made another very striking discovery, a discovery concerning the regular rectilinear solids. For a rectilinear solid, that is, one whose edges are straight lines, to be perfectly regular, it is necessary (i) that the solid angles formed by its faces shall be all alike, (ii) that its faces shall be all alike, and (iii) that these faces shall be equiangular and equilateral. Now Pythagoras found that he could construct five different sorts of these solids and no more. Using equilateral triangles as faces, he could make three different sorts of solids, namely, the regular tetrahedron (or triangular pyramid) with four faces, the regular octahedron with eight faces, and the regular icosahedron with twenty faces; whilst if he used squares as faces, he could construct another, but only one sort of regular solid figure, namely the cube. These figures may have been—the pyramid and cube certainly were—known before Pythagoras. The important point, however, is that Pythagoras found that, using other rectilinear figures as faces, he could not make a regular solid at all, save only in the case of the pentagon, by means of which the regular dodecahedron, with twelve faces, was obtained.

If we think ourselves into the mental atmosphere of the times in which he lived, we shall be able to understand somewhat the emotions which the contemplation of this figure produced in the mind of Pythagoras. It was a figure of mystery and wonder, holding within itself the secret of the Universe.

The Greeks believed the world to be compounded of four elements. To the mind of Pythagoras, it seemed certain that their forms, being perfect, must be those of the regular solids. There were, as I have pointed out, four—shall I say?—ordinary regular solids, having triangles or squares for their faces. These, then, were the forms of the four elements; whilst the mysterious dodecahedron, the fifth form which involved in itself the number five, and exhibited twelve faces (the number of the Zodiacal Signs), must be the form of the Universe.

It is easy enough to criticize this as bad reasoning. Judged by modern standards, it is. But a future generation may pass a similar judgment on much of our reasoning. We must judge the reasoning of Pythagoras in relation to the thought of his age—in relation to what was then known and believed concerning the Universe. The assumptions concerning the forms of the elements and the Universe which seemed good to him (and later on seemed good to Plato also), fitted in very well with the rest of Greek philosophy and, as we shall see, served a very useful purpose in the advancement of human knowledge.

The dodecahedron was, for Pythagoras, the most perfect of all forms. The pentagram or five-pointed star—the Star of Perfection was its plane symbol, and was adopted as the badge of the philosophical Brotherhood which he established, to pass therefrom into popular belief as a magic symbol of power.

From the time of Pythagoras to the Middle Ages, throughout these and beyond, the pentagram played an all-important part in magical belief and practice. It was a symbol of power to conjure up the dead, a symbol of protection to guard one against evil spirits. It appears on many early Greek coins and was extensively employed in early ornamental arts. During the Middle Ages it was, accompanied by the sign of the cross, placed above doorways to prevent the entry of witches; and I have by me, as I write, an interesting talisman, dating from the seven tenth century, on which the pentagram appears—as it did on many talismans—accompanied by other magical symbols.

Eliphas Levi traced resemblances between the form of a man or a goat's head and the pentagram according to whether it had one or two points in the ascendant; and he regarded it, in consequence, as a symbol of the microcosm, or alternatively as an instrument of black magic. This seems a departure from the original tradition, a not surprising occurrence in the writings of this brilliant but very unreliable genius.

I believe there to be a heart of truth embedded within the seemingly fantastic theories and practices of magic. But even if I am correct in this belief, the fact remains that the history of Magic embraces many records of human cruelty, stupidity and ignorance. The pentagram, it would seem, has hardly justified its title of "The Star of Perfection." There is, however, another side to the story.

It was imperatively necessary to the Pythagorean theory that the possibility of the existence of a sixth regular rectilinear solid should be disproved. Moreover, the dodecahedron being the most perfect of all forms, the form which "the Deity employed in tracing the plan of the Universe," it was essential that its properties be fully understood and that its method of construction be formulated in the most rigorously logical terms. What an incentive there was here for mathematical research. The Pythagorean theory inspired Euclid to compile his Elements of Geometry and thereby lay the foundations of the science. Without this incentive, Euclid might never have accomplished his great work. The Greek mind cared little for practice, but everything for theory. It is just because of this that the world is so deeply indebted to the Greek thinkers, because always the gaining of theoretical knowledge has made advancement in practical achievement possible.

Diverse are the significations, which have been and are attached to the mystic pentagram; but to me it is the symbol of the conflict of the human mind with experience—the symbol of the triumphs and failures of human thought in its efforts to understand. And it is, indeed, the Star of Perfection, because only through the work of the mind, only through the power of thought, shall man solve the problems that beset him and win Perfection for himself and for the world.

AN ALCHEMICAL BANQUET

In the days before the War, it was usual for me to dine with the late Professor Ferguson on the occasion of his visits to London, and, after dinner, we would sit up into the early hours of the morning talking on numerous subjects, especially alchemy and alchemical books, concerning which Ferguson had a vast store of knowledge. He was a delightful conversationalist, a broad-minded, tolerant thinker of the very best type. He told me how for years he had endeavored to arouse interest in the early history of chemistry in Glasgow without success, and expressed a pleasurable amazement that I had been able to find sufficient folk interested in the subject in London to make possible the running of the Alchemical Society, of which he was Honorary President throughout its three or four years of existence.

Looking over some reviews of the Society's Journal, I notice one in which the reviewer—who ought to have known better, since his profession was that of imparting knowledge to others—writes, apropos of a paper by Mr. A. E. Waite, in which the desirability is urged of distinguishing the alchemical texts which are contributions to the mystical side, from those whose concern is purely with material things. "Even Browning's Grammarian might well ask, 'Is it worth it?'"

These words are worth preserving as the final utterance of an age of obscurantism. Today we live in a clearer mental atmosphere.

It is, indeed, a remarkable sign of the times—the very real interest now taken in the many problems which alchemy presents, and the realization that the solution of these problems is vitally necessary to the understanding of the evolution, not only of chemical science, but, indeed, of human thought itself.

H. Stanley Redgrove

Dr. E. J. Holmyard has just written an excellent little book, intended both for the general reader and for college students, in which the story of chemistry is woven round the lives of some of its greatest exponents. Nearly a quarter of its pages are devoted to alchemists, the men specially selected as the greatest adepts in the science in alchemical days being Geber (Jabir ibn Hayyan), Rhazes (Abu Bakr Muhammad ibn Zakariyya), Roger Bacon, and Paracelsus, truly a quaternary of alchemical giants.

Geber is a man of quite exceptional interest, since it is possible that he was the originator of the famous sulphur-mercury theory of the metals—a theory in the genesis of which it seems certain that the mystical concept of man as a being of body and spirit, and ideas connected with sex, played a large part. Towards the close of the fifteenth century, certain Latin works appeared claiming to be translations from Arabic MSS. of Geber. They were many times reprinted and were translated into English by Richard Russell, "a Lover of Chymistry," and published in London in 1678, under the title of the "Works of Geber," the works in question being of the *Investigation or Search Of Perfection, Of the Sum of Perfection* (two books), *Of the Invention of Verity, or Perfection, and Of Furnaces.*

These works have now been re-issued, with the addition of illustrations taken from the Latin edition published at Berne in 1545, in a delightful volume edited by Dr. Holmyard.

In the whole history of alchemy, few works are more important than these. Not only do they contain a very clear exposition of the sulphur-mercury theory and of the concept of the Philosopher's Stone as the perfect medicine for metals; but, in addition, a wealth of knowledge is displayed concerning chemical substances and the technology of chemical operations.

Nowadays, of course, it is easy to scoff at the sulphur-mercury theory as absurd; but the theory provided a real impetus to research, as did also the hope of confecting the Stone of the Wise. Dr. Holmyard, in the book previously referred to, having used the word "unfortunately" in connection with the lure of transmutation, immediately adds a correction: "Yet perhaps we should not say 'unfortunately'; a vivid inspiration of some kind was essential if men were to labor at such a difficult, exacting and—in those days—unhealthy occupation."

The authenticity of the works ascribed to Geber was seriously called in question by Professor Berthelot, who brought forward weighty evidence for regarding them as having been written not earlier than the fourteenth century. Further facts, however, brought to light by Dr. Holmyard and others, have shaken Berthelot's conclusions; and for reasons stated in his introduction to the new edition, Dr. Holmyard is inclined to regard them as translations of the genuine works of the great Arabian experimentalist and thinker.

Whoever wrote them, they provide an insuperable answer to the two opinions concerning alchemy current, previous to the publication of my Alchemy: Ancient and Modern. These were: (1) the commonly accepted view that the alchemists were a set of knaves and fools; and (2) the view held by a small school of thought, that the alchemists treated purely of mystical matters—the transmutation of man's soul—under the veil of chemistry.

In point of fact, whilst under the term "alchemist" are gathered knaves and fools and also certain mystics who used a chemical symbology, the main body of alchemists were searchers into natural secrets—secrets of minerals and metals—in a word, the secrets of chemistry. But, as made plain in *Alchemy: Ancient and Modern*, their philosophy had its roots in mysticism. Alchemy was the product of mysticism applied to metallurgy. I am glad to find Dr. Holmyard, although less sympathetic to the mysticism of the alchemists, perhaps, than myself, concurs. "Alchemy," he writes, "defined as the art and philosophy of making gold by occult methods, dates from the beginnings of the Christian era, and its twofold origin—metallurgical facts and mystical speculation—cannot be doubted."

The question of alchemy's historical roots remains. Egypt is usually assigned as its birthplace; but from time to time there have been intimations of a quest and a doctrine like that of Western alchemy far back in the history of China.

A very interesting contribution on this subject by Mr. F. Hadland Davis was published in The Academy in 1913, and an equally interesting paper, written in China itself, by Professor Herbert Chatley, B.Sc., appeared in *The Journal of the Alchemical Society* in the same year. A more complete study of the subject, by Dr. O. S. Johnson, has recently been published, containing a mass of relevant information and raising many points of the greatest interest.

Chinese alchemy had its roots in Taoism; and Tao, the eternal principle of Perfection, closely resembles that Hermetic "One Thing "which" is the cause of all perfection throughout the whole world," and by means of which "were all things created."

The Taoists of China seem to have sought perfection in exactly the same two directions as that in which the quest was pursued by the alchemists of the West. They sought gold, the perfect metal; they sought the perfection of life in a medicine which would endow man with immortality.

The lofty philosophy of Lao Tzu soon became sullied with superstitious notions, and Taoism degenerated into a species of magic of the most absurd type. But as Dr. Johnson indicates, the influence in other directions of the alchemical quest or quests was of a salutary character. It encouraged metallurgical and medical research; and, although the Chinese have failed to evolve any coherent body of science concerning drugs and metals, in the manufacture of certain articles they early achieved a degree of technological perfection which, in some respects, has not been surpassed.

Forgotten Essays

"Their skill in metallurgy," Dr. Johnson writes, "their brilliant dyestuffs and manifold pigments, their early knowledge of gunpowder and pyrotechnics, their asphyxiating and anaesthetic compounds—all bear eloquent testimony to this fact." The mystical philosophy of Taoism, it would seem, has borne some very practical fruit.

The doctrine of Yang and Yin, the eternal male and female principles of the Universe, played a large part in the development of Chinese alchemy. These principles closely correspond to the sulphur and mercury of the alchemy of the West. Moreover, it is interesting to note, "Mercury was . . . regarded by the Chinese as the soul of metals,": and cinnabar, a compound of sulphur and mercury, was the chief agent used by them in their endeavors to perform transmutation.

These are significant facts, and Dr. Johnson thinks that Western alchemy may have had its origin in the infiltration of ideas derived from China.

This is possible, but has not been demonstrated; and the independent genesis of similar ideas concerning the nature of metals and the possibility of transmutation seems, when the true character of these ideas are taken into consideration, not unlikely—a matter to which I shall again refer.

The part England has played in the evolution of alchemy is of interest. The first alchemical book to be translated from Arabic into Latin was a treatise ascribed to Morenius, and the translation was the work of an Englishman, Robert of Chester, who completed the task in 1144. Roger Bacon, one of the really great figures in the history of alchemy, was also a native of these isles.

Thomas Norton, who lived in the fifteenth century, was an English alchemist of a somewhat different type. In a previous book, Dr. Holmyard described him as "in all probability a charlatan." This judgment is too harsh. Certainly, however, Norton was no great chemist, and he does not appear to have enriched science by a single observation of importance. Nevertheless, his book, *The Ordinall of Alchimy* very readable on account of its sprightly style and atmosphere of romance, is of considerable interest for the light it sheds on alchemy in England of the fifteenth century. The attractive facsimile reproduction of the book from Elias Ashmole's *Theatrum Chemicum Britan nicum*, and of Vaughan's curious and beautifully executed engravings, which has just been published, is, therefore, very welcome indeed.

In this book, Norton tells us that the great secret of transmutation can only be learnt orally from an adept. He gives an account of his own initiation (his Master in Alchemy is supposed to have been Sir George Ripley) and how his labors were twice brought to nought by the cupidity of dishonest persons who stole the completed Magistery from him. In the course of his book he indulges in many curious speculations, one of his peculiar notions being that metals were produced in the earth, not, as was generally supposed, by a process analogous to sexual procreation, but as the result of astrological influences. *The Ordinall*, however, contains little or nothing of a practical character and is very unlike *The Works of Gober*.

Indeed, by the fifteenth century the concept of the Philosopher's Stone had served its purpose and reached, or rather passed, the term of its utility. A new impetus to research was required—an alchemical revolution was called for.

Paracelsus supplied the impetus and made possible the revolution. Without in any way denying the possibility of metallic transmutation, he turned the minds of alchemists in a new direction—the perfecting of medicines. Moreover, Paracelsus, more than anyone else, was responsible for the gradual supersession of the sulphur-mercury theory. He lent his authority to the newer hypothesis—some say he initiated the idea—that the metals were threefold in constitution. This, the Sulphur mercury-salt theory, may be envisaged as not very different from Geber's notion, and in some ways an improvement on it; but the new theory had a much shorter life than the older one. Was this because it lacked the universality of the latter?

The origin of error, perhaps, is more mysterious than that of truth. At any rate, if the sulphur-mercury theory were true, the fact that different schools, separated by time and space, have adopted it would occasion no surprise.

And, after all has been said, does not the theory contain a real heart of truth? Turn where we will, we are confronted with duality. In the moral sphere, we meet with the duality of good and evil. Life manifests duality in its sexual dichotomy. There is the duality of force and inertia without which motion is impossible, and the duality of electron and proton without which matter could not exist.

What are these seemingly opposed though really complementary pairs, but sulphur and mercury?

It may be said that the duality of Nature is but seeming, being a creation of the mind which can think only of a thing in so far as it is contradistinguished from its opposite, light being inconceivable apart from darkness, darkness inconceivable apart from light. And it may be said that this duality is the duality of Nature, for Nature is the manifestation of Mind.

H. Stanley Redgrove

THE KABBALAH AND WORD-MAGIC

THE belief in the magic power of words is of extreme antiquity. By some, this belief is supposed to have originated in the fact that words are amongst those things which issue from living men and women, thereby serving to distinguish them from the dead. Hence, words were thought to be "givers of life," possessed of magic power. Interesting and suggestive as this theory is, it seems sufficient, in order to account for the belief in the magic of words, to postulate a failure on the part of the mind of primitive man to distinguish between the word and the thing which it symbolized.

That a similar failure is not unknown even at man's present stage of evolution is evidenced by those who, as it is so graphically expressed, "lose themselves in a maze of words." In the early days, more especially amongst those races adopting a picture-writing, confusion between words and things, or words and ideas, must have been so easy as to have been almost inevitable. The Englishman, for example, has no excuse for confusing a dwelling with the word "house," for the simple reason that there is no similarity between them. The ancient Egyptian, who expressed words by means of hieroglyphics—little pictures of the things symbolized—had every excuse if he committed a like error of thought.

Hebrew is not far removed from hieroglyphical writing. Moreover, since all the Hebrew letters are consonants, any and every combination of letters can be pronounced, in this sense forming a word; and, since the same signs express both letters and numbers, every word is also a number.

That these peculiarities in the structure of Hebrew as a written language played a part in the evolution of that strange body of doctrine known as the Kabbalah, there can be no doubt. They led to that fantastic species of logic—using this term to denote a method of reasoning, but not necessarily one which leads to truth—comprised under the terms, "Gematria," "Notariqon" and "Temuria." It is true that one can operate with symbols without being aware of their meaning, and arrive at a result which, translated into meaning, yields truth. But it is necessary to operate in accordance with laws determined by the nature of the things represented. Deductive logic is a case in point. Mathematics is an even more remarkable one. It is, however, one thing to assert that, if, for example, x and y are measurable quantities similar in character, x being the greater, $x — y$ always equals $(x — y)(x + y)$, no matter what their magnitudes may be. It is quite another to say that, if two things or ideas are expressed by words symbolizing equal numbers, then these two things or ideas are also equivalent; or, alternatively, that if one word can be split up into two others, then the thing or idea expressed by the whole word is somehow the result of the things or ideas expressed by the two parts.

This may appear in the light of a destructive criticism of the Kabbalah, and it is intended as a destructive criticism of a phase of it, which certain mystery-mongers, pleased with puerilities, have seized upon as being one of the most important aspects of its Mystery.

Gematria, Notariqon and Temuria: these may, indeed, be recommended as alternatives to cross-word puzzles, and of no more significance and importance, except as remarkable instances of the aberrations of the human intellect. The real mystery of the Kabbalah lies deeper than these.

It is sometimes necessary to express a truth by means of overstatement. Let me, then, describe logic as an afterthought of the mind. Intuition plays a more important part in our thinking than we are wont to credit. Again and again, we reach conclusions intuitively, but invent reasons for them so rapidly that we deceive ourselves into the belief that we are logical beings. Not less true is this of the pseudo-logic of Kabbalism; and we may justly consider the fantastic thought-apparatus I have just criticized as merely the means adopted to fit a system of philosophy in with the words of the sacred scriptures of Jewry. We must dismiss this apparatus and evaluate the system on its own merits. It is an extraordinarily interesting system, marred, it is true, with much that is puerile and fantastic, but containing also many things that are illuminating and impressive. It is a philosophy of light and shadow, or, to vary somewhat the metaphor, let me say that it is like a land where there are quagmires and dark woods in the valleys, wherein the explorer may easily be lost, but also lofty summits, soaring into the empyrean.

Emphatically, we need a guide in this strange land.

There are many books on Kabbalism; but, considered as glides, not a few may be described only as traps for the unwary. Two books, however, may be singled out as being of real value to the student. These are Mr. A. E. Waite's *The Doctrine and Literature of the Kabbalah*, a relatively elementary introduction to the subject, and *The Secret Doctrine in Israel*, a more advanced study. Both are out of print, and second-hand copies of them, as of all Mr. Waite's books, are difficult to obtain. It is with great pleasure, therefore, that I welcome the publication of a new work on the subject by this author, in which these two older books have been incorporated. It may be confidently recommended to those who wish to explore the Mystery of the Kabbalah; not, let me add, the mystery of its puerilities, if indeed there is any mystery concerning these, but of those matters lying at the heart of this strange philosophy, which, whoever first committed it to writing, certainly contains the thought of ancient Jewry, tinctured, as the Jew came into contact with influences outside those of his own land, with Neo-Platonism and Sufism.

I do not propose, nor would such a project be practicable, to attempt any summary of Kabbalistic philosophy in this necessarily short article. It is not a system which lends itself to a summary statement by one who has any regard for accuracy. Mr. Waite's large volume treats the whole subject in a masterly fashion. Not only has the author very successfully endeavored to get at the heart of the Kabbalah and to lay it bare for our inspection, but he also deals very thoroughly with the knotty question of its origin and adequately sketches its later developments, the works of the chief Christian students of the Kabbalah from Raymond Lully to Eliphas Levi being surveyed, as well as the connections between the Kabbalah and other channels of secret tradition, such as Alchemy, Magic and Freemasonry.

In Mr. Waite's view, the central Mystery of the Kabbalah is a mystery of sex. This is a point of outstanding interest. The mental fear—I can think of no more appropriate expression with which civilized man has, on the whole, tended to regard the phenomenon of sex is one of the most amazing things in the whole history of human thought. Sex is of such fundamental importance in the life of mankind that one would naturally expect to see it playing a central part in every system of thought, claiming to be sane. Such, however, is not the case. Religious systems, perhaps in order to divert the sexual energy to their own ends, have, too frequently, done all that was possible to degrade sex, treating it as a sign of mankind's sinful nature which somehow must be transcended if he is to enter into a state of glory. Sterile philosophically and with most disastrous results in practice, such systems are gradually passing away.

The Kabbalah, on the other hand, treats sex as essentially a phenomenon of the soul, regarding marriage as a sacrament in a very real sense, to which the Roman Catholic church, in spite of its verbal recognition of the sacramental character of marriage, has never even remotely approached.

I do not think the Kabbalah provides, either on the theoretical or practical side, a complete solution to the problem of sex, which perhaps is the fundamental problem of existence. But it exhibits the temper in which this problem must be approached if a real unveiling of the mystery is to be achieved. Sex may indeed be described as the road to heaven and the road to hell. No roads are more important. And, in the duality which, in the light of modern science, is seen running through all existence, we may, perhaps, glimpse something of that fundamental reality of which sex is the manifestation.

THE FOUNDATION OF MAGIC

MAGIC has its roots in animism, "the conception of spirit everywhere," as Edward Clodd has aptly called it. Now there is a quality of inevitability about animism; man in his attempt to explain the Universe to his mind had to start by explaining it in terms of himself. I think he will end as he began, but with a knowledge enriched and ever increasing of the Universe as a world of experience. Professor Eddington has declared his belief, to which he has been forced by a profound study of the implications of recent advances in the mathematical and physical sciences, that the primary stuff of the Universe is "mind-stuff," though he warns us that by "stuff" he does not exactly mean stuff and by "mind" he does not exactly mean mind. That is well. The new animism will be a vastly different affair from the old. Nevertheless, the fact that we are beginning to realize that we cannot construct a universe with mind left out may make us a little more tolerant in our treatment of the primitive animist. If he was, indeed, a child who believed in fairy stories, the materialist of the century that has passed was a youth at college, who, having done a first year's course in chemistry, physics and biology, was prepared to explain everything from his vast store of profound knowledge.

Out of animism, primitive man created myth and magic. The very close relationship between myth and poetry has been admirably dealt with by F. C. Prescott in his book, *Poetry and Myth*. "The imagination," he writes, "working spontaneously, produces a fictitious concrete, a story, the burden or efficacy of which is not so much a meaning for the understanding as a feeling for the heart. Like myth, poetry can be apprehended only by the imaginative faculty, by which it was first produced."

The world of Imagination! Well, that, says the materialist, is just . . . imagination; which does not get us any farther. In this world of imagination, every poem, every work of art, is conceived; and which of us would care for a life devoid of poetry, of music, of painting? Moreover, it is equally true to say that of it, too, is born every scientific hypothesis. Man lives, must live, in two worlds, the world of experience wherein the will meets with resistances external to itself, and the world of imagination, where it is limited in its activities only by its own nature.

We might describe primitive magic as the first attempt to bridge the gap between the two worlds. Faced with dangers and difficulties, innumerable, primitive man appealed for help to the spiritual beings with which his imagination peopled the Universe. He appealed to them by symbolic prayers, by magic. Sometimes his prayers were answered; or, if this mode of expression is preferred, let me say that sometimes he made discoveries, such as how to make fire, which he explained animistically.

A distinction has been drawn between the religious attitude towards the beings of the spiritual world as propitiative, and the magical attitude as coercive; but, in point of fact, religion and magic are too closely intertwined to make this distinction of any value. It would, perhaps, be more correct to describe religion as "official magic."

The priest has always endeavored to monopolize magic, and, in light of this fact, the extreme hostility of the Latin Church to all forms of magic other than her own rituals, which, of course, are magical, becomes easy to understand. In the past, this hostility was not directed merely towards practices of a psychical character. There was a time when any delving too deeply into Nature's secrets was liable to be regarded as partaking of magic. Perhaps the Church was right in this view, for every physical enquiry ends in a spiritual one, and the term "magic" embraces far more than merely "dealings with the dead." In any case, the world is deeply indebted to those real enquirers who dared to face the Church's terrors; and, if the history of magic contains an abundance of names of impostors, dupes and lunatics, amongst the magicians must also be reckoned some brave investigators and notable thinkers.

I have referred to the magic-working symbolic prayers of primitive man. A good example of such a prayer, which has persisted to this day, is the practice, found especially in Italy, of extending the fore-finger and little finger, the rest of the hand being closed, to ward off the effects of the evil eye. The sign is that of the crescent moon, and, as F. T. Elworthy has pointed out in his Horns of Honor, is thus a mute appeal to the moon goddess for her protection. The use of horseshoes to bring good luck has a similar significance.

Analogy, wherefrom symbols arise, is one of the most primitive organons of thought. It is at the heart of magic, as it is at that of alchemy, with which magic has close associations. "What is above is as that which is below, to achieve the miracles of the One Thing." Analogy has led man to make some grand generalizations; it has also led him deep into the region of fantasy.

A peculiar fantasy based on the notion of the efficacy of symbols, which, as C. J. S. Thompson points out in his *Mysteries and Secrets of Magic*, is to be found practically all over the world, is the idea that an enemy can be injured and caused to die by making a waxen image of him and sticking pins in it, or causing it slowly to melt in front of a slow fire. Closely connected with magical beliefs of this character is the notion very prevalent amongst primitive races that by acting on part of a thing one acts thereby on the whole. For this reason, it is considered to be dangerous to leave hair-cuttings or nail-pairings about, or even to allow one's real name to be known.

These aberrations, however, must not lead us to conclude that analogy is always worthless, and symbolism invariably destitute of efficacy. Indeed, language itself is nothing but a system of symbols, and without analogy we could never compare one event with another. Thought and its expression would be impossible.

According to Christian (Histoire de la Magie), magic was "the synthesis of those sciences once possessed by the Magi or philosophers of India, or Persia, of Chaldea, and of Egypt"; and Ennemoser, in his History of Magic, also treats the word as a synonym for the secret wisdom of the ancients. We shall be correct, perhaps, in saying that in the days of which these authors write, the distinction between science and magic did not exist. Science had yet to be born. But its birth did not mean the death of magic; it meant its persistence as superstition.

The history of magic, despite books bearing this title, remains to be written, and its author will need to range over almost the whole of human thought. The questings of primitive man, his attempts to grapple with his experiences and to satisfy his desires, the play of his imagination, the knowledge he gained and the myths he created—here must be the starting-point of the book if it is ever written. It will pass to a consideration of the growth of human knowledge, seemingly intertwined inextricably with human superstition and tinctured with a belief in the reality of spiritual powers and the efficacy of symbols as a means for invoking their aid. It will tell the whole story of this development, and of how science gradually shook itself free from the entanglements of superstition, and, in the achievement of this task, lost some things of value as well, including the belief in the fundamental reality of mind or spirit. Finally, it will relate how these began slowly to be regained, man learning once more to feel the wonder of the Universe, to value aright the things of the Imagination, and to believe in Magic.

To write such a book as this would be to achieve a task of the greatest magnitude. Moreover, for its successful accomplishment, it would be necessary to avoid any one-sided point of view and the temptation of running any particular theory to death. I feel sure, for example, that Ennemoser's History would have been a better book had he been less certain that "animal magnetism" was the key to unlock all the mysteries of magic. Eliphas Levi, one of the most interesting and suggestive of all writers on the subject, commits a like fault with his theory of "astral light." These writers are amongst those who are, so to speak, on the side of magic. On the other side, we have many books by those who can see in magic nothing but the record of human credulity and folly in its most childish forms.

It is necessary, so it seems to me, to be able to visualize both the sublimities and the follies of magic. We must not allow the brilliance of the former to blind our eyes to the existence of the latter, nor the amazing futilities of magic to prevent us from realizing that magic is not all folly.

Well, did the poet Blake say, "everything possible to be believed is the image of truth." At the heart of magic there is truth. Our task must be to purge it from the dross. Amongst the many illuminating passages in Eliphas Levi's works is the statement that "superstition is the sign surviving the thought ... the dead body of a religious rite." Regarded in themselves, most superstitions seem positively unintelligible; but set them in their right relations in the mythologies of which they originally formed part, and their significance appears.

The philosophy of magic reached sublime heights in the writings of the Neo-Platonists, whose theory of emanations is essentially a magical theory of the Universe, and a development of the doctrine of "as above, so below." "Nature," writes *Iamblichus*, "in her peculiar way makes a likeness of invisible principles through symbols in visible form."

He is writing on the Egyptian mysteries, in which magic and astronomy or astrology are inextricably mixed. This is easy to understand. Amongst the earliest observations made by the ancients were observations of the stars, and one of their earliest scientific discoveries was the fact that astronomical phenomena could be predicted. It is not surprising that they concluded that the stars governed all mundane events. From this hypothesis the art of astro-prediction or astrology was borne.

To Plato, the stars were quasi-spiritual beings, and the idea persisted, in one way or another, for ages.

When Greek learning was rediscovered by the Christian world, the youthful Cornelius Agrippa essayed a vast synthesis of magic in his Three Books of Occult Philosophy. He had drunk deeply of the waters of Neo-Platonism, and his synthesis is essentially a system of astro-correspondences, in which all things are magically connected with the stars.

We may smile at many of the details of his philosophy; yet are we entitled to reject its underlying idea, that the Universe forms a magical unity? The theory of universal correspondences is to be found in a more highly-developed and philosophical form in the writings of Swedenborg. Here, however, everything is interpreted theologically; and to many minds, Swedenborg's interpretation of the symbols of nature are as little acceptable as Agrippa's.

Nevertheless, I suggest that here in Agrippa and in Swedenborg is to be found a fundamental truth, which is the truth of magic in, so to speak, its static aspect. Let me express it in Carlyle's words: "All visible things are emblems; what thou seest is not there on its own account; strictly taken, it is not there at all: Matter exists only spiritually, and to represent some Idea, and Body it forth."

H. Stanley Redgrove

I have referred to Eliphas Levi's doctrine of the Astral Light. As I have pointed out before, I consider his hypothesis to be at once too indefinite and too wide in its applications. Moreover, this quasi-material agency appears to have been based, in its inventor's mind, on scientific concepts now more or less obsolete. Nevertheless, it provides the clue to the discovery of the truth of magic in what I may, perhaps, call its dynamic aspect. For the "astral light" was a universal force governed by the will.

Will is not a mere epiphenomenon of material forces—it is the fundamental dynamical reality of the Universe. Imagination is not just imagination—it is the explanation of reality.

Imagination can kill a man through fear, several cases of this phenomenon amongst primitive races being on record. It can conjure up in the mind of the superstitious all the terrible and absurd beings of black magic. As Eliphas Levi has well said, "he who affirms the devil creates . . . the devil." This is one aspect. On the other hand, imagination can create the sublimest works of art and the most profound theories of science and philosophy. It is the only creative energy we know. The forces we assume to exist in the world of matter are no more than symbols of the activity of will. They are like the spirits with which primitive man peopled the Universe. In the last analysis, we can say nothing more than that it is a will-determination, and that is what I mean when I say that we are inhabitants of a magical world.

A NEW PLEA FOR MYSTICISM

THE world of human experience is threaded through by lines which are traced out by the passage of each individual life through it, so that it is honeycombed by myriads of parallel strands, which enter it on the one side, cross it, and leave it on the other, all pursuing the direction of the individual journey towards the unknown. "Let us call this individual threading of the world the direction of the warp. Seen along the warp, the world appears to consist of a community of fellow-travelers whose identifies remain permanent whilst the scenery around them keeps changing as they pursue their way from birth to death. . . ." The other way of looking at the world is along the weft. The weft is the direction that lies wholly within the world of sensual experience. The fibers of the weft do not mysteriously appear out of the unknown at one point and disappear into it at another. Their origin is lost in the mists of an unfathomable past, and their destiny lies in the womb of a future which is incalculably remote. Seen along the weft, the world presents a permanent substratum providing a solid environment which is subject only to a slow change, or evolution, caused by the passage of a mysterious agency called 'time'." I have quoted these passages from a new book by a new writer, just published by Messrs. Rider & Co., which presents several features of interest.

Mr. Tyrrell's theme is not a new one—it is, indeed, a very old one—but it is approached and handled in a novel manner and with a knack of felicitous illustration that adds much to its value. Mr. Tyrrell thinks, perhaps with some measure of justice, that today we tend to regard the world too exclusively along the weft. "The politician, the sociologist, the economist, the eugenist, the doctor, and even to a large extent the priest, are looking at life along the weft". As it so happens, the mathematical physicist, of all seemingly unlikely persons, together with the mystic, emphasizes the need for the other point of view.

The Theory of Relativity endows the observer with an importance equal to that of the thing observed. Regarding the world as a System of metrical relationships, it assures us that, whilst each individual's System may be unique for him, it has just the same claim to validity as that of anybody else. As a result of recent developments in mathematical physics, the scientist has come to believe in the existence of a world which is utterly different in almost every possible way from that of the plain man of common sense. Now it is pretty useless going to the plain man of common sense and telling him that he must give up believing that he is living in a world of material objects, having definite shapes, sizes, colors, positions in space, and so on—that he has got to imagine himself in a world of electrons, or irregularities in the geometry of space-time, or waves of probability, or something even more abstract. He will reply that he is quite satisfied with his common-sense view of things, for the simple and perfectly satisfactory reason that it works. Nor would it serve any useful purpose to bid the mathematical physicist give up his theories and equations, so utterly opposed to common sense, and for precisely the same reason. He would triumphantly point to the fact that his theories work, that his equations give the correct result as determined by experiment.

The plain fact is that both views of the nature of the universe, that of common sense, that of modem science, are true within their appropriate spheres of application. And if it is hard to understand how theories which seem utterly to contradict each other can both be true, I would say that theories are mental tools and their truth the measure of their utility. A hacksaw and a microtome are both extremely useful tools for cutting; but the latter would be pretty useless to the woodsman, and the former equally lacking in value to the botanist engaged in identifying a plant. We may say, if we so please, that reality has many faces or aspects; and it is precisely this mode of envisaging the universe which appeals to Mr. Tyrrell and which he has developed in his book.

The world of sense, he holds, is not an unreal world, but it does not comprise the whole of reality. It is, rather, an aspect of a deeper, richer reality, which cannot be attained, at any rate in any complete sense, by the unaided intelligence, but calls for the exercise of an intuitive faculty to which the term "mystical" is applicable. "To become aware of a deeper, as distinct from a more complex, meaning in anything, or of a degree of significance higher than the one usually assigned to it, is—to apprehend it mystically... Mystical knowledge of values and meanings... is of the same direct kind as... awareness of the self".

Although, no doubt, mysticism has been taken to mean a variety of things other than this, I think most serious students of the subject will agree that Mr. Tyrrell has accurately seized upon what is the really characteristic quality of mysticism, serving to mark it off, in its diverse manifestations, from all other modes of thought. To the mystic, the world of sense is a symbol; and that is only another way of saying that it is an aspect of something else. This is why I have described his theme as a very old one. Those who would know in detail how it is rehandled are referred to the book itself. There is one very apt illustration, however, which I cannot forbear quoting:

"To an animal, a book is merely a colored shape. Any higher significance a book may hold lies above the level of its thought. And the book is a colored shape; the animal is not wrong. To go a step higher, an uneducated savage may regard a book as a series of marks on paper. This is the book as seen on a higher level of significance than the animals, and one which corresponds to the savage's level of thought. Again, it is not wrong, only the book can mean more. It may mean a series of letters arranged according to certain rules. This is the book on a higher level of significance than the savage's. It might be that for an intelligent being who had never heard of the art of writing. Or finally, on a still higher level, the book may be an expression of meaning."

Have we exhausted the full significance of existence when we have fully explored the universe from the scientific point of view, and determined the whole of its metrical relationships? Are there not meanings and values beyond this? There is an interesting and able chapter on Presuppositions, in which Mr. Tyrrell fully exposes the fact that most of our beliefs, including those which we fondly imagine are based on undeniable facts and irrefragable logic, owe not a little to our presuppositions. This chapter forms an introduction to a study of Psychical Research, a domain where the activity of presuppositions has been particularly manifest.

Were it not for these, Mr. Tyrrell thinks that telepathy would be universally recognized as a fact. And, as he indicates, a point to which I called attention many years ago, in a little book I wrote as a young man, *Matter Spirit and the Cosmos*, no physical theory of telepathy is adequate to account for the facts, since what is so often transmitted is not the actual mental image, but the idea or meaning underlying it. Mr. Tyrrell's own presuppositions incline him to accept, in a general sense, the spiritist explanation of psychic phenomena; but he deprecates the attempt of the spiritualists to base a religion on the experiences of the séance room, he criticizes the credulity which too many of them manifest, and he is well aware of the difficulties in the way of attempting to establish human survival by means of mediumistic experiments. Until we know more concerning the limits of telepathy and cryptæsthesia, they can always be stretched to cover any phenomenon. But immortality, he holds, joining hands with Dean Inge, is something greater than mere survival. It is a fact of mystical consciousness.

FINIS

H. Stanley Redgrove

Other Books by the Managing Editor

Manly P. Hall All-Seeing Eye Series:
Book First, Second, Third

Manly P. Hall Seeker of More Intelligent Life Series:
Book I-IV

Hiram E. Buttler Exoteric Christianity

Arthur Waite Forgotten Essays

The Initiates Speak

George Oliver Masonic Writings

Walter L. Wilmshurst Forgotten Essays

Joseph Fort Newton Masonic Writings

Freemasons – South Dakota Territory, Book A – K

Freemasons – South Dakota Territory, Book L - Z

For latest books, please visit:
Parallel47North.com/collections/esoteric-books
Contact: Info@Parallel47North.com

Forgotten Essays

About Author and Managing Editor

Darrell Jordan is an acolyte of the August Fraternity, former Noble Grand-IOOF and Freemason.

He is also a member of the Theosophical and Philalethes Societies.

Darrell Jordan

www.ingramcontent.com/pod-product-compliance
Lightning Source LLC
Chambersburg PA
CBHW020311010526
44107CB00001B/66